PAKISTAN:
Military Rule or People's Power

TARIQ ALI

Jonathan Cape
Thirty Bedford Square London

First published 1970
© 1970 by Tariq Ali
Reprinted 1970

Jonathan Cape Ltd, 30 Bedford Square, London wc1

ISBN 0 224 61864 4

Printed in Great Britain by
Ebenezer Baylis and Son Ltd
The Trinity Press, Worcester, and London
bound by James Burn and Co Ltd, Esher, Surrey

CONTENTS

ILLUSTRATIONS

ABBREVIATIONS

C.S.P.	Civil Service of Pakistan
C.O.P.	Combined Opposition Parties
C.P.I.	Communist Party of India
C.P.P.	Communist Party of Pakistan
D.P.R.	Defence of Pakistan Regulations
D.A.C.	Democratic Action Committee
D.A.S.	Development Advisory Service
E.B.D.O.	Election Bodies Disqualifying Order
E.P.R.	East Pakistan Rifles
E.P.S.L.	East Pakistan Students' League
E.P.S.U.	East Pakistan Students' Union
E.P.W.F.	East Pakistan Workers' Federation
G.T.S.	Government Transport Service
N.A.P.	National Awami Party
N.D.F.	National Democratic Front
N.S.F.	National Student Federation
P.D.M.	Pakistan Democratic Movement
P.K.I.	Parti Kommunist Indonesien (Communist Party of Indonesia)
S.A.C.	Student Action Committee

For Hasan Nasir, Communist militant of
Karachi, tortured to death in Lahore.
Also for the hundreds of workers,
peasants and students in both parts of
Pakistan who fell before police and army
bullets in the struggle against capitalist
and feudal oppression.

PREFACE

This book is an unabashed and straightforward polemic against the feudal and capitalist class of Pakistan which has ruled the country since 1947 in varying guises. It will, I hope, go a small way towards balancing the reactionary and paternalistic assessments of Pakistan which are made from time to time in the bourgeois press in Britain and the United States, and also in the books written on the subject by learned academics in these two countries. More important still is that this book should be read in Pakistan by those who can read, so as to make a start on correcting the imbalanced view of Pakistani politics which has become current because few Pakistanis have bothered to write the truth.

I would like to stress that most of the facts cited in this book have been verified; there may be some inaccuracies with regard to individual roles, but these will have arisen because the different sectors of the Pakistani ruling class compete with each other in telling lies.

I would like to thank those politicians and student militants who saw me in connection with this book, but who are in no way responsible for any of the views expressed in it:

Student militants
Raja Anwar (Rawalpindi), Qazi Anwar (Peshawar), Karim Yar Abbasi (Multan) and many others in Lahore, Karachi, Lyallpur. Also Mahbubullah, Rashed Khan Menon and many other militants of the East Pakistan Students Union in Dacca, Mymensingh, Bogra, Dinajpur, Tangail, Gaibandha, Rangpur.

Political leaders
Mian Mumtaz Daultana (Muslim League), Mian Mahmud Ali Qasuri, Professor Mozaffar Ahmed, Saif Khalid (pro-Moscow National Awami Party), C. R. Aslam, Maulana Bhashani, Major Ishaq, Afzal Bangash (pro-Peking National Awami Party), Sheikh Mujibur Rehman (Awami League) and Zulfiqar Ali Bhutto (People's Party).

13

In addition I would like to thank many journalists and ex-journalists whose advice and newspaper files were invaluable. My thanks are due in particular to Mr Nizam Din, the librarian of the *Pakistan Times*, Lahore, for his assistance in collecting data on the depth of the upsurge and the casualties of police and army firing, and to the proprietor and editor of *Holiday* for *all* their help. For their kind hospitality and help in Dacca (East Pakistan) I would like to thank Mr and Mrs Sayeedul Hassan, and also Maulana Bhashani, who allowed me to accompany him on a tour of the East Pakistani countryside and who proved that despite his eighty-six years he was more energetic than I was.

In Europe I would like to thank my comrades of the International Marxist Group for their advice on certain issues. The last chapter was checked and many of its errors corrected by political associates of the Fourth International, Ernest Mandel and Pierre Frank.

Readers will notice that I have quoted liberally from the *Pakistan Times* in its pre-Ayub days. The reason for this is that it was my only radical source of information in Pakistan.

April 1970   TARIQ ALI

A NECESSARY INTRODUCTION

As the year 1968 drew to a close, political analysts and sociologists from both sides of the barricades began to draw their conclusions. Would the struggle continue or had the "student hooligans" been decisively defeated and "democracy" vindicated? Many thought that the struggle had temporarily been contained, and that the betrayals of the reformists had succeeded in preserving the status quo indefinitely.

No one doubted that the events of May 1968 in France had left their mark on the most complacent and self-satisfied social class in the world (outside the U.S.A.): the bourgeois class in Western Europe. The spectre of a French May repeating itself elsewhere in Europe frightened people, and every street demonstration in the cities of Europe acquired a new significance. Even the world's oldest and most experienced ruling class, the British bourgeois, displayed unease, not to say distinct signs of panic before London's largest pro-Vietcong demonstration in October 1968.

Towards the end of October it seemed that there had been a lessening of momentum in the world-wide upsurge of young people, and that the movement had entered a period of decline. Mexican workers and students had suffered a temporary defeat. Street demonstration in Italy and West Germany had not succeeded in sparking off a general uprising and confrontations had been successfully isolated by the authorities. In Czechoslovakia, despite the brave and sometimes heroic resistance of the Czech workers and students, the Soviet bureaucracy had succeeded in destroying all immediate hopes for a maturing political, anti-bureaucratic revolution.

And then, in the second week of November 1968, news of massive student demonstrations in West Pakistan began to seep through into the foreign press. It almost seemed as though the Pakistani students had timed their revolt to dispel the growing feeling of gloom which was pervading Western Europe. The upsurge in West Pakistan spread to the eastern part of the country, a thousand miles away. After a month of determined and sustained struggle by the students

15

against the police and the army, battle was joined by the urban proletariat, by the huge army of unemployed and by some of the professional, petit-bourgeois sections of society.

The impetus of the uprising was such that though the government tried its favourite trick of closing down all the universities and schools, the students continued to mobilize and fight on the streets. The struggle continued until its main aim – to bring down the dictator – had been achieved.

On February 21st, 1969, President Ayub Khan announced his departure from the political scene. The Pakistani students and workers had succeeded beyond their wildest dreams and had accomplished in the short term what their counterparts elsewhere in the world had failed to bring about. True, the overthrow of Ayub did not end the system he represented, but it remained nevertheless an important political victory, and its psychological effect on the consciousness of the students and workers was extremely valuable. Even this limited success, won by mass action on the streets of Pakistani cities in a completely disorganized and uncoordinated fashion, suggested what an organized force could achieve; the lesson has not been lost on either the reactionaries or the progressives in Pakistan.

In Asia students have always played an active part in politics. Even a cursory glance reveals the power which students have wielded in China, Japan, Korea, Vietnam, Indonesia, to name but a few, over the last few decades. In the countries of the un-free world, ruled by comprador oligarchies under the command of United States imperialism, the political strength of the students has been recognized and they have been dealt with accordingly: mass arrests, vile tortures, brutal murders of student leaders are not uncommon in the unliberated parts of Asia.

The puppet rulers in Asia could afford to smile condescendingly at the "troubles" facing their capitalist masters in Europe and the United States, and at their inability to deal with the students as they were dealt with in Asia or Latin America. The contradictions of late-capitalist societies prevented the ruling class from employing the methods their clients in the exploited parts of the world were able to use. The Pakistani dictator Ayub was extremely sympathetic to the troubles facing de Gaulle, and there is some evidence to suggest that messages were exchanged soon after May 1968. Certainly, the Pakistani ruling class put forward the view that the May revolt in France was merely the result of a "Jewish conspiracy" to punish de Gaulle for his "pro-Arab" sympathies. It is a sad reflection on the political consciousness of students in West Pakistan that in many cases this story was accepted at face value, and I was questioned about it closely by many student militants.

There were certain similarities between the May revolt in France and the November uprising in Pakistan. In both countries a strong man had held power for ten years with the support of the army, and the political system was such that defeat at the polls was improbable. The political atmosphere in both countries was oppressive and harsh (though of course in differing degrees), and both de Gaulle and Ayub had a "Left" face in their attitudes to Vietnam and China respectively. Also, de Gaulle's "friendship" with the Soviet Union had made the French Communist Party and its supporters even less capable of opposition, and Ayub's "friendship" with China had succeeded in immobilizing the "pro-Peking" elements in Pakistan. In both France and Pakistan the orthodox opposition parties had not succeeded in providing a militant opposition to the authoritarian regimes within the limits prescribed by the state. An extra-parliamentary opposition was therefore the only way out, but in both countries it was thought that the political structures were such that a sustained revolt was well nigh impossible.

But despite the political similarities of the two countries there were considerable differences in other fields, the most important of which was their respective development of productive forces. France is an advanced capitalist country where the proletariat is the largest and most powerful social class, and almost the entire population can read and write. Pakistan is a semi-colonial, feudal society with a rising comprador capitalist class; out of the population of 120 million less than fourteen per cent are literate, and the majority of these are students, ex-students with no jobs, lawyers, clerks, doctors and teachers. The largest social force in the country is the peasantry. In France the student revolt was linked to the economic contradictions inherent in late-capitalist society; it reflected the general crisis of bourgeois ideology and also the conflict between the needs of the capitalist economy in relation to the university and the bourgeois institutions inside the university system. Universities in many advanced capitalist countries are beginning to express and reflect all the contradictions of capitalist society, but students have no real political or organizational autonomy and power compared, for example, to the power of the working class. However, this is changing rapidly

2

with the increase of the number of students and the general development of technology.

In France the workers' movement was dominated by the French Communist Party and its trade-union bureaucracy. In other countries the forces of social-democracy controlled large sections of the workers. Thus the weakest link in the political domination of both Stalinism and social-democracy was the student movement, whose political sensitivity could discern the crisis of bourgeois ideology and act much more quickly than other sectors. This crisis deepened in France with the First Vietnam War and the Algerian War; and the latest and most important factor in mobilizing the student movement was the heroic and unprecedented resistance of the Vietnamese people to United States imperialism. This reached its height with the Tet offensive of February–March 1968, and was directly responsible for the revolt at Nanterre.

In Pakistan the student movement is in a completely different position. The students consciously see themselves as a force of political opposition, as new political parties have not been allowed to develop and the existing parties have failed hopelessly to fight even for demands concerning civil liberties. And, of course, during periods when political parties were banned the student movement was the only organized force in the entire country. The low level of literacy is also an important factor, and almost impels the students to participate in politics. Even when the students have decided not to articulate political demands for tactical reasons, their actions have always been related to the political life of the country, and they have linked the struggle against oppression at the university to a struggle against the Ayub regime. The question of posing demands related to the university alone has never arisen as the students have frequently been forced to put forward demands on behalf of the petit-bourgeoisie and the urban and rural proletariat in West and East Pakistan. Any programme for the student movement in Pakistan would therefore be part of a general programme for the Pakistani masses. I have outlined a plan of this kind in the last chapter of the book.

The links between the Pakistani student movement and the workers are extremely strong, for they have been built by common actions and not by distributing leaflets outside factories (which might not be possible in Pakistan for legal reasons even if the workers could read). The absence of a strong social-democratic or semi-fascist grip on the workers facilitates common actions between them and the students.

Most of the right-wing trade-union bureaucrats are so thoroughly discredited because of the money they receive from the capitalists and the government that they do not constitute any threat at all. In fact workers in Pakistan usually welcome the students who go and explain political developments to them or help them to organize strikes and raise money for the strikers. The very fact that an "educated" person is bothering to talk to them, let alone discussing ways of helping them, is welcomed enthusiastically by the workers.

For ten years Ayub ruled Pakistan with the backing of the army and the bureaucracy, and with the support of the feudal and capitalist interests in Pakistan. Opposition movements, whether led by students or initiated by workers in the form of strikes, had been ruthlessly suppressed and even a gentler form of opposition by bourgeois political parties had not been tolerated. The press had been effectively silenced and the radio was controlled by the Ministry of Information and Broadcasting. The propaganda of the regime was so crude and blatant that it alienated the people, and one of Ayub's last gimmicks – the setting up of the Green Guards and the publishing of a little Green Book containing his "thoughts" – had not even amused the students; it had simply disgusted them. The lack of any firm opposition coupled with the artificially developed "popularity" of Ayub had made the ruling class in Pakistan complacent and self-satisfied. Nothing, they felt, was strong enough to shatter their security, and they began to half believe the myths which they had constructed around themselves.

When the students of Rawalpindi emerged on the streets of the country's political-military capital in November 1968 to demonstrate against what was specifically a non-political grievance, not much attention was paid to them. The regime's initial reaction indicated quite clearly that they thought the demonstration could be crushed at will. It was difficult to imagine that this small beginning could lead to a major conflict between the people and the state. But when the objective conditions are ripe, even a small spark can light a flame which is difficult to extinguish. In this case the repression was completely counter-productive, and in combination with other factors it created a situation which led to a virtual student uprising. The fires of revolt had been lit and the only way to snuff them out was for the oligarchy to sacrifice the leader who had led it for the last ten years.

These ten years they had designated the "Decade of Development", and as far as the capitalists were concerned they certainly were the years during which properties were developed, fortunes amassed and the Ayub family emerged as one of the twenty richest families in the country. For the people of Pakistan they were ten years of darkness, oppression and increasing material poverty—and of intellectual poverty, the result of the rigorous political and cultural censorship imposed by the regime.

Unfortunately for the ruling clique, their leader was a mediocrity in every way (as a casual glance at his ghosted autobiography will confirm). He was completely lacking in political imagination, and even in the barrack-room horse sense which he was supposed to possess and which endeared him to the readers of the *Daily Telegraph*. Any sense he may once have possessed had been sucked out of him over the years by the abject sycophancy of his courtiers, who had succeeded in isolating him from the political realities of Pakistan. In the end the army had no option but to dump him. A few of his loyal bureaucrats tried to devise methods for salvaging him politically, but these ended in failure and did not have the backing of the army.

The thirty-three days which elapsed between Ayub's speech announcing his withdrawal from politics and the military take-over by General Yahya Khan saw the political processes of Pakistan in full play. The right-wing political forces and the pro-Moscow groupings were mobilized into a hurried united front to negotiate with Ayub at two successive conferences. These were known as the Round Table Conferences, a title obviously inspired by the conferences which took place in London during the 'thirties when the representatives of the Indian bourgeoisie negotiated India's political independence with the British ruling class. During these thirty-three hectic days the civilian representatives of the landowners and upper petit-bourgeoisie argued desperately to be allowed to participate in the running of the state, but their own differences and the predetermined decision of the army to take over power after Ayub frustrated them. The army was worried that a civilian government coming in the wake of a mass popular upsurge would be forced to make radical concessions; and also a civilian government posed a threat to the financial autonomy of the army, which had become a jealously guarded preserve. Therefore no civilian government could be tolerated immediately after Ayub.

I paid two visits to Pakistan in 1969. The first, in February, was on the invitation of student militants in West Pakistan; I spoke at meetings attended by students and workers, and observed first-hand the struggle which was taking place. Although Ayub had already made his retirement speech, the urban proletariat was continuing its strikes against the low wages and bad working and living conditions, thus demonstrating very clearly that it was the social system which was defective and had to be smashed and not simply one powerful individual. The atmosphere was extremely heartening and optimistic. Large meetings of workers openly attacked the capitalist and pro-imperialist structure in Pakistan, and every attack on the landlords was greeted with thunderous applause. The poetry of Habib Jalib (the Poet of the Revolution), who had been imprisoned many times by the dictatorship, was in great demand. It reflected the moods and aspirations of the masses engaged in struggle, and though effete critics attacked the literary merit of his poems they themselves stayed aloof from the struggle.

The fact that the masses felt that they, and only they, had brought down Ayub gave them a feeling of confidence that they could act in a similar way with any future regime which sought to oppress them. But they lacked an organization, and this made the army take-over on March 26th, 1969, a comparatively easy affair. After a historic struggle lasting over three months by the Pakistani students, workers and peasants, there had merely been a change of dictators and the Pakistan army had emerged clearly and unmistakably as the main defender of bourgeois law and feudal order in Pakistan.

However, there were some important differences between the Martial Law of 1958 and the take-over of 1969. Though the army was numerically much stronger in 1969, politically it was in a much weaker position and the second Martial Law was not feared as the first one had been. Even though the Martial Law regulations were in many instances exactly the same, the attitude of the masses was different.

Martial Law was first defied in East Pakistan in 1969 the day after it had been imposed: workers in Chittagong came out on strike, and work in the entire city came to a halt. True, the army arrested some trade-union leaders and left them on the streets after whipping them, but in some cases masses of workers surrounded army trucks and rescued those who had been arrested. Slogans daubed on many walls in East Pakistan read: "We oppose the second Punjabi occupation of Bengal." In North Bengal many peasants defied Martial Law by demonstrating and attacking police stations. In some cases arms and ammunition were liberated by the peasants. Despite the fact that no political party gave a lead, the workers in both East and West

Pakistan demonstrated their opposition to the new regime by ignoring its regulations and codes. The workers in Karachi came out on strike and defied the army to open fire and kill them, but in this instance the army gave way. In Quetta (Baluchistan) the coal miners' strike ended in bloodshed when at least two miners were shot dead by army units and many others injured. They had refused to call off their strike after Martial Law had been declared.

The East Pakistani student militants were also defying the new regime by holding semi-public meetings in their colleges. The revolutionary student leaders told their followers that the new government was a perpetuation of the old class rule, and warned students not to be deceived by the "flirtation with China", but to prepare for a continuation of the struggle (the new regime's "Leftist" Air Marshal Nur Khan had been sent to Peking where he had been welcomed by Chou En-lai, who had proposed a toast to "the health of His Excellency Yahya Khan, President of Pakistan"). Some student cadres had been arrested and whipped, but the regime was forced to release them after a few weeks. In addition, students had been allowed to hold public meetings to commemorate specific occasions, and East Pakistan's Mujibur Rehman (the Bengali equivalent of Chiang Kai-shek) was beginnings to demand "free and democratic elections".

The Yahya regime has been forced to make concessions on various crucial constitutional questions. The centralized structure of West Pakistan has been dismembered, and the provinces given back their original status. The demand of one man, one vote, has been accepted, and a general election on this basis promised for October 1970. Whether or not this election takes place depends on how the situation develops, but even if it does, although it will be an important step forward, it will not solve the basic problems which confront the Pakistani masses. These can only be solved by a socialist revolution, and for this the most important prerequisite is a revolutionary party capable of leading the masses to a seizure of state power. A revolutionary student leader of East Pakistan, Mahbubullah, expressed it to me in this way: "If there had been a revolutionary party we would have made a revolution in East Pakistan. Even now the objective conditions are very ripe ... Our task is to denounce all collaboration with the regime. Even if the Chinese government tells us that there is not a revolutionary situation we will disagree with them. We know there is a revolutionary situation and we will exploit it. We will not let our generation rot."

The lessons of the November 1968 uprising in Pakistan have undoubtedly been studied in detail by both the Pakistani ruling class and the U.S. State Department, which feeds it and keeps it alive. The oppressors have no doubt made the necessary preparations for dealing with the next wave of the revolutionary upsurge. It is necessary that the oppressed, too, learn the lessons and prepare.

TARIQ ALI

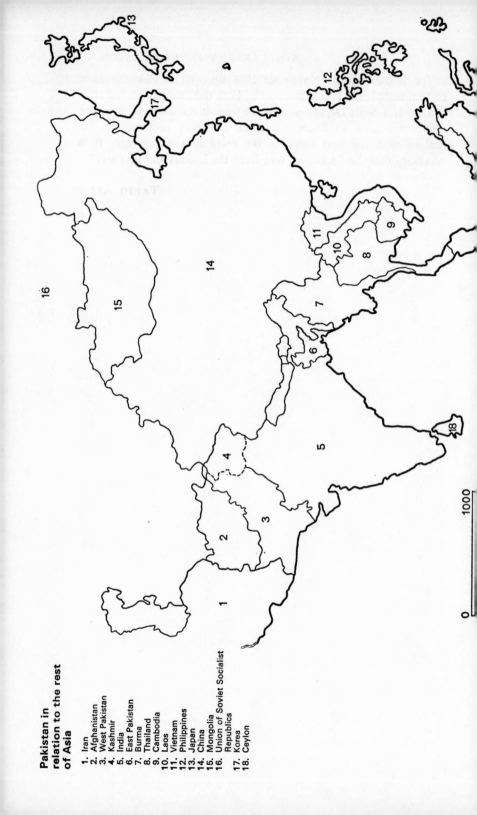

Pakistan in relation to the rest of Asia

1. Iran
2. Afghanistan
3. West Pakistan
4. Kashmir
5. India
6. East Pakistan
7. Burma
8. Thailand
9. Cambodia
10. Laos
11. Vietnam
12. Philippines
13. Japan
14. China
15. Mongolia
16. Union of Soviet Socialist Republics
17. Korea
18. Ceylon

0   1000

CHAPTER ONE

Parliamentary Façade: First Phase, 1947-53

> "Our endeavour should be to uphold in full force the (for us fortunate) separation which exists between the different religions and races, not to endeavour to amalgamate them. *Divide et impera* should be the principle of Indian government." Lieutenant-Colonel Coke, Commandant of Moradabad, 1860

> "When religion becomes the back-bone of reaction and anti-progressive forces seek refuge under its cloak, when religion becomes only a farce of particular dogmas and ceremonies and its inborn spirit of revolutionary change is dead, then such a religion becomes only a tool for perpetrating all the sins of injustice. When religion as the dominant creed of a particular society loses its fervour and revolutionary spirit of changing itself and changing others, then to vest such a religion with governmental powers is equivalent to placing dangerous authority in the hands of Reaction to be ultimately used against the people." Maulana Obeidullah Sindhi, radical religious leader

The Muslim landlords have a country

There are only two countries in the world today whose sole reason for existence is religion, and Pakistan is one of them.[1] After a referendum, the Indo-Pakistan sub-continent was divided on the basis of religion, the areas whose inhabitants were mostly Muslim being combined to form Pakistan. The North West Frontier Province, Sind and Baluchistan, became part of Pakistan; the Punjab was divided into two, East Punjab being part of India; and Bengal was split—this division provides the key to Pakistani politics.

The reasons for Partition are many and varied, and a proper explanation of them would require a lengthy analysis that is not, strictly speaking, relevant to my purpose in writing this book. But the geographical peculiarities of Pakistan are crucial to an understanding of Pakistani politics, and a glance at a map will at once reveal one of the most striking: the two parts of Pakistan are separated from each other by a thousand miles of Indian territory.

[1] The other country is of course Israel and though this analogy will undoubtedly annoy chauvinists in both countries it remains an historical fact.

The political implications of this unique geographical quirk will reverberate throughout this book; in fact the two parts of the country will have to be dealt with separately, so deep is the gulf between them. The political party which first put forward the demand for Pakistan was the Muslim League. It is difficult to assess whether the demand was initially meant as anything more than a means of putting pressure on the Indian Congress Party and on the British on behalf of the landed Muslim interests, and at a later stage on behalf of the rising Muslim bourgeoisie. At all events, in October 1906 seventy leading Muslims led by the Aga Khan[2] were granted an audience by the British Viceroy, Lord Minto, at his summer retreat in Simla. They carried with them a petition signed by "nobles, ministers of various states, great landowners, lawyers, merchants, and many others of His Majesty's Mahommedan subjects". It was clear that these groups were interested only in protecting their own class interests. They feared the competition of the non-Muslim bourgeoisie. "Lord Minto assured the delegation that he was entirely in accord with their case."[3] Of course he was. He jumped at the opportunity of using religion to divide the two groups who, if united, could pose a serious threat to British imperialism. Accordingly, in December 1906, several weeks after Lord Minto had given his blessing to the deputation, the All-India Muslim League was created.

Plainly, one of the reasons for the creation of the League was the pressure of British imperialism. A large number of those present at the founding conference belonged to landowning families from different parts of India, and their influence as poodles of British imperialism was exerted towards making the Muslim League adopt as its main objective: "To foster a sense of loyalty to the British government among the Muslims of India." It couldn't have been spelt out more clearly than that. A sprinkling of Muslim lawyers were also present; they concerned themselves with the interests of the Muslim middle classes and promised to "look after the political interests of Indian Muslims". The Muslim League was initially, therefore, an alliance of Muslim landlords and British civil servants, and in the first decade of its existence it was to remain a loyal upholder

[2] The Aga Khan was the leader of the powerful Ismaili community which was probably the richest group amongst Indian Muslims in industry and commerce. The Aga Khan's son, Prince Aly Khan, later became Pakistan's representative at the United Nations, though he was best known for his non-political exploits.

[3] Khalid bin Sayeed, *The Political System of Pakistan* (Oxford University Press, Pakistan Branch, 1967).

of British interests. Any fears that the middle-class elements in the League might gain preponderance were soon dispelled and the Governor of the United Provinces wrote to Lord Minto in 1910:

> I have felt frightened lest the lawyer party, mainly consisting of young and irresponsible persons, would attain a predominant position in the League, and that they might at some time coalesce with the advanced Hindu politicians against the government on one or more questions and later on rue the fact that they had done so. I think that the Aga Khan has put an effectual check to this, and that the League may be expected to be much more conservative and stable than it once promised to be.[4]

It was quite obvious that the British policy of "divide and rule" had fallen on fertile ground, and its pernicious effects were to be felt in the following years. In discussions with the Muslim leaders Lord Minto used to stress that the aim of Muslim political activities should be to combat the increasing economic power of the Hindus. The Aga Khan was only too pleased to agree and sent directives to League branches asking Muslims "to apply all their energy to furthering British prestige and instilling respect and affection for the British in the public mind".[5]

The feudal landlords continued to retain their grip on the Muslim League, but they realized full well that they would never be able to make the League a powerful political force; at least, not on their own. So they began to welcome members of the Muslim bourgeoisie – the lumpen-bourgeoisie of India. Though they could never win over anti-imperialist Muslim radicals of the calibre of Mahmud Hasan and Obeidullah Sindhi,[6] they managed to draw to their ranks some Muslim lawyers, liberal in training and constitutionalist in outlook. The

---

[4] Ibid.

[5] Gankovsky and Polonskaya, *A History of Pakistan* (Moscow, 1964).

[6] Mahmud Hasan and Obeidullah Sindhi were both religious leaders "consumed with an overpowering desire to end British rule". Hasan and his group established contact with various terrorist groupings consisting of Hindus and Sikhs to try and organize an uprising against British imperialism. British agents arrested Hasan's messenger and captured silk scrolls containing details of the uprising. The plan was that the Muslim masses should rise and overthrow the British at a prearranged signal and proclaim India a democratic republic. However, the lack of even the embryo of a revolutionary organization resulted in the conspirators' failure. They were arrested, and Mahmud Hasan was exiled to Malta.
The Muslim League had its counterpart in Hasan and Sindhi's radicalism – a fact which should induce those who hold that all Muslims were reactionary to change their minds. Hasan and Sindhi had their counterparts in the worker-priests of France and also in latter-day Latin America, where the slain guerrilla priest Camillo Torres had much in common with Obeidullah Sindhi.

most articulate and brilliant of these was Mohammed Ali Jinnah.

Unlike the other League leaders, Jinnah had no contact with the feudal landlords. The son of a businessman belonging to the Ismaili community, he received his legal training at Lincolns Inn in London and the first political party he joined was the Indian Congress. The only language he spoke fluently was English, the language used in the courts of bourgeois law where Jinnah soon acquired a brilliant reputation, and where he usually championed the interests of the business community with whom he was associated in Bombay. When he joined the Muslim League just before the First World War his reasons had nothing to do with religion; Jinnah was completely secular in outlook. He joined the League because the Congress was getting too "extreme": it was going beyond the limits prescribed by law, and Jinnah's constitutionalism could not tolerate this heresy. He soon became the most popular spokesman of the League, but at the same time remained a member of the Indian Congress.[7] Jinnah realized that the interests of the Muslim and Hindu propertied classes were basically the same; he worked hard for Congress-Muslim League unity and was described by a leading Congress leader as the "ambassador of Muslim-Hindu unity". It was Jinnah who encouraged Congress and League leaders to attend each other's annual conferences, which led to both organizations meeting in Lucknow in 1916 and concluding a Congress-League Pact which came to be known as the Lucknow Pact. The pact accepted the principle of separate electorates for Muslims, but, more important, it brought wider sections of Muslims into the movement against the British.

The euphoria did not last long. British policy, combined with Hindu and Muslim bigotry and an extremely shortsighted attitude on the part of the Hindu bourgeoisie, ensured that moves towards separatism would increase. Though the class interests of both Muslim and Hindu bourgeoisies were identical, the competitive struggle between the different groups became confused with religious and caste differences. The struggle for two states thus reflected the

[7] There is no contradiction here. Jinnah represented the bourgeoisie, which dominated the Indian Congress. A section of it was too unconstitutional for Jinnah's liking so he also joined the Muslim League, which was just beginning to welcome representatives of the Muslim business community. Jinnah could therefore retain his membership of both parties and still remain loyal to his class. Indian politics at this stage were clear cut and simple, unlike European politics with their elaborate façades.

uneven and combined development of two national bourgeoisies. In 1937 the Muslim League revised its elitist constitution and opened its doors to the petit-bourgeois and to the peasants. The latter never joined in any numbers, but the influx of the petit-bourgeois, while influencing the League towards independence, did so within a framework of a separate Muslim state. (Although the establishment of Pakistan was the final demand after the Congress leadership had clearly demonstrated that they were not interested in sharing political power, and after the Muslim desire for autonomy had been scorned by Congress intellectuals.) In provinces where there was a Muslim majority the League became powerful, and the Prime Ministers of the Punjab and Bengal[8] had to join the League themselves. Jinnah was prepared for an Independent India, but with safeguards for the Muslim minority and the right to secede guaranteed. The Hindu bourgeoisie refused to concede this, and as a result the independence movement was divided on communal grounds. The banner of Islam was thus raised and effectively used by Jinnah. The Muslim masses responded, and overnight the Muslim League found itself at the head of a mass movement.

With the exception of Jinnah the League leaders were mediocrities. They were forced to overcome their repugnance of mass movements and take part in limited civil disobedience. It is often said in Pakistan that the short period of struggle by the Muslim League against the British imperialists threw up leaders who had not really participated in the freedom movement but whose country was won for them by the autonomous action of Muslim peasants. The landlords, who were in the vanguard of the party, had nothing but contempt for these peasants.

Jinnah was the first to realize the low calibre of the leadership which would rule Pakistan after him: it reflected the low level of development of the Muslim bourgeoisie economically, and hence also politically. They were attracted to the idea of a separate Muslim state because it meant a territory where there would be no non-Muslim competition and where they could develop unhindered by Hindu commerce. For them all other avenues were closed. "Long live Pakistan" really meant "Long live free enterprise". The subsequent

---

[8] The Prime Minister of the Punjab was a Muslim, Sir Sikandar Hyat Khan, who had succeeded in holding together the province by a united front of Muslim, Hindu and Sikh landlords. In Bengal Fazlul Haq held sway, but both were forced to come to terms with the League.

economic pattern which emerged in Pakistan clearly justified the policy of the Muslim middle classes.

In other parts of the country local class and national contradictions played their part in the move towards Pakistan. For example, the Bengali peasant saw Pakistan as an end to his problems because most of the landlords were Hindus and the entire commerce of the province was in Hindu hands. In a letter to Lord Minto, the Lieutenant-Governor of East Bengal (now East Pakistan) reported: "In Mymensingh and in Sylhet the Hindu landlords are persecuting all Mahommedan tenants ... [because] they have given evidence in the Courts with respect to them."[9]

In other parts of what is now West Pakistan, class differences were distorted by reactionary League politicians and presented in such a way as to increase friction between the communities. In the Punjab the League leadership enlisted the Khaksars into their volunteer detachments. The Khaksars were founded in 1931 by Allama Mashriqi and were modelled on fascist lines with their own para-military organization. They consisted mainly of the lumpen-proletariat gathered from Lahore, Peshawar, Rawalpindi and other West Pakistani cities. The League was to receive an influx of radical new members when in 1942-6 it was inundated with Muslim members of the Communist Party of India.

Let us pause to see how the various groups in India lined up on the question of Pakistan. The attitudes of the Muslim League and Indian Congress are well known, though the pro-Pakistan attitude of right-wing Congress leaders is sometimes underestimated. The extreme right-wing Hindu Mahasaba, of course, supported the demand for Pakistan, but in much the same way as the fascists in the United States support the demand for a separate Black State inside the United States. The two groups whose policies should be considered in some detail are, first, the Indian Communist Party and, second, the orthodox Islamic groups.

The Indian Communists supported the demand for Pakistan on the grounds that each nationality had the right of self-determination. The Communist leaders had been released from their prison cells after Hitler attacked the Soviet Union, as they had agreed to support the war effort. Theoretically, and indeed in their public speeches, they were strong opponents of British imperialism, but in practice their efforts were devoted to pressuring Congress to cease the anti-British

[9] Khalid bin Sayeed, op. cit.

struggle and help the war effort. By enforcing this policy on the party as a whole, the Comintern destroyed what chances there were of the Indian Communists seizing the leadership of the anti-imperialist struggle. It was ironical that while Congress leaders were in prison and refusing to call off the anti-British struggle, the Indian Communists were moving about freely helping the British both militarily and politically. It was in this context that they put forward the line of Congress-League unity to unite and aid the war effort, and could best be fostered by accepting the demand for Pakistan. A crude distortion of Lenin on the national question was served up in the C.P.I. pamphlet entitled *Pakistan and National Unity*, in which Communist theoreticians confused religion with nationality and finally came up with a mixture advocating self-determination for all nationalities.

With this demand we have no quarrel. The right to self-determination is crucial and necessary, but the C.P.I.'s treatment of the question almost caused the disintegration of the Marxist cadres. Once again theory had nothing in common with practice.[10] The Indian Communist Party was from the very beginning a party of middle-class revolutionaries, and the major influence on a significant section of these "revolutionaries" was not Marx or Lenin or Trotsky, but Gandhi. The party was formed in 1921, but till 1934 it worked as part of the Congress and had no independent life. Instead of the Communists influencing Congress ideology the exact opposite happened, and many Communists remained in the Congress.

The party had become a strong force when in 1938 a large number of Indian revolutionaries were released from prison in a general amnesty. Many of them had been connected with the terrorist movements. They attempted to mobilize the peasantry and the working class and succeeded partially, but after the invasion of the Soviet Union they again became isolated from the mass. Their slogan was: "Freedom of India depends on unity of Congress and Muslim League"; in effect: Let the feudal lords and the bourgeoisie unite and win independence. This co-called revolutionary party did not visualize an independent role for itself in the Indian freedom movement. The most grotesque decision was to send its Muslim members to enter the ranks of the Muslim League. This resulted in many of the militants who were involved in working with the peasants

[10] As this particular phase of Communist politics is important for understanding the degeneration of the Communist movement in India I have included the Party document on Pakistan, *On Pakistan and National Unity* as Appendix I.

joining their local League branches and rapidly becoming Branch Secretaries. The President of the branch was always the local land-lord, so small wonder that the peasants stopped trusting them.[11] Also because of the extremely low theoretical level of the Indian C.P. many of its Muslim cadres found themselves quite at home in the League. Their class background was a further link, and many of these "mili-tants" never came back from the League. Some of them became the leading forces of reaction, and because of their past experience knew exactly how to deal with, in the words of a former militant, "Com-munists, fellow-travellers and suchlike". The C.P.I. had entered the Muslim League in order to strengthen the bourgeois faction in the League against the feudal landlords, a plan perfectly in keeping with Stalin's theory of revolution by stages. Instead they had lost some of their best cadres. There was opposition to this inside the Indian Communist Party, but it was soon suppressed and dealt with on the advice of the Comintern, which was experienced in such matters.

The religious leaders of Indian Muslims were, by and large, opposed to the very idea of Pakistan as being alien to Islam, which, they argued, was a universal religion whose adherents should aim to convert the entire world and not to build enclaves. There could be no Islam in one country. There were a number of different schools of Muslim orthodoxy in India. The Aligarh school was based at the University of Aligarh, the first Muslim University in India. This school was led by Sir Sayyid Ahmed, an arch-reactionary whose aim it was to make the Indian Muslims appreciate the benevolence of British imperialism. In the initial stages he succeeded, but the strength of the nationalist movement was too much for his followers to resist. His influence, however, lingered on. Then there was the Deoband, a Muslim seminary which achieved great prominence under the direc-tion of Mahmud Hasan and established links with Muslim radicalism throughout the Arab world. One of its leading scholars, Obeidullah Sindhi, developed radical theories of Islamic socialism. However, it also contained many orthodox Muslims. Thirdly, there was the Jamiyyat al-Ulema-i-Hind, a religious-political movement set up by Muslim divines in 1919. It believed in "composite Indian nationalism". The last two bodies were strong opponents of the theories of separatism and of the "loyalist" school which argued that

[11] For instance in Dacca a local militant, Shamsudin, became Secretary of the Dacca Muslim League. The President was the Nawab of Dacca, who was also the richest Muslim landlord in the area!

Muslims had to be loyal to the British. The "composite nationalists" argued that Islam did not reconcile itself to national slavery and that is what being ruled by British imperialism meant.

> If non-Muslims occupy a Muslim land, which India was under the Mughals, it becomes the obligatory duty of Muslims of that land and of others to strive and regain independence. This *jihad* in India has to be non-violent: and it can be fought only in alliance with the Hindus, who constitute the majority community. In independence thus gained Muslims and non-Muslims would be co-partners in creating a society and administration which, though not modelled entirely on the conception of an Islamic state, would comprise effective and influential Islamic elements in it.[12]

This was the view of some of the most respected and authoritative Muslim divines in India. These same views would have been considered heresy in 1947 when Pakistan was established.

In 1941 Abul-Ala Maududi set up the Jamaat-i-Islami with the intention of opposing the secular nationalism of the Deoband group. Maududi was an orthodox fundamentalist in religious matters. He viciously attacked Jinnah and the Muslim League, whom he accused of being motivated not by pure religious beliefs but by the "worldly socio-economic interests of the Muslims".

> Not a single leader of the Muslim League from Jinnah himself to the rank and file has an Islamic mentality or Islamic habits of thought, or looks at political and social problems from the Islamic viewpoint ... Their ignoble role is to safeguard merely the material interests of Indian Muslims by every possible manœuvre or trickery.[13]

He was opposed to Pakistan; there had to be a Muslim world or nothing.[14] His attitude was that of a Menshevik within the confines of Islam.

Only a few religious leaders supported Pakistan. Shabbir Ahmed Usmani was their ablest spokesman and he split from the Jamiyyat

[12] Aziz Ahmed, *Islamic Modernism in India and Pakistan, 1857–1964* (Oxford, 1967).

[13] Ibid., quoting Maududi.

[14] The debate on what exactly an Islamic state is continues to this very day and all the bourgeois parties in Pakistan take part. We shall touch on this debate in later chapters—but only briefly: we are nearing the twenty-first century, and man has reached the moon.

3

al-Ulema-i-Hind, which was pro-Congress, and founded a splinter organization called the Jamiyyat al-Ulema-i-Islam, which supported the demand for Pakistan. In Pakistani politics today this group represents the progressive section of the religious groups, and Maududi the extreme right wing.

The struggle for Pakistan continued unabated, and the man who came to represent Pakistan in the eyes of the world was Jinnah, now referred to as Quaid-i-Azam (The Great Leader) by his followers. After the war there was undoubtedly a pre-revolutionary situation throughout India. The naval mutiny of February 1946 symbolized the new spirit of the Indian revolution, and the British authorities must have been reminded of the *Potemkin* and the *Aurora*. The spectre of revolution haunted them, and it also began to haunt the leaderships of the Muslim League and the Congress. The rebellion matured in Bombay and spread to Madras and Karachi. Sailors hoisted the red flag on their ships with the slogan: "Inquilab Zindabad" (Long live revolution). They appealed to the Congress and Muslim League but received neither moral support nor any practical help. The sailors elected a Central Naval Strike Committee and maintained a model form of discipline.

The British, for once caught off balance, resorted to repression and dispatched naval and military units to Bombay and Karachi; but Indian soldiers refused to open fire and British troops had to do their dirty work themselves. On February 21st, 1946, the British Admiral Godfrey threatened to destroy the whole navy unless the strike was called off. The Strike Committee responded by calling on the civilian population to strike in sympathy. The Congress leaders refused to endorse this call for strike action, but the Communist Party, recovering from its initial surprise, supported it and the workers of Bombay held a general strike in Bombay on February 22nd. British imperialism decided on a massacre. According to the official figures 250 people were killed between February 21st and February 23rd. The unofficial figures were five times as high. A British officer described the scene thus:

> ... There were a good many people in the street though they did not make up a crowd, much less a mob. *On the advice of the Communist Party none of them was armed,* not even with sticks or stones [italics mine].

Suddenly, without the slightest warning, an open lorry loaded with British troops, drove across Elphinstone Road with rifles and one Bren gun. As the people ran into the doorways, myself included, the troops turned their fire in that direction. Twenty people were wounded and four killed ...

The trade-unions had called for a general strike in support of the naval ratings. The strike was 100 per cent effective in textile mills, factories and railway workshops. Someone in high position had decided to "teach the wogs a lesson". So armed patrols in full battle-order moved about the streets in lorries firing at random ... Later, on DeLisle Road, I saw the troops enter the slum tenements and fire on people in their own houses ... [15]

On February 23rd the Congress and Muslim League leaders, upset by this revolutionary manifestation of working-class unity, advised the naval ratings to surrender and a Congress leader, the reactionary Vallabhai Patel, promised that "Congress will do its level best to see that there is no victimization." Feeling isolated, and with no lead from the Communist Party, the Naval Strike Committee decided to surrender. Within two days the leaders were arrested. Their last statement was, "We surrender to India and not to Britain."

Little did they know how true this was: that the Indian bourgeoisie would see to it that none of the leaders of the revolt were employed by the Indian navy. The naval strike and its effects revealed quite clearly that the armed forces were with the people. A revolutionary leadership could have posed the question of seizing state power, but none existed. The Communist Party, despite opinion in its rank and file, was too closely integrated with Congress and the Muslim League, and the theory of revolution by stages meant that this *had* to be merely a struggle for political independence from Britain. The feudal and bourgeois leaderships of the League and the Congress thus aligned themselves with British imperialism against the masses. The Congress President, Maulana Azad, stated that strikes were "out of place" and Gandhi was worried by the "unholy combination" of Hindus and Muslims in opposition to his creed of non-violence. In his newspaper *Harijan* he wrote on April 7th, 1946, that accepting this combination would have meant "delivering Indian over to the rabble. I would not want to live up to 125 to witness that consummation. I would rather perish in flames."

The situation in India prompted the British Labour government to

[15] Quoted in R. P. Dutt, *India Today* (London, 1940).

accelerate independence. When it became clear that there could be no League-Congress agreement on a united India it was decided to accept Pakistan as a separate state. On August 14th, 1947, Pakistan became independent and Mohammed Ali Jinnah became its first Governor-General, with virtually unlimited powers.

There can be no doubt that Jinnah represented the progressive wing of the Muslim League and he was in a minority. As long as he lived this was irrelevant, as no one dared question his authority, but the landlords could afford to wait. Jinnah was ill, and could not live long. After his death the mask could come off completely: the Muslim landlords would have a country. But what of the millions of Muslim workers and peasants who were promised that Pakistan would be a "heaven"? What of the millions of refugees who left their homes in India to come to the Promised Land? For the feudal barons this "riff-raff" were now superfluous. There is no established record of how many Muslims, Hindus and Sikhs died during the Partition of the sub-continent, slaughtered in a frenzied and senseless carnage: a massacre which neither side seemed able or willing to prevent. The protection guaranteed by the two armies turned out to be a complete farce. A Muslim officer named Ayub, of whom we will hear more later, was responsible for a time for the protection of Muslim refugees. He did not acquit himself very well and was almost sacked from the army.

Political groups

> The system of political parties in Pakistan bears little resemblance to that of most other democratic countries. Politics has begun at the top. Pakistan has neither a two-party system, in which the political struggle is waged between fairly stable groups, one of which is in office and the other in opposition, nor a multi-party system, in which clear differences of programme or ideology separate a variety of opponents. In Pakistan politics is made up of a large number of leading persons who, with their political dependents, form loose agreements to achieve power and to maintain it. Consequently rigid adherence to a policy or a measure is likely to make a politician less available for office. Those who lack fixed ideas but who control legislators, money or influence have tended to prosper in political life.
>
> Keith Callard[16]

That Mohammed Ali Jinnah was largely responsible for the establishment of Pakistan was recognized by all his subordinates. It

[16] *Pakistan: A Political Study* (London, 1957).

is possible that had Jinnah lived the country would have proceeded calmly on the path of a constitutional govenment, based on adult franchise and the parliamentary system. But even if this had happened, judging by the example of India, Pakistan would still have been in the same economic predicament as it is today.

Jinnah's death in 1948, just over a year after independence, deprived the Muslim League of the only leader who could have held it together. His illness prevented him from playing an active role in Pakistani politics, but on one thing he was quite clear: Pakistan should be a secular state. He argued that there were no longer Muslims, Hindus or Christians in Pakistan, only Pakistanis, and there is evidence to suggest that he was thinking on these lines with regard to Pakistan's first Constitution.

Pakistan was a largely agricultural country at the time of Partition, and had inherited from the British a feudal, colonial economy. Forty-one per cent of the industrial establishments were devoted to the processing of agricultural raw material and were in seasonal operation. Out of the 1,414 industrial enterprises which Pakistan inherited only 314 were situated in East Pakistan. Pakistan's economy was in the grip of Indian capitalists (Tata, Birla and Dalmia) and British imperialism, the latter holding dominating interests in trade and in the credit system of Pakistan.[17] This control enabled Britain to determine the pattern of economic growth in Pakistan by preserving it as an agrarian and raw-material-producing country tied closely to the metropolitan country by extensive economic links. A large proportion of the population lived on the land, where agriculture was dominated by feudal property relations. The land was tilled in the most primitive manner by peasants who were exploited by cruel and tyrannical landlords. Six thousand landlords in West Pakistan owned more land than the 3·3 million peasant households. In this situation it was hardly surprising that agriculture was stagnating.

[17] "Ninety per cent of the banking capital of Pakistan was in the hands of British banks, such as Lloyds and Grindlay's Bank. Roberts, Gill & Co., Imperial Tobacco and other British firms controlled over eighty per cent of Pakistan's import ... The insurance business was also dominated by British capital ... Pakistan's holdings of sterling in London and the organization of currency control within the sterling area, of which Pakistan was a member, restricted the country's opportunities of developing economic relations with states outside the sterling area, and helped to uphold British influence." Gankovsky and Polonskaya, op. cit.

But to return to the state of the Muslim League: its leaders acted in the belief that Pakistan was destined to be a one-party state, and that that one party was the Muslim League. While Jinnah was alive this was a fair assumption, though he himself was disgusted by the bickerings and the scramble for power which disfigured the League leadership in the Punjab and in other provinces. The Communists and progressives who had joined the League were adept at writing manifestoes, but even this radicalism on paper became too much for the League leadership. The Manifesto of the Punjab Muslim League was written by a well-known Indian Communist lawyer, Daniyal Latifi, and contained large sections suggesting drastic land reforms, nationalization of public utilities, progressive taxation, public control of private industry and other left-wing social-democratic measures. But this was utopianism gone mad. To expect a party with a strong feudal base to carry out these demands reflected a crude idealism.

The progressive elements inside the League were either amalgamated or were forced by circumstances to leave the League. Once Jinnah was dead, the landowners who represented the largest grouping on the Muslim League National Council were unfettered.[18] He had represented the only barrier to their unmitigated greed for wealth and political power. A well-known Sindhi leader, G. M. Syed, expressed his disgust at the League leadership in no uncertain terms. Bitterly attacking the entire feudal structure of Sind, where the League leaders branded every progressive idea as "un-Islamic",[19] he wrote:

> Do not forget also that Islamic society actually in existence is that in which the religious head is an ignorant Mullah, the spiritual leader an immoral Pir, political guide a power intoxi-

[18] Sayeed, op. cit.: "Out of a total membership of 503 members, there were as many as 163 landlords. Proportionately, Sind's share was the highest in the sense that out of twenty-five members in the Council, fifteen were landlords ... The next largest group was lawyers, about 145 in number.'

[19] The word "un-Islamic" has the same connotation in Pakistani politics as the word "un-American" in the politics of the United States. Both represent a neo-fascist, McCarthyite trend and both words are used when political "argument" fails. In Pakistan even today the word is used fairly often and the regime of General Yahya Khan "legalized" the concept by establishing a Special Martial Law regulation to deal with those who indulged in "un-Islamic activities". In September 1969 some of the most highly respected lecturers and professors were dismissed from their teaching posts because of "un-Islamic" activities. The dismissals could only have taken place under the cover of Martial Law as in normal conditions the students would have come out on strike.

cated feudal landlord and whose helpless members are subjected to all worldly forces of money and influence ... their cry of "Islam is in Danger" became a cloak for dark deeds and reactionary moves, complacency and tyranny ... Such is the extent to which mockery can be made of Islam in these days of capitalist subterfuge and commercialized politics.[20]

In the North West Frontier Province the Muslim League was led by landlords and tribal leaders and also by merchants and contractors associated with British firms and rapidly getting richer. The Nawabs of Hoti, Teri and Tank were names which disgusted every nationalist-minded Pathan. They were well known as the men who had collaborated with the British to crush the nationalists. Other leaders included Abdula Latif (an army contractor), Shah Pasand (responsible for recruiting Pathans to the police and army) and Khan Abdul Qayyum Khan, a lawyer who was later to distinguish himself by ordering the massacre of Pathan peasants and workers and who, after the establishment of Pakistan, was to become Chief Minister of the North West Frontier Province.

In Baluchistan a feudal system prevailed; tribal leaders, who were all-powerful in their different localities, were consulted when the wishes of the people had to be ascertained. The system of "tribal consultation" begun by the British in all their colonial territories was taken over by the Central government of Pakistan. A national movement existed in Baluchistan which demanded complete provincial autonomy and an equality of opportunity for Baluchis as far as official nominations were concerned. The Baluchis who were prominent in the national movement also demanded an end to the cultural and economic backwardness to which British colonialism had consigned them. Like many others they, too, thought that the establishment of Pakistan would be an end to their problems. Like many others they, too, were wrong.

In the princely states of Dir, Chitral and Swat, which were ruled directly by their respective "royal families", slavery was still legal and the royal chieftains ruled with an iron hand: the number of political prisoners they tortured and the number of peasants they killed is still unknown.[21]

[20] G. M. Syed, op. cit., pp. 216–18.
[21] In August 1969 the Martial Law regime decided at long last to "abolish" these slave-states as a gesture to liberal public opinion. Their rulers were demoted and political changes carried out, but the social structure remains the same.

West Pakistan was in the grip of the landlords, and to expect these robber barons to become Robin Hoods was sheer utopianism on the part of the left. The landlords' main aim would obviously be to preserve the existing system of feudal property relations. The Muslim bourgeoisie, which was extremely weak, could not hope to challenge them in the initial post-Partition period. In the Punjab, for instance, the Muslim League government displayed an extraordinary sense of class-consciousness when they issued a directive making it a crime for a tenant to read in "public or in private" the Muslim League manifesto of 1944 which, as we noted earlier, was drafted by a Communist and contained quite a few radical ideas. The punishment for a peasant caught in the act was ejection from the land he tilled by his local landlord. In brief, the tenant was told: Either you support your local landlord or out you go.

During the first few years the Pakistani bourgeoisie was represented by Muslim businessmen who had left their homes in India after Partition and settled in Karachi. They were more experienced than their native counterparts in West Pakistan, but because they did not yet feel fully secure and were still developing their roots in West Pakistan, they sided with the landlords and preferred to keep out of politics. They concerned themselves mostly with foreign trade, where they collaborated with British firms, and the easy profits they made discouraged them from capital investment. A further barrier to investment was the refusal of British banks to advance long-term loans on credit which would have advanced the industrialization of the country. Accordingly, the first measure advocated by the bourgeoisie was to bring the transactions of foreign banks under the control of the State Bank of Pakistan, and early in 1950 a tariffs commission was set up which imposed protectionist duties and implemented various other measures to safeguard Pakistani industry and industrialists.

The importance of import and export licences in the development of the Pakistani bourgeoisie should not be underestimated; these licences became one of the privileges bestowed on loyal supporters by successive Pakistani governments. The role of the civil servants also became much more insidious because in cases where the government Ministers were dismissed or governments were sacked, the economic power remained with the civil servant. In many cases civil service intrigues even led to the fall of a government or the dismissal of a particular minister.

The reactionary policies of the Muslim League, defended so aggressively and with so much self-confidence by some of its brasher leaders, led to a situation where the less reactionary and progressive members began to leave the party. Mian Iftikharudin, a well-known left-wing leader who was close to the Communist Party, resigned as Minister for Refugees and Rehabilitation in the Punjab government when they rejected his suggestion that Muslim refugees from India should be housed on the estates of the landlords, who should be compelled to give up some of their land. He set up a new, radical party called the Azad (Free) Pakistan Party. Opposition came also from the Awami (People's) League, which had been set up in East Bengal by H. S. Suhrawardy, and the Jinnah Awami League, set up by the Khan of Mamdot, a rich landlord who had lost out in a faction fight with other landlords in the Muslim League, and had subsequently been removed as Chief Minister of the Punjab in 1949.

In the Punjab election of 1951 the Muslim League retained control by winning 52·0 per cent of the votes. The largest opposition group was the Jinnah Awami League, with 18·3 per cent. Mian Iftikharudin's Azad Pakistan Party won only two per cent of the total vote. However, if we consider that the bulk of the population lived in the countryside, which was completely under the thumb of the landlords who were by and large supporters of the Muslim League, the result is not surprising. In the cities the civil servants saw to it that League candidates were elected, but even their powers of intimidation could not prevent the Jinnah Awami League from spending enough money to buy five seats out of twelve in the capital city of Lahore. The Communist candidate was a trade-union leader, Mirza Ibrahim, and his opponent was a Muslim League yes-man named Ahmed Saeed Kirmani.[22] Mirza Ibrahim was contesting in the constituency where the railway workers amongst whom he worked were in the majority, and despite the fact that he had been conveniently arrested before the election it was clear that he would win. However, the civil servant supervising the counting[23] disqualified a large number of

[22] Kirmani later became a provincial Minister for Labour under the Ayub regime and Mirza Ibrahim (now a pro-Peking supporter) accompanied him to address a railway-workers' meeting during the rail strike of 1966. Mirza appealed to workers to give him a hearing. History plays strange tricks on us all.

[23] The civil servant involved was the Deputy Commissioner of Lahore, S. S. Jafri. The election was known in the coffee and tea houses of Lahore as 'Jafri's election'. Mr Jafri's climb to the top in the civil service of Pakistan is part of another story and another book.

votes cast for Mirza Ibrahim on the grounds that they were dirty. The railway workers could not afford to clean their hands with perfumed soap before they came to vote. And so Kirmani was elected. This was one, typical, example of how the landlords fought an election. In the countryside these subtle manœuvrings were not needed, and brute force or the threat of it was sufficient.

In the other provinces of West Pakistan the elections were also won by the Muslim League. It is not necessary to describe in detail the corruption and intimidation of these "elections" in the North West Frontier Province and in Sind. Suffice it to say that the League remained in office. But in East Bengal the story was to be different.

The Left in West Pakistan

The Partition of the Indo-Pakistan sub-continent resulted in the dislocation of many of the Communist cadres in what was to be designated West Pakistan. A large proportion of Communists in West Pakistan had been Hindus and Sikhs,[24] and their departure for India left West Pakistan depleted overnight. Many of them had been involved in the leadership of the C.P.I. in this area, but even more significant, most of the cadres active in the trade unions and the peasant committees had been forced to leave as well. This gap had somehow to be filled, and it was clear that it could not be filled all at once; there would have to be a slow and steady process of building up new cadres.

It was only rational to assume that once the Communist Party of India had accepted the fact that it had to support the creation of Pakistan some sort of a perspective for Pakistani Communists would be planned. This was not done. Instead of instructing its contacts and members to build the Party, the Communist Party of Pakistan was set up by a decision of the C.P.I. in 1948 and a leadership was sent from the Indian Party to "lead the movement in Pakistan". It was a classic Stalinist operation culled from the textbooks of the Comintern. Thus the general thesis regarding political parties in Pakistan, namely, that they were established from the top, applies equally well to the C.P.P.

[24] There had been a strong terrorist movement in the Punjab under the leadership of the Sikhs, symbolized by the heroism of Bhagat Singh. Many of the Sikhs who joined the C.P.I. had received their political education in the terrorist milieu.

The first General Secretary of the C.P.P. was a well-known Indian Communist leader, Sajjad Zaheer, who came from a notable Muslim feudal family of the United Provinces in India. He was a respected poet and critic of Urdu literature, but, alas, his commanding position in the realm of Urdu literature far surpassed his grasp of those organizing abilities so necessary in constructing a political party. The perspectives of the C.P.P. were essentially reformist.[25] Yet they were forced into adventurism by the "Left turn" taken by the C.P.I. in 1948-9.

Building a revolutionary movement virtually from scratch in a semi-feudal environment is by no means an easy task. It requires enormous patience and a disciplined, revolutionary leadership. This the C.P.P. could not provide. The leadership was faced with a contradiction which they could never resolve: their reformist perspectives were hampered by the fact that they called themselves the Communist Party of Pakistan. They insisted that they were struggling for bourgeois democracy and bourgeois democratic rights, and they were telling the truth. Their enemies, however, refused to believe them, and they were caught in a web of their own making. They looked for short cuts to get out of it, but chose to try in collusion with certain groups in the army. Putschism could not provide an answer; in fact it proved to be counter-productive. The role of the C.P.P. is in itself insignificant. In a conversation with me in September 1969 in London, Sajjad Zaheer admitted that the membership had never been higher than two hundred (it was probably a great deal less). However, at least the C.P.P. existed, and this alone was an important fact.

It was unfortunate that the C.P.P. could not even operate as a successful reformist group, and doubly unfortunate that there was no organized revolutionary cadre in West Pakistan; the economic situation was such that even a minimum amount of reasoned planning could have led to the development of an influential trade-union network. The economic dislocation resulting from the Partition of the sub-continent had left a large army of unemployed in the cities of West Pakistan, and now that there was a border to cross they could

[25] In so far, of course, that they can be said to have any perspectives. It was not easy to find a manifesto of the Communist Party of Pakistan. Readers should understand that when I refer to the C.P.P. I am discussing its existence, numbers, etc. in West Pakistan. The party in East Pakistan had virtually no contact with its West Pakistani counterpart and though Sajjad Zaheer was nominated to be the Secretary of the C.P.P. his writ did not and could not run to East Pakistan.

not move freely to areas where there was a possibility of work.[26] Neither the C.P.P. nor the Azad Pakistan Party could organize and defend the class interests of the workers — employed or unemployed.

The Azad Pakistan Party was formed because a number of progressives decided that they could not stay on in the Muslim League. As we have seen, they were led by Mian Iftikharudin, the founder and spokesman of the new party. He was a leading landlord of the Punjab, but was in favour of drastic land reform and other radical measures. In the years to come his voice was the only one in Parliament to speak on behalf of the oppressed, but Mian Iftikharudin was on his own, and he was a social-democrat. The Azad Pakistan Party made some progress, but in an isolated and disjointed fashion, and it was later merged with various other groups which called themselves the National Awami Party.

Undoubtedly, Mian Iftikharudin's greatest contribution to Pakistani politics was Progressive Papers Limited. This was a chain of radical newspapers, including the *Pakistan Times, Imroze* and *Lail-o-Nahar*. The *Times* and *Imroze* made rapid progress, the former becoming the largest-circulation English daily in the country, the latter pioneering new techniques in Urdu journalism and becoming immensely popular. This Company employed known radical journalists and became the strongest left-wing force in the country. The newspapers were miles ahead of their readership, and their role in radicalizing sections of the petit-bourgeoisie is incalculable. But although they played an important role in the vanguard in Pakistan, those who controlled them were never able to develop an organizational base which could utilize them. This was a major weakness. The papers became an end in themselves.

The 1951 Rawalpindi "Conspiracy Case" was used as an excuse to start an anti-leftist witch-hunt. Most commentators on Pakistani

---

[26] *Pakistan Statistical Year Book*, 1955 (Karachi, 1956) p. 182. The number of skilled and unskilled workers topped the six million mark. But in previous years almost as many had been unemployed, particularly the artisans and the workers of small-scale industries, as production virtually came to a halt in the years following Partition. The railway workers comprised the largest single trade union. In 1947–8, owing to the dislocation, unemployment among the railway workers increased sharply and even the Pakistan Finance Minister admitted that "there are more than 2,000 workers in the railway who are redundant." But the real figure was at least ten times larger. The huge numbers of unemployed, together with the growth of the agrarian population, kept wages at an extremely low level, and though businessmen were forced to increase the wages of skilled workers even the increase only amounted to a subsistence wage.

politics claim that "not enough is known of the case", but they may not have made allowance for the fact that there was nothing much to know in the first place. The Rawalpindi "conspiracy" was bungled from the very start. The mastermind was Major-General Akbar Khan, Chief-of-Staff of the Pakistan army. Akbar had fought in the war to "liberate" Kashmir and felt that he had been betrayed by the political leadership. He was considered to be progressive, a pre-Nasserite army radical, and the officers who supported him were a mixed bag ranging from neo-fascists to national chauvinists. The tiny Communist Party of Pakistan also got embroiled in this mess. Sajjad Zaheer told me that he had met Akbar at a cocktail party, and the general had broached the subject and "requested help" to draft manifestoes and a possible plan of action. The C.P.P. leadership accepted the offer and participated in various meetings with army officers. Eventually it was decided to shelve the plan for some time, but a conspirator, fearing that the truth might be revealed at a later stage, turned informer and the "conspiracy" was unveiled. The army officers and Communist leaders involved were arrested.

It soon became clear that very little had in fact been planned, though they had undoubtedly discussed the allocation of ministries, and had drawn up a list of those who had to be shot — including the Commander-in-Chief of the army, who was none other than Ayub Khan. The amateurishness of the "conspirators" ensured that they were given light sentences, but as a result of the disclosures the government later banned the Communist Party and purged a number of army officers who had "doubtful antecedents". General Ayub was extremely disturbed by the conspiracy. The future military dictator wrote in his memoirs:

> The whole affair came as a great shock to me and to all right-thinking people in the army. The prestige of the army had received a serious blow. *The army had inherited a great tradition of loyalty, sense of duty, patriotism, and complete subordination to civil authority* ... I shudder to think what would have happened to the country and the army if the conspiracy had succeeded ... [27]

It seems that General Akbar's mistake was that he acted before his time. If he had waited another seven years things could have been different.

[27]Italics mine. From Mohammed Ayub Khan, *Friends Not Masters—A Political Autobiography* (Oxford, 1967).

Many of the members of the banned C.P.P. joined the Azad Pakistan Party, while others remained active in the trade unions; but from now on they were to submerge their identity as Communists and work inside "progressive parties". The Pakistani Communists had no historical sense. They had not learnt a single lesson from the experiences of the C.P.I., first with the Congress and later with the Muslim League. They had deliberately consigned themselves to the reformist dustbin.

The economic situation in West Pakistan was appalling. People were literally dying of starvation or were resorting to desperate measures to stay alive. The *Pakistan Times*, commenting editorially, informed the public that "an unemployed worker in Jhelum was driven to sell his son for the paltry sum of twenty-two rupees [approximately two pounds] in order to pay off a loan incurred to keep himself and his family alive." It continued:

> If we remember the not infrequent Press reports of suicides or other inhuman crimes, committed by men and women made desperate by hunger, and also that only a small percentage of such cases is reported, a grim picture emerges of what the present state of Pakistan's economic affairs means for a large section of our people.[28]

It was a grim picture indeed. The Muslim League was in a state of disarray and disintegration throughout West Pakistan. The bourgeois opposition parties were more interested in power than politics and were completely unable to take advantage of the Muslim League's failure. And there was no revolutionary socialist force in the province to give a lead and speak unequivocally on behalf of the workers and peasants of Pakistan. Things were to continue in much the same way for the next decade.

East Pakistan

East Pakistan, or East Bengal, is completely unlike the western part of the country: it has a different cultural tradition, a live and vigorous revolutionary nationalist background and, most important of all, a different language. Geographically it has more in common with South-East Asia than with West Pakistan, and at the time of Partition economic development was much further advanced in

[28] *Pakistan Times*, July 22nd, 1953.

Bengal than in West Pakistan, where key areas were still under tribal control. These differences are emphasized by the fact that it is physically separated from West Pakistan by one thousand miles of Indian territory.

The only common link between East and West Pakistan is religion, and in Chapter 5 we will discuss how this particular bond faded into insignificance beside a succession of momentous political and economic events. The other factors which supposedly unite the two parts of the country are the English language and Pakistan International Airlines; but they are relevant only to the military-bureaucratic interests, and completely bypass the needs of the toiling masses in both East and West Pakistan.

The problem facing the Muslim League was how to keep the two parts of the country together. The majority of the people of Pakistan were Bengalis, and the refusal of the Muslim League politicians and the bureaucracy to recognize this constituted the most crucial electoral problem for Pakistani politicians. From the very start the civil service of Pakistan, led by bureaucrats trained by British imperialism to protect and safeguard British interests, came to the fore. They had been taught by the British to be disdainful of politicians, especially nationalist politicians, and the only Pakistani leader capable of overruling them was Jinnah. But his ill health made impossible any meaningful exercise of political power. Chowdhuri Mohammed Ali, the first boss of the Pakistani bureaucracy, and Aziz Ahmed, appointed the Chief Secretary of East Bengal, virtually dominated the Muslim League politicians and made the crucial decisions.

Though Pakistani politics were based on the "Westminster" model, and the form of government was technically described as a parliamentary democracy, this was a mere façade and not a very carefully constructed one at that. The members of the Constituent Assembly had been elected before the establishment of Pakistan, and most of them were aware that in a new election they might not retain their seats because they lacked a feudal base, and could not be certain of enough votes in the cities where large amounts of money were required for campaigning and for the inevitable bribery. Also, the fact that Jinnah had decided to become Governor-General instead of Prime Minister did not exactly help the cause of "parliamentary democracy". When it became clear that even this completely unrepresentative Constituent Assembly was virtually powerless in the face of Jinnah and the bureaucracy, it became a centre of intrigue and the scene of constant bickering over the appointment of ministers and ambassadors. Relations between Pakistan's first Prime Minister, Liaquat Ali Khan, and the Governor-General also remained strained throughout the last few months of Jinnah's life.

In East Pakistan the leader of the Muslim League was Sir Khwaja Nazimuddin, knighted for his services to the British raj, and a leading landowner in East Bengal. He also became the first Chief Minister of East Bengal. Nazimuddin was a weak man, not very intelligent and easily manipulated. Thus as far as the non-Bengali politicians were concerned he was an ideal person to deal with. His brother Khwaja Shahabudin was supposed to be one of his main advisers.[29]

The first signs of unrest in East Bengal appeared only a few months after Partition, and were provoked by the decision to impose Urdu as the official "national language" of Pakistan. The census of 1951 showed that Urdu was the mother tongue of only 2·4 million citizens in Pakistan, which constituted 3·3 per cent of the population, and that only 7·3 per cent of the total population could speak Urdu at all. Each province in West Pakistan spoke its own language, and in East Pakistan the language was Bengali. On the basis of population alone Bengali should have been the national language, but this was quite clearly a ludicrous idea and no Bengali nationalist proposed it seriously. What they did demand was that Bengali should be one of the two state languages. This the Central government in Karachi refused to accept. Bengali members of the Constituent Assembly were not allowed to speak in Bengali, and when a protest was made the country's first Prime Minister replied: "Pakistan is a Muslim State and it must have as its *lingua franca* the language of the Muslim nation ... It is necessary for a nation to have one language and that language can only be Urdu and no other language."

The innuendo that Bengali was a non-Muslim or anti-Muslim language was exploited to the full by large sections of the ruling class who, of course, just happened to be non-Bengalis. In February 1948 agitation in favour of Bengali spread throughout East Bengal. Students were in the vanguard, but they were supported by other sections of Bengali society. The students set up an Action Com-

[29] Shahabudin later became a Cabinet Minister in Ayub's government, and no doubt advised his new patron along the lines which had proved so disastrous in his brother's day.

mittee, and elaborated a series of demands which, while being radical in the context of the existing political situation, were basically petit-bourgeois.

Agitation continued unabated, causing a great deal of alarm in provincial government circles, and undoubtedly worrying the Chief Minister Khwaja Nazimuddin. The latter was even more panicky than usual because Jinnah was scheduled to visit Dacca on March 19th. It was his first visit to East Pakistan — and was to be his last. In an attempt to defuse the situation, Nazimuddin arranged a meeting with the Student Action Committee on March 15th, 1948 where the student leaders put forward the following demands:

1. The East Bengal Assembly should adopt a resolution making Bengali the official language in East Bengal and the medium of instruction in schools and colleges.
2. The East Bengal Assembly should by another resolution recommend to the Central government to make Bengali *one* of the state languages.
3. All political prisoners arrested during the movement should be released.
4. Bans on newspapers which gave support and publicized the movement both in East Bengal and in Calcutta should be lifted. (This meant that Calcutta newspapers should be allowed into East Pakistan).
5. A commission should be set up immediately to investigate the atrocities committed on the students by the police and their commanding officers.
6. It should be declared that the movement was inspired by highly patriotic motives and sentiments, and the Chief Minister should broadcast this over Dacca Radio.
7. All warrants of arrest against workers of political parties who had joined in the movement should be withdrawn.
8. The Chief Minister should withdraw his previous statements in which he called the agitators Communists and agents of the enemies of the state.

While the Chief Minister accepted *all* the demands of the Student Action Committee the bureaucrats were not pleased — the old British attitude that the natives were inferior was adopted by many non-Bengalis towards Bengal.

The political situation was returning to normal when Jinnah arrived. He had obviously decided to take the advice of the bureaucracy

4

not to accept the demands. At his first meeting in Dacca large numbers of people left when he reaffirmed his policy that Urdu must be the only state language, and in many schools and colleges angry students removed Jinnah's portraits. In his convocation address at Dacca University he repeated his earlier remarks, and the ensuing chaos made it impossible for him to finish his speech. At a later discussion with the Student Action Committee the atmosphere became heated, and the meeting ended in stalemate. Jinnah was well known for his obstinacy, and the Bengali students for their part, having won an initial victory, were not interested in compromise. For a time the struggle was shelved, but it exploded once again in 1952 when the Central government attempted to introduce an Urdu script for the Bengali language. A number of students were killed, and the government was forced to withdraw its proposals. February 21st is still observed regularly in East Pakistan as Shaheed (Martyrs) Day.

Meanwhile the influence of the Muslim League, which had naturally increased during the struggle for Pakistan in East Bengal, began to wane considerably. The blatantly reactionary policies of the provincial League government, and their complete impotence in the face of dual pressure from the bureaucracy and from West Pakistani landlords and businessmen to fight for provincial autonomy, caused them to be hated.

To the surprise of everyone the national question had been raised almost immediately after political independence had been established. In March 1949 the veteran Bengali leader, H. S. Suhrawardy, had returned to Pakistan from Calcutta. He had been Prime Minister of Bengal before Partition, and had nurtured hopes of an independent Bengal. He had decided not to leave West Bengal immediately after Partition, giving as his reason that his presence would tend to ease the fears of the large Muslim majority in Calcutta. Suhrawardy, like Jinnah, was a liberal constitutionalist, and an extremely able lawyer. According to one of his supporters, he "was disturbed to find that the Muslim League government had become almost a fascist government, and decided to set up an opposition platform, but Prime Minister Liaquat Ali Khan had openly declared that he would not tolerate an opposition party in Pakistan. Suhrawardy, however, decided to accept the challenge."[30]

[30] Kamrudin Ahmed, *The Social History of East Pakistan* (Dacca, 1967), p. 116. Banned by the Yahya regime in December 1969.

Suhrawardy had ultimately set up the Awami League in collaboration with Maulana Abdul Hamid Khan Bhashani, a Bengali peasant leader. The Muslim League government tried to suppress the new party by a policy of mass arrests, government-sponsored disruption of political meetings, and so on, but these measures only increased the Awami League's support, which came largely from the Bengali middle class. It was from the very beginning a bourgeois-nationalist party, and to this day has retained its middle-class base. It provided the first serious opposition to the political monopoly of the Muslim League, and it should be noted that the main reason for the opposition was the importance of the national question. Many Bengalis felt that they were being ruled by West Pakistani landlords and by anti-Bengali civil servants. They were, of course, absolutely right.

The Left in East Bengal

It was mentioned earlier that many non-Muslim Communists left East Bengal after Partition. But the position of the Communist Party was much stronger there than it was in the provinces of West Pakistan. After Partition East Bengal still had a Hindu population of well over nine million who decided to stay and many of them were Communists. It was all too easy for successive Pakistani governments to denounce these Hindu Communists as "enemy agents".

Deciding to ignore the odium in which they were held, in December 1948 the underground C.P. in East Bengal accepted the "Randive thesis" of immediate armed struggle, which had been first propounded by the C.P.I. leader Randive, and accepted by the party in 1948. It was put into practice in the districts of Rangpur, Dinajpur, Mymensingh and Jessore. The local C.P.s began by raiding local police stations and seizing arms, but they lacked adequate preparation and political education and the movement was crushed. Their about-turn from supporting the bourgeois-based Muslim League to advocating an immediate armed struggle against the bourgeois government was too sudden and, inevitably, failed. The local militants — predominantly Hindu, and experienced in struggling for the demands of the peasant movement — were uprooted and dispersed, and the areas were repopulated with refugees from India. These refugees were in most cases fanatic Muslims, and they became a powerful bastion of reaction. In the years from 1948 to 1954 there were over three thousand political prisoners in East Bengal's jails;

among them was the leader of the Mymensingh peasants, Moni Singh, whose feudal background had not influenced his political beliefs; the lands of his entire family had been confiscated because of his radicalism.

The Mymensingh district had been the scene of an important peasant struggle in 1945–6. The struggle was known as the Tebhaga movement, and its main slogan was that the share of the landlord be reduced from one-half to one-third of the crop. The movement arose as a result of the terrible famine in Bengal in 1943, when over three million peasants had starved to death. The militancy of the peasants increased, because there was a labour shortage in the countryside; apart from those killed by the famine, many share-croppers had drifted to the cities and did not return. Although the movement assumed massive proportions, it was contained by the landlords, in collaboration with the politicians belonging to both the Congress and the Muslim League.[31]

It is important to understand that the underground C.P. in East Bengal, because of its geographical proximity to West Bengal, was affected by the decisions of the C.P.I. In 1949 there was a discussion among the leadership of the C.P.I. on whether to draw a balance sheet on the 1948 "line", and different views emerged.

In April 1950 a leading Indian Stalinist, Ajoy Ghosh, wrote an open letter to the members of the Indian C.P. from a jail in South India where he had been imprisoned because of the C.P.I.'s "Left-deviation". It was written with the knowledge of the Indian government, and it called on Communists to abandon the present line of struggle and return to their former policies. India needed a bourgeois revolution, and this could only be accomplished in collaboration with the national bourgeoisie. The stage was not set for a socialist revolution. It was not a new argument. It had been used by the Menshevik leaders who had been opposed to the seizure of power by Lenin and Trotsky in Petrograd in 1917, and had been adapted by Stalin in his theory of building "socialism in one country".

The Ghosh letter increased the factionalism in the top ranks of the

---

[31] The reasons for the failure of the movement have never been analysed in detail, and the lack of information on the subject makes the task difficult. An excellent article appeared in *Socialist Register*, 1965, "Peasants and Revolution" by Hamza Alavi, which touched on the question, but only as part of the general perspective of the article. A detailed analysis of the Tebhaga movement is still needed. One may have appeared in a Bengali publication, but it has been impossible to trace it.

party, and "international advice" (i.e. Stalin's) was sought. Stalin summoned the leaders of the three factions to Moscow and gave formal approval to Ghosh's line. Indian Communists were to adopt the parliamentary road to socialism. Peaceful coexistence with the bourgeoisie and class-collaboration was the order of the day, and as a result, the leadership in India and East Bengal was changed.

After the Ghosh line had been formalized by Stalin a problem arose for East Pakistani Communists. It was all very well for countries like India, where the party was legal. There it was easy to collaborate with the ruling class; but how could Pakistani Communists collaborate with a bourgeoisie which refused to allow them to function?

A group in the underground East Pakistani C.P. had argued that the Communists should work through the Awami Muslim League, whose President was Maulana Bhashani, but this had been opposed on two grounds: first, because it was a bourgeois party and secondly, because it was restricted to Muslims, and many Communist militants were non-Muslims.

In 1951, however, a political note appeared in the Cominform journal, *For a Lasting Peace, For a People's Democracy*, suggesting that in East Pakistan the progressive forces were fighting through the Awami Muslim League. The appearance of this political note provoked intensive discussion amongst the leadership, some arguing that this was a political line inspired by Stalin, and should be accepted. The habit of accepting without question the dictates of Stalin was so deeply ingrained that it never occurred to anyone to analyse the political situation and act on that.

Two main groups of the underground C.P. were held in Rajshahi and Dacca jails. The Cominform line was accepted by those in Dacca jail, but the group in Rajshahi jail submitted an alternative thesis: the party, they claimed, should continue as an underground movement and work in the trade unions and the peasant organizations. The Stalinist faction argued in favour of the Cominform line, that as the working class was numerically weak there should be a multi-class leadership for a patriotic-democratic revolution. The Rajshahi faction countered by saying that only the working class could lead a democratic revolution; but they had the weight of Stalinist orthodoxy against them. The official line was accepted and all the "Muslim comrades" were asked to work in the Muslim League, while the non-Muslims were asked to work with the peasantry and the trade unions,

— to a large extent an academic request, as most of the non-Muslim cadres were in prison.

After the 1952 language movement large numbers of political prisoners were released, among them many Communists. In July 1952 the party decided on two types of organization: the first underground; the second, legal, organization was to include those who had entered the Awami League.

Even after December 1952 the C.P. could not officially declare itself, and most of its leaders were still in prison. The first public meeting of the C.P. in East Bengal after Partition was held in Chittagong on November 7th, 1953, to celebrate the anniversary of the Russian Revolution. When local Muslim-League thugs supporting Fazlul Quader Chowdhury[32] tried to break the meeting up, five thousand railway workers surrounded the platform and fought back.

At about the same time the C.P. and the Youth League issued a call for a united front of all anti-Muslim League forces to contest the next provincial election, and despite initial disagreements one was set up. And, significantly, in September 1953 Sheikh Mujibur Rehman, the Secretary of the Awami Muslim League, suggested that the word Muslim should be removed and that the League should become a secular party. This was agreed, and by December 1953 the entire activities of the progressive forces in East Pakistan centred round the forthcoming elections, in which the C.P. played an important role.

The Muslim League government in East Pakistan was a decadent institution, typifying the decaying, semi-feudal contradictions of the East Bengali countryside. It even lacked a strong social base, unlike its counterparts in West Pakistan where feudalism was still strongly entrenched. This government had come to represent the interests of alien landlords; it could not even begin to represent and fight for the interests of the disinherited Bengali bourgeoisie, who were preparing to inflict on it a blow from which it would never recover. The whole of East Bengal awaited with impatience the collapse of the League, and when it came there was rejoicing throughout the province.

In Pakistan as a whole the Muslim League was losing support as it proved entirely incapable of inaugurating even bourgeois-democratic reforms. In 1951, the first Prime Minister had been assassinated

[32] Fazlul Quader later became a member of Ayub's government as Minister for Education.

by a fanatic named Said Akbar, a supporter of the Jamaat-i-Islami.[33] Khwaja Nazimuddin, who had succeeded Jinnah as Governor-General, now became Prime Minister. He was every West-Pakistani bureaucrat's favourite Bengali and his many weaknesses made him the ideal Prime Minister, as he could be manipulated at will.

In December 1952 another political party came into existence. The Ganatantri Dal (Democratic Party) was the Bengali counterpart of Iftikharudin's Azad Party in West Pakistan. The main forces behind the Ganatantri Dal were Left-liberals, fellow-travellers and those Communists who had refused to join the Awami League because of its restricted membership.

From now until the promulgation of Martial Law by General Ayub in 1958, politics were governed by party intrigues and a blatant lust for office. No agreement was reached on a constitution for Pakistan, and the country was still ruled by laws laid down by British imperialism. In the field of foreign policy the country moved from a passive position to become an active stooge of the United States. The Prime Minister, Mohammed Ali, was a one-time ambassador to Washington. In July 1953 while opening, very appropriately, a General Motors assembly plant in Karachi he declared:

> We sincerely hope that we will be in a position to give further and greater incentive to accelerate the pace of such investments. It is through mutual friendship and co-operation, not only in the field of culture and politics, but also in the field of commerce and industry that ties of goodwill and friendship can be forged on a *permanent basis* [italics mine].

The United States responded by sending wheat shipments to Pakistan as "aid". The fact that it was part of the American government's domestic price-support scheme to ıeduce a big wheat surplus, which would have tended to drive wheat prices down in the United States, was of course passed over. The Pakistan government was humbly grateful and Dulles put out a statement acclaiming Pakistan as "a bulwark for freedom in Asia". The *Pakistan Times*, commenting editorially on July 27th, 1953, spoke on behalf of the Pakistani masses:

---

[33] A mystery surrounds Liaquat's murder. The assassin was beaten to death a few minutes after he shot Liaquat, despite the presence of large numbers of police and C.I.D. Many claimed that anti-Liaquat factions inside the Pakistani ruling class were responsible for the assassination, but now the truth may never emerge.

They [the Pakistani masses] will find it somewhat difficult to understand the meaning of the Prime Minister's assertion, on the occasion of the arrival of the first U.S. wheat ship, reiterated later by the Food Minister that Pakistan and America speak "the same language regarding the ideals of freedom and democracy". They will indeed find it hard to work out a common factor between their ideals of freedom and such concrete expressions of American foreign policy as innumerable strategic bases round the globe, open support to the crumbling Western Empires and their indigenous puppets in the Orient, alliance with such retrograde elements as the Kuomintang and the Rhee gang, and the strengthening of Wall Street's hold on various Middle Eastern economies. They will also wonder how to reconcile their cherished dreams of a democratic political and social order with such cruel realities of American life as racial discrimination and the lynching of Negroes, persecution of intellectuals and witch-hunting. It would have been much wiser for us to purchase the wheat needed than to get it as a charity from benefactors who make no bones about the political price they ultimately expect for their aid ... And, lastly it is perfectly obvious that if the solemn guarantee given by the Prime Minister that every single grain of American wheat would be protected against "leakage, wastage, smuggling and pilfering", could have been applied to Pakistan's own wheat during the last few years, we would not today be accepting a humiliating gift which carries with it the danger of involvement in political policies which are abhorred by the vast masses of our people.[34]

But this was a voice in the wilderness. The merry-go-round of Pakistani politics continued to whirl. In the first six years of Pakistan's existence none of the problems affecting the mass of workers and peasants, or even the petit-bourgeoisie, had been solved. The Muslim League was tottering, but it tried to distract attention from its decay by engaging in a policy of repression. In East Bengal and the North West Frontier Province many political prisoners were detained without trial under laws promulgated initially by the British to curb the freedom movement in India.

When the Pakistani ruling class celebrated the sixth anniversary of Pakistan's independence they were probably too busy congratulat-

[34] *Pakistan Times*, July 27th, 1953.

ing each other to review the state of the nation, and to consider the bitter disillusion of the people who had been promised that Pakistan was going to be a "paradise". Exploitation of the peasantry and the workers continued; one child in every five died from malnutrition, and no efforts were being made to counteract tuberculosis, which was claiming the lives of many workers every day. Once again it was left to the *Pakistan Times* to raise its voice against the stagnation and retrogression of the last six years:

> Inside the country, the last twelve months have witnessed a disturbing intensification of political confusion and further dis-integration of our economy, with no planned effort on the part of those in authority to grapple with either crisis and no concerted political campaign by the Opposition parties to force the Muslim League either to reform its regime or surrender its monopoly of power. Public discontent and frustration have now reached the verge of despair; the people are to an alarming extent, becoming cynical and apathetic or responsive to the maudlin appeals of charlatans eager to fill the political vacuum with theories culled from the history of fascism's rise to power ... [35]

It is Pakistan's tragedy that no organized revolutionary socialist party has made regular analyses of political and economic developments and provided a scientific theory for the country's workers, students and peasants. This is as true today as it was in 1953. From 1953 to 1958 the situation was to deteriorate even further, until, on the pretext of restoring "law and order", the army was to move in with the active support of the bureaucracy.

[35] *Pakistan Times*, August 14th, 1953.

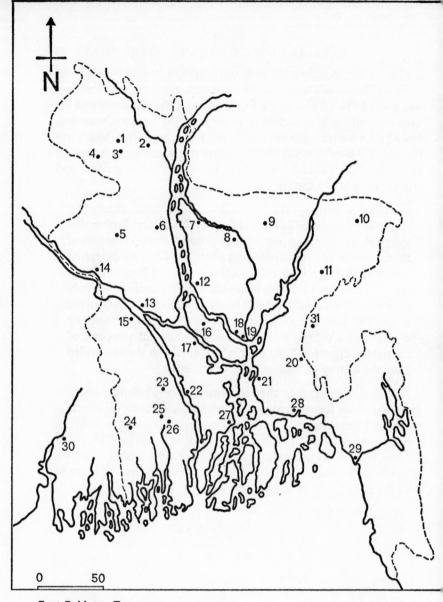

East Pakistan Towns

1. Saidpur
2. Rangpur
3. Parbatipur‡
4. Dinajpur
5. Naggaon
6. Bogra
7. Jamalpur‡
8. Mymensingh‡
9. Mohanganj
10. Sylhet‡
11. Srimangal
12. Tangail‡
13. Pabna‡
14. Rajshahi‡
15. Kushtia‡
16. Manikganj‡
17. Faridpur
18. Dacca‡
19. Narayanganj‡
20. Comilla‡
21. Chandpur‡
22. Gopalganj‡
23. Narail
24. Satkhira
25. Daulatpur‡
26. Khulna‡
27. Barisal‡
28. Noakhali‡
29. Chittagong‡
30. Calcutta
31. Agarthala (in India)

KEY: All the towns marked on these maps were affected by the struggle. Deaths occurred in the towns marked with a double dagger.

CHAPTER TWO

Parliamentary Façade: Second Phase, 1954-8

> "Pakistan represents to us Americans a new Land of Promise."
> U.S. Consul-General in Lahore (quoted in *Pakistan Times*, October 22nd, 1955)

There is no parliamentary road

In *State and Revolution* Lenin describes how "Marx splendidly grasped the essence of capitalist democracy when he said, *the oppressed are allowed once every few years to decide which particular representative of the oppressing class are to represent and repress them in parliament.*" In Pakistan the ruling class did not even allow the Pakistani people their choice of oppressors. They inflicted on the people any government they wanted.

The absence of a viable revolutionary opposition to the system undoubtedly made their task much easier. The few active socialists seemed to be involved in merely tinkering with the system by getting absorbed in petit-bourgeois constitutional struggles. The power of the bureaucracy, the West Pakistani landlords and the army went unchallenged until the coup d'état of 1958, when the army felt secure enough to do without the façade and govern the country directly in alliance with the bureaucracy. However, the last four years of "parliamentary government" did not proceed smoothly for the forces of reaction. Opposition was on the increase in both East and West Pakistan in the years before the imposition of Martial Law.

East Pakistan

Since 1951 the opposition parties had been clamouring for an election on the basis of adult franchise in East Pakistan, and had been regularly thwarted. There had been large-scale arrests of opposition political workers, and civil liberties had been curtailed.

The economic situation was worsening. After the boom associated with the Korean war, when Pakistan's refusal to devalue had paid

59

off, there was a sharp drop in the prices of agricultural raw materials, government permission was required to sow jute and "extraneous" jute was destroyed by the authorities. A poor harvest in 1952–3, coupled with a chronic deficiency of food, had developed into a famine, and the short supply of food was cruelly exploited by West Pakistani merchants and speculators, often in league with the bureaucracy. To make matters worse, large numbers of Muslim refugees from India had helped to swell the army of the unemployed.

In this situation drastic measures were needed and the Muslim League government in East Pakistan proved hopelessly inept.[1] It merely increased the rates and taxes in East Pakistan. The Central government was uninterested in East Pakistan, except as a colony whose agricultural raw material could be used to earn foreign exchange to help develop West Pakistan.

The economic exploitation of East Pakistan began immediately after Partition, and by 1956 economists had worked out that at least 300 million rupees were being extracted annually.[2] In addition, the balance of trade between the two parts of the country worked out unfavourably as far as East Pakistan was concerned. Exports from West Pakistan had exceeded imports from East Pakistan to the tune of 909 million rupees between 1948 and 1953.[3] Thus the Muslim League government and the bureaucracy made full use of both external and internal trade to use East Pakistan's resources in order to develop certain areas in West Pakistan.

This is clearly illustrated by comparing the sums of money granted for development projects by the Central government. Between 1948 and 1951 a sum of Rs. 1,130 million was sanctioned for development. Of this only 22·1 per cent of Rs. 250 million went to East Pakistan.[4] Between 1948 and 1955 the gap had increased and East Pakistan was given 12·6 per cent of the total sum; that is, the Central government granted West Pakistan Rs. 10,000 million and East Pakistan Rs. 1,260 million. A study of industrial enterprises set up in East Pakistan would show also that the large majority were controlled by non-Bengali businessmen financed by West Pakistani capital. East Pakistan, therefore, gradually became a complete

---

[1] For further details of economic situation see Gankovsky and Polonskaya, *A History of Pakistan* (Moscow, 1964).

[2] *Pakistan Times*, February 8th, 1956.

[3] *Statistical Bulletin*, February, 1959.

[4] Gankovsky and Polonskaya, op. cit., p. 190.

colony; its raw material, which brought in badly-needed foreign currency, was used to develop Karachi and the Punjab. The reverse of the coin was that East Pakistan also became a market for industrial commodities produced in the industrial centres of the Punjab.

The bureaucracy quite rightly feared that if a national bourgeoisie were allowed to develop in East Bengal, its economic strength united to its political power would make it a dominating force in Pakistani politics. They were, therefore, determined to prevent this happening. Besides being subjected to political and economic discrimination, the East Bengalis were not welcomed into the ranks of the bureaucracy, and all the major posts were occupied by Punjabi civil servants whose attitudes were distinctly racist. So well had they absorbed the ideology of their former British masters that they felt that the Bengalis were an inferior race.

The language controversy can be seen as symbolizing the cumulative nature of Bengali grievances; a mass demonstration by students on February 21st, 1952, had been "dispersed" by the police who had opened fire, killing twenty-six and wounding four hundred.

In September 1952 the Youth League, together with the Communist Party, had issued a call to all the East Bengali political parties to form a united front against the Muslim League government, though the Communist Party, to preserve its independence, decided to put up ten of its own candidates, who would campaign on a basis of principled class struggle. The united front produced a programme known as the Twenty-One Points. It was a bourgeois-democratic programme whose chief demands were for equality between the provinces and provincial autonomy for East Bengal and which aimed to clear the path for an unfettered development of capitalism in East Pakistan. Thus point 2 demanded that all incomes derived from rent should be ended without compensation, and that surplus land be handed to landless peasants. Points 4 and 7 required that irrigation be improved, agricultural co-operatives be set up and measures to boost agricultural production be implemented; point 3 demanded that the jute trade be nationalized and that jute be purchased from producers at fair prices. Other points included requests that discrimination against Bengalis in the armed forces should cease and that the naval headquarters be transferred to East Pakistan; that the vicious Safety Acts which allowed for imprisonment without trial be repealed and all political prisoners released; and that the I.L.O. conventions regarding labour be put into practice.

It was a radical programme in any context. For the bureaucracy and the ruling clique at the centre it amounted to a virtual revolution. The Muslim League was unable to counter it politically, so with the co-operation of the government at the Centre they sent mullahs and other religious fanatics round the countryside to propagate rumours that the united front was controlled by Hindus and Communists.

The elections in East Pakistan were finally scheduled for February 16th, 1954. The government postponed them for a couple of weeks to start on a policy of repression against the Left, and in the course of forty-eight hours 1,200 persons were arrested, most of them supporters of the Communist Party. Thinking that the people would be impressed by the new alliance with the United States, the government persuaded its masters in Washington to announce the decision to grant military aid to Pakistan just before the election. This Eisenhower did on February 21st, 1954.

Voting finally took place from March 8th to March 12th, 1954. The result was a crushing and humiliating defeat for the Muslim League. Out of 309 seats it gained only ten! All the provincial ministers, including the Chief Minister Nurul Amin, failed to get elected. Within the united front the Awami League had a majority of Muslim seats (elections had taken place on the reactionary basis of separate electorates whereby seats were reserved for members of different religions). Accordingly, a united front government with Fazlul Haq (of the Krishak Sramik Party) as Chief Minister was formed in East Pakistan in April 1954. The bureaucracy had suffered its first real defeat since Partition.

It was, of course, a right-wing government, but in the context of Pakistani politics at that stage the election had a radicalizing effect on the whole of Pakistan. The Communist Party had won 4 seats out of the 10 they had contested. All the Muslim Communists had lost and the Hindu Communists had won 2 seats in Chittagong, 1 in Sylhet and 1 in Barisal. Twenty-two members of the C.P. who were working within the Awami League and the Ganatantri Dal were also elected. So the real strength of the Pakistani C.P. in the East Pakistan legislature was 26. After the election the C.P. office was constantly overcrowded and the C.P. used this opportunity to reorganize its bases in the trade unions and the countryside.

As the influence of the C.P. increased, big business began to panic and an anti-united front campaign was started. To appease the business interests the government re-arrested many Communists who had been released immediately after the victory. But the businessmen and the bureaucracy were not to be mollified so easily. Police provocation in factories became common, and the employers provoked clashes between Bengali and non-Bengali workers at Adamjee's jute mills. Maulana Bhashani alleged in public that this was a conspiracy to discredit the united front government, and the Communist Party warned that these provocateurs had as their aim the downfall of the government. A false report claiming that Fazlul Haq had put up the idea of an independent East Pakistan while visiting Calcutta, succeeded in stirring up more trouble. The Central government blamed the Communists for riots in the factories and asked the East Pakistani government to take immediate measures against them. However, the government refused.

On May 30th, 1954, the Central government dissolved the Legislative Assembly of East Pakistan under Section 92A of the Constitution and proclaimed Governor's rule in the province. An old semi-fascist bureaucrat, Major-General Iskandar Mirza, who had distinguished himself by aiding the British to crush the Pathans, was appointed Governor. He ruled East Pakistan with an iron hand and in his first week he arrested 659 activists of the united front, including 13 members of the dissolved assembly. Fazlul Haq and several provincial ministers were kept under close house arrest. Apparently even the parliamentary road was too dangerous for Pakistan.

(This was also the time when the Central government was about to sign a bilateral military pact with the United States. One hundred and sixty-two members of the provincial Assembly in East Pakistan had signed a motion denouncing the proposed pact. The pact had been signed after the dissolution of the assembly.)

The new Governor had a special place in his heart for the Communist Party. On July 5th, 1954, he banned it and instigated the setting up of police committees in the industrial areas whose job it was to discover the Communists and their sympathizers in the factories and report them to the employers. Employers were warned that they must dismiss Communists or face the wrath of the government. This was used as an excuse to dismiss many non-Communist militants in the factories. In this period of repression it became difficult for the Communist Party to function at all.

In September 1955, after a series of shoddy compromises had been made by the Central government and members of the united front, Governor's rule was ended and the provincial Assembly was restored.

Once again political prisoners were released. In the Constituent Assembly of Pakistan even a right-wing Bengali leader was forced to speak up for Bengal:

> Sir, I actually started yesterday and said that the attitude of the Muslim League coterie here was of contempt towards East Bengal, towards its culture, its language, its literature and everything concerning East Bengal ... In fact, Sir, I tell you that far from considering East Bengal as an equal partner, the leaders of the Muslim League thought that we were a subject race and they belonged to a race of conquerors.[5]

On November 21st, 1955, the Dacca police struck for more wages, and their strike was broken by the East Pakistan Rifles (E.P.R.). The government used the strike as a pretext to arrest all the known members of the Communist Party, who were accused of planning to take over the province, and the entire Central Committee of the party went underground.

After the 20th Party Congress a debate opened up in the C.P. The main opposition was not to the de-Stalinization, but to the reverse side of the coin – the formulation of the theory of "peaceful coexistence" and the "peaceful transition" to socialism. Once again the opposition was led by the comrades in Rajshahi jail, but on this occasion a vocal minority emerged inside Dacca jail. During these discussions there was another mass upsurge after the government had opened fire on and killed some hunger marchers. Over twenty thousand people led by the Awami Leaguer, Sheikh Mujibur Rehman, attacked Dacca jail. The Communists imprisoned there could not help but feel elated. The next day (July 6th, 1956) the government fell and the Chief Minister, Ataur Rehman, rushed to the jail immediately after being sworn in and ordered the release of all political prisoners. For some time after the release, the Communist Party was to act on the thesis of peaceful co-existence contained in the Khrushchev report to the 20th Party Congress.

The crisis of 1954–5 proved quite conclusively that in East Pakistan there was need of an extra-parliamentary mass opposition which could continue to struggle even if the constitution was suspended, and even if the parliamentary façade was replaced temporarily by the real face of the Pakistani ruling class. If the lessons of 1954 had been learnt and digested, the situation in October 1958 when the generals

[5] Keith Callard, *Pakistan: A Political Study* (London, 1957), p. 173.

took over might well have been different. It was to be expected that the right-wing members of the united front would rely on bureaucratic and inter-parliamentary manœuvring in the struggle for provincial autonomy, and they did in fact have secret negotiations with their "opponents" in West Pakistan. It was up to the left-wing elements, whatever their numbers, to continue to rely on the masses and to keep up the campaign even after the united front government had gained power. This they failed to do, and as a result when the bureaucracy and the feudal landlords and the bourgeoisie of West Pakistan united to attack the national movement in East Bengal, it crumbled.

West Pakistan

The result of the 1954 election in East Pakistan succeeded in revitalizing the political atmosphere in West Pakistan. The Communist Party was banned in West Pakistan as well, and its General Secretary, Firozudin (Dada) Mansur, together with trade-union leaders and other activists, was arrested. Over 1,300 persons were imprisoned. Despite the repression, the candidates of the Muslim League continued to be defeated at successive by-elections.

Taken together with the deteriorating economic situation – there was a food shortage, and many essential commodities were available only on the black market – it was a serious situation for the ruling groups. The bureaucracy had the additional worry that if a Bengal ruled by the united front combined electorally with the smaller units of West Pakistan they would be in a permanent majority, and the privileged Punjabi elite, comprising landlords, businessmen and bureaucrats, would stand to lose political and economic control. They conceived of the One Unit scheme, which would abolish provincial autonomy in West Pakistan and bring landlords of the Punjab, Baluchistan, Sind and the Frontier Province together. Also a "united" West Pakistan would be better able to combat the demands of East Bengal.

However, the contradictions involved in the One Unit plan were enormous. Many provincial political leaders (i.e. landlords) did not want to strengthen the hand of their Punjabi peers too much. They saw One Unit as a threat to the development of their own areas. As a result, when the unification proposals were discussed by the Muslim League Parliamentary Party they were turned down by a majority

5

of Muslim Leaguers belonging to Bengal, Sind and Baluchistan. When the plan came up before the Constituent Assembly, the Chief Minister of Sind, Pirzada, spoke against it, obviously with the support of the majority of the members of the Sind Assembly. The deputies from Bengal also opposed the plan, and it was defeated. A new plan was suggested, diametrically opposed to One Unit but in favour of a re-organization of West Pakistan into six provinces. This proposal was carried, and it was somewhat naively expected that it would be carried out.

The Punjabi landlords, who were Muslim Leaguers, held somewhat different views. If they had accepted the decision of the Constituent Assembly they would have been signing their own political death warrant. On the other hand, the Muslim Leaguers from Bengal (Nazimuddin, Nurul Amin, Tamizudin), from Sind and Baluchistan were not prepared to capitulate as they saw this as an opportunity to wrest political power from the Punjabi ruling clique. Nazimuddin had been nursing a grudge ever since he had been dismissed as Prime Minister by the Punjabi Governor-General, Ghulam Mohammed, a foul-mouthed bureaucrat closely in league with the United States.[6] According to one source the struggle had international aspects in that:

> it also reflected imperialist contradictions and the competition of the American and British monopolies for decisive influence in Pakistan. The representatives of East Pakistan in the Muslim League turned towards Britain because of their old connections with it, while the leaders of the Muslim League in the Punjab, headed by Ghulam Mohammed, the Governor-General, considered a further rapprochement with the U.S.A. more advantageous. Inter-imperialist rivalry and the direct support which the Punjabi clique received from the American monopolists undoubtedly affected the outcome of the internal struggle waged in Pakistan in 1954.[7]

When the Bengal-Sind alliance decided to attack the Ghulam Mohammed group again, and attempted to take away some of the Governor-General's powers, he and his coterie decided to act. The

---

[6] Before Nazimuddin was removed as Prime Minister he complained to Ghulam Mohammed, "When I was Governor-General I never interfered with Liaquat." To this Ghulam Mohammed replied, "Ah, but you see I am not Nazimuddin and you are not Liaquat."

[7] Gankovsky and Polonskaya, op. cit., p. 212.

Prime Minister, Mohammed Ali Bogra (a former ambassador to the U.S.A.), and the army chief, General Ayub Khan, were sent off to Washington where they negotiated a long-term military and economic aid pact. On their return to Karachi they were taken straight to the Governor-General's residence, where it was decided to dissolve the Constituent Assembly and to proclaim "a state of emergency" in the country. Ayub described the scene in his memoirs:

> The Governor-General was lying in his bedroom upstairs ... He was bursting with rage, emitting volleys of abuse ... I was about to step out of the room when the nurse attending the Governor-General tugged at my coat. He then beckoned me with a peculiar glee in his eye ... He then pulled out two documents under his pillow ... [8]

According to Ayub, these documents offered him the power to take over the country with the army and produce a constitution. He refused to do so, perhaps because his superiors in Washington had forewarned him and advised him to bide his time.

After the dissolution of the Constituent Assembly the country was ruled by a semi-insane Governor-General. He asked Mohammed Ali Bogra to form a new cabinet with Ayub as Defence Minister, and in December Mr H. S. Suhrawardy also joined the cabinet; it was he who was to draft the One Unit Bill. Suhrawardy, who had fought for provincial autonomy in East Pakistan, was to fight for its abolition in West Pakistan. The plan to force through One Unit was put into immediate effect. In the Sind Assembly the anti-One-Unit Chief Minister was dismissed and replaced by an old hand at strong-arm politics, M. A. Khuhro. The latter ordered the police to surround the Sind Assembly and forced the members to accept One Unit. Even Suhrawardy was forced to exclaim some months later, "You [Khuhro] struck terror—and I say this with confidence—that you struck terror into the hearts of the Members of the Sind Assembly when they came to vote."[9]

The Central government wanted to "unify" West Pakistan under the Emergency Powers Ordinance, but the Supreme Court intervened to inform the Governor-General that his powers did not allow him to amalgamate provinces and that this would have to be done by

[8] Mohammed Ayub Khan, *Friends Not Masters—A Political Autobiography* (Oxford, 1967), p. 52.
[9] Callard, op. cit., p. 191.

the Constituent Assembly. The new Assembly was elected by the members of the provincial Assemblies in June 1955, and despite a spirited opposition to One Unit by the Bengali deputies the Act was passed. On October 14th, 1955, the new province of West Pakistan came into existence in an atmosphere of frustration, bitterness and anger. From now on the struggle to undo One Unit was to dominate West Pakistani politics.

In August 1955 ill-health had forced Ghulam Mohammed to resign, and Iskandar Mirza had replaced him as acting-Governor-General. A new Premier, Chowdhuri Mohammed Ali, was appointed, another bureaucrat turned politician, who was also a Muslim fanatic and violently anti-leftist. He was responsible for producing the new constitution for the country which came into effect on March 23rd, 1956, when Pakistan became an Islamic Republic.

The new constitution succeeded in resolving none of the basic contradictions within Pakistan. On the contrary, it institutionalized political discrimination against East Pakistan by not allowing East Bengal the weight due to it by virtue of its population, and established One Unit as a "balance" to contain East Pakistan. The wide-ranging powers it gave to the President and the Central government made autonomy seem a complete farce. Article 15 of the Constitution read:

(1) No person shall be deprived of his property save in accordance with law.
(2) No property shall be compulsorily acquired or taken possession of save for a public purpose, and save by the authority of law which provides for compensation thereof and either fixes the amount of compensation or specifies the principles on which and the manner in which compensation is determined to be given ... "property" shall mean immovable property, or any commercial or industrial undertaking, or any interest in such undertaking.

The class nature of this particular law needs no elaboration. The new Constitution gave the President far-reaching powers. This would have been unfortunate in the most healthy circumstances, but in the political atmosphere prevailing in Pakistan it was disastrous, particularly as President Iskandar Mirza thrived on political intrigue.

Despite changes in the cabinet, policy remained very much the same. On August 14th, 1956, the country celebrated its ninth year of "freedom". The sole dissenting voice, the *Pakistan Times* bewailed:

On this day, nine years ago, Pakistan became a free country. How much longer will it be before our people become a free people ... the gentlemen who found themselves in power when independence came immediately set about dinning it into the people's ears that since Pakistan had been freed, the freedom of Pakistan's citizens mattered not one jot ... Anyone who maintained otherwise, anyone who objected to the curtailment of civil liberties or the promiscuous use of emergency laws was either a fool or a traitor ...

Every time the ruling gentry manage to reduce national affairs to a particularly unholy mess, and they do it with almost clocklike regularity, the cry that goes up from numerous interested quarters is not for more freedom for the people, but for less, not for greater democracy, but for greater dictatorship. It is necessary to remind our people, therefore, and to keep them reminded, that they can never hope to be rid of their besetting ills until they can personally attend to them, that their house will never be put in order until they take charge of it themselves.

It seems strange indeed that nine years after independence it should still be necessary to explain that freedom is a good thing and that democracy is neither dangerous nor undesirable. The phenomenon is easily understood, however, in the context of the direction or rather misdirection, of our political life since independence. On the one hand, the core of our ruling class have steadily moved themselves further and further away from the danger of political contamination by contact with the masses, have come to rely more and more on the sanction of force rather than the sanction of popular opinion, and in consequence have almost completely divorced State policies domestic and foreign from national sentiment and the wishes of the people. Whether these policies are good or bad is beside the point. The point is that these policies are the brain-children of bureaucratic scribblers in the Secretariat, of foreign experts, of big or small fry in the Government and not a practical codification of popular desire. On the other hand, the bulk of the intelligentsia and the politically conscious elements, at least, in West Pakistan, have either given up the fight or have become more and more resigned to the inevitability of a long period of waiting before better days come round again. And the people have been left out in the cold by both sides ...

... The prospects of a general election are as shadowy as ever, feuds and squabbles among the ruling gentry have grown fiercer, and the perversions of constitutional provisions and proprieties become nearly as constant as sunset and daybreak. It would be pointless to catalogue proofs; the events are too well known. Any vestige of doubt that the authors and custodians of the new Constitution still attach some sanctity to this document will be removed by the latest performance of Governor Fazlul Haq. To save a few partisan skins the East Pakistan Assembly has been prorogued twice within a few weeks with a shamelessness that must be unique in the annals of constitutional bodies ... [10]

In September 1956 Mr H. S. Suhrawardy had won the confidence of President Mirza and had been nominated Prime Minister; the necessary support in the Assembly had not been long in coming. In the meantime a number of big landlords in the Muslim League believing that the League could no longer defend their interests, had decided to set up a new party called the Republican Party. Undoubtedly the party had been formed on the initiative of President Iskandar Mirza to provide him with a pawn which would increase his political manœuvrability. One of the new leaders of the Republican Party, while addressing a party convention in Abbotabad, was quoted as saying that "the Republican Party was the outcome of the Muslim League Party during the last nine years".[11] The Muslim League split in the West Pakistan Assembly and a Republican bloc held a majority of the votes in parliament (189 out of 306). The West Pakistan government, therefore, became a Republican Party government. Like its parent body, the Republican Party defended the status quo, and many landlords who controlled the local Muslim League organizations changed the signboard above the party office and became Republicans.

Whatever else may be said about the Pakistani ruling class, one has to acknowledge that in the defence of its class interests it displayed a refreshing honesty. The break-up of the Muslim League in West Pakistan combined with the break-up of the united front (or what was left of it) in East Pakistan, and the resulting "victories" of the Republican Party in the West and the Awami League in the East

[10] *Pakistan Times*, August 14th, 1956, editorial entitled "How Far is Freedom Yet?"
[11] Ibid., July 29th, 1956.

also helped to make Suhrawardy Prime Minister. Suhrawardy presided over an Awami-League-Republican coalition. The aspiring bourgeoisie of East Bengal combined with the most reactionary landlords and businessmen in West Pakistan. Hence from the very beginning it was out of the question for Suhrawardy's government to solve the national question in East Bengal. During his tenure of office, however, there was an increase in the ranks of the East Bengali bourgeoisie.

In the provinces the hunt for winning over Members of the Legislative Assembly continued with a new vigour. The baits, lures and seductions of the parliamentary political parties became a well-known feature of the political game.

This spectacle, which has now become a regular prelude to every session of the West Pakistan Assembly, would be excellent entertainment if it belonged to the fictitious world of stage or screen. Unfortunately this is not so. The gentlemen of easy virtue involved in the game are our legislators and their seducers are actual or prospective rulers of this half of the land. The immoral traffic in M.L.A.'s is not amusing: it is very degrading and very sad.[12]

U.S. aid and Pakistan's foreign policy

In addition to the charade of Pakistan's domestic life the Pakistan government had become one of the most grovelling supporters of United States imperialism in Asia.

Once the United States government had realized that the Indian bourgeoisie was not prepared to enter into open military alliances, it shifted its interest to Pakistan, and invited Pakistan's first Prime Minister, Liaquat Ali Khan, for an official visit in 1950. On his return from a ticker-tape welcome and a triumphal tour in the land of the all-powerful dollar, Pakistan had veered sharply towards a pro-American position in international affairs. He had been greeted by a barrage from the *Pakistan Times* on his return. In an editorial headed, "Return of the Native", the newspaper castigated his refusal to attack America's Korean policy and suggested a few of the things he could have said to the State Department:

[12] *Pakistan Times*, September 8th, 1957, editorial entitled "Of Straws and Wafer Cakes."

... he did not say that the American aided colonial war in Vietnam should end, that the British troops in the Middle East and American warships round Formosa, were deeply repugnant to national sentiment in Asia; he did not say that our economic structure apart from foreign assistance also needs revolutionary internal reform which we shall put through irrespective of the economic theories held sacred by Wall Street; he did not say that the Truman doctrine as it works in Japan and Korea and Turkey and Iran, that American support for corrupt, autocratic Asian regimes, is a violation of both freedom and democracy. If he had said all this he might have given the cocky American policy makers a better appraisal of the situation in Asia and who knows it might even have aroused in some corner of their mind a realization that everybody is not as stupid as they think and that at least in Asia, the gilt of American policies barely hides the metal underneath.[13]

But if Liaquat had said all this he could not have claimed to be speaking on behalf of the ruling class of Pakistan.

In February 1951 and February 1952 Pakistan received an increasing amount of aid from the United States, with the stipulation that it was to be used only in consultation with the American government and with their approval. The agreement also made it clear that Pakistan could not accept technical assistance from other countries "without the consent of the United States government". With the aid came the "experts" and "advisers" who were to supervise its use.

By 1953 the United States had made its presence strongly felt in Pakistani politics, and from then on it was to play an important role in guiding the policies of successive Pakistani governments. A wheat shortage was, it seems, exaggerated beyond all reasonable proportion by the foreign experts and sections of the press and was built up into a crisis.[14] The price of getting part of America's unwanted wheat

[13] *Pakistan Times*, July 14th, 1950.

[14] The crisis served the ends of the United States as the scare succeeded in panicking many people, prices soared and large stocks of wheat were hoarded and sold on the black market. By February 1953 the government was appealing for "wheat aid" to the United States. For two months the United States avoided committing itself. In May 1953 the Nazimuddin government fell a victim to pro-American and anti-British intrigue. Once the new Prime Minister had been installed, the United States announced its offer of aid, but it was nearly the end of the year before the first shipments arrived. A previous shipment of wheat from America had been welcomed by government spokesmen at the Karachi docks with hordes of camels wearing placards round their necks which read: THANK YOU AMERICA.

surplus was the installation of Mr Mohammed Ali Bogra, the Pakistan ambassador to the United States, as Prime Minister of Pakistan.[15]

In foreign affairs, too, the government was now moving firmly behind the United States under the pressures of the Eisenhower administration, whose foreign policy was fostered by Dulles. While Pakistani bureaucrats and government Ministers have always stressed the "philanthropic" nature of American aid, and the fact that it did not have "strings attached", the United States officials have, in the main, not pandered to these illusions. An official American paper laid down certain guidelines for foreign aid:

> Technical Assistance is not something to be done, as a Government enterprise, for its own sake or for the sake of others. The U.S. Government is not a charitable institution, nor is it an appropriate outlet for the charitable spirit of the American people. That spirit finds its proper instrumentality in the numerous private philanthropic and religious institutions *which have done so much good work abroad* [my italics]. Technical Assistance is only one of a number of instruments available to the U.S. to carry out its foreign policy and to promote its national interests abroad. Besides Technical Assistance, these tools of foreign policy include economic aid, military assistance, security treaties, overseas information programmes, participation in the U.N. and other international organizations, the exchange of persons programmes, tariff and trade policies, surplus agricultural commodities disposal policies and the traditional processes of diplomatic representation.[16]

Besides supporting American policy in Korea, the Pakistan government in 1952 recognized the puppet regime in South Vietnam. It was only a matter of time before Pakistan was brought into a military alliance against the Soviet Union and against People's China.

In September and October 1953 the Prime Minister and the Commander-in-Chief of the army, Ayub, visited the United States and negotiated military aid for Pakistan and the conditions which went with it. As neither Afghanistan nor India were prepared to enter into a military alliance with America, or hence with Pakistan,

---

[15] "The Burden of U.S. Aid," *Pakistan Today* (Autumn, 1961).
[16] Ibid., quoted from *Technical Assistance: Final Report of Committee on Foreign Relations*, March 12th, 1957.

it was decided to make the first moves through Turkey. On April 2nd, 1954, the Pakistan-Turkey military alliance was signed in Karachi. These two countries would help the United States to "contain" the Near and Middle East. The United States had achieved three aims: it had widened its spheres of influence to the southern borders of the Soviet Union; it had weakened Britain's position in the oil lands of the Middle East; and it had isolated India.

A month later, on May 19th, 1954, the United States and Pakistan signed the Mutual Aid and Security Agreement in Karachi. As many socialist writers have pointed out, there was nothing to justify the use of the word "mutual" in the agreement. It was completely one-sided: the United States would decide on its own initiative how much military aid Pakistan was to get, and most of the clauses in this "mutual security pact" were impositions on the government of Pakistan to act faithfully as a trustee of American interests in the region. American military personnel were given "diplomatic immunity" and, more important, had direct access to the Pakistan army. Under American strategy Pakistan was simply a jumping-off point for an invasion of the Soviet Union.

Once the Pakistani ruling class had decided to become puppets there was no stopping them. In September 1954, Pakistan, Thailand and the Philippines signed the South East Asia Defence Treaty (SEATO). The other Asian countries were, of course, Britain, the United States, Australia, New Zealand and France. The purpose of the treaty was to prevent social revolution in Asia or, in American parlance, "Chinese aggression". The complete impotence of the treaty has been demonstrated to us by the successes of the guerrillas in Vietnam and in Laos. Thailand, a SEATO country, is at the moment engaged in fighting a war in its north-eastern provinces; its capital, Bangkok, is known as America's favourite brothel in Asia after Saigon. SEATO became a pact of paper tigers.

The next pact which Pakistan entered into, in September 1955, was the Baghdad Pact, under which the Pakistani ruling class agreed to permit the armies of member countries to use Pakistani territory if the circumstances demanded it. Unfortunately for the countries who signed the pact (Pakistan, Iran, Turkey, Iraq and Britain), an army coup in Iraq resulted in the execution of its monarch and his advisers and the withdrawal of Iraq from the Baghdad Pact. This forced the defenders of the "free world" to change its name to the Central Treaty Organization (CENTO). Membership remained the same, minus one.

At the same time as the United States was harping on the worn-out theme of supporting Pakistan against attack, other U.S. spokesmen were repeating that these alliances would not be operative in any Indo-Pak conflict. The principal aim of the pacts was to make the Pakistan army a mercenary force ready to defend United States interests in the Middle East.

However, it became increasingly clear that the pacts were concerned with combating "subversion" at home as well as abroad. A study group of the Royal Institute of International Affairs reported: "The [SEATO] Council representatives were directed as one of their first tasks to arrange meetings of experts to consider means of strengthening co-operation in combating subversion and infiltration. The Council was obviously much preoccupied with this particular question ... [17]

An American liberal, Professor Ralph Braibanti, presented a paper on SEATO at the Lahore "Pacific Relations Conference"[18] and went on to remark, "Hence any kind of subversion could be interpreted as endangering the peace of the area. The danger lies in the possible use of this power to depose the government of a nation when that government is not acceptable to the treaty powers."

One result of United States military and economic aid is seen quite clearly by the whole world when the recipient country becomes a camp-follower of the United States on even the most petty question debated in the United Nations and elsewhere. But the insidious, less obvious, effects of aid on the internal regime of the country have been grossly underestimated. Military aid produces a change in the balance of socio-political forces in the receiving country in favour of semi-fascist, ultra-reactionary elements. In countries like Pakistan, where there is neither a strong trade-union movement nor a powerful peasantry, this results in the army becoming tainted with the ideology of American imperialism. As a document on the Mutual Security Programme admitted, "From a political viewpoint, U.S. military aid has strengthened Pakistan's armed services, *the greatest single stabilizing force in the country*, and has encouraged Pakistan to participate in collective defence agreements."[19]

[17] Ibid.
[18] The conference which took place in Lahore in the mid-'fifties was supposed to be a conference of regional C.I.A. operatives. The United States government has neither confirmed nor denied this.
[19] Ibid.

It is difficult to pinpoint differences between military and economic aid as both have one fixed purpose: political and economic domination of the receiving country. It is not difficult for a country to divert economic resources to military uses, though admittedly it has to be done in league with the "donor" — the United States of America.

The development of Pakistan's foreign policy from 1954 onwards held no surprises. Whenever there was a reactionary cause to be supported, the Pakistan government supported it. The climax of the decadent foreign policy followed by successive Pakistani governments came when the British, French and Israeli governments decided to invade Egypt on October 29th, 30th and 31st, 1956.

On July 26th, 1956, Nasser had nationalized the Suez Canal Company after Britain and America had decided to stop financing the building of the Aswan Dam. The imperialists, he had declared, could "choke in their rage". The nationalization of the Canal had been welcomed by the Pakistani masses; Nasser's action had stirred a chord in the soul of every country in a similar economic situation. Then imperialism and Zionism decided to attack Nasser for his impertinence, and a wave of anger gripped Pakistan. The horror of the people knew no bounds when the Prime Minister, H. S. Suhrawardy, justified the invasion. All the talk about "Muslim brotherhood" was forgotten, and the Pakistan government gave uncritical and shameless support to the imperialists. It is surprising that this particularly disgraceful act is ignored by most of the commentators who have written on Pakistan.[20]

The reaction was immediate. Once again the students gave a lead and mass demonstrations took place in both East and West Pakistan. In Lahore some of us who were still at school saw university students march into the school and order the Principal (an Irish Jesuit) to close it immediately in protest against the imperialist aggressors; when this was done, they asked us to join them in a march to the British High Commission office. A few of us were only too pleased to join the demonstration, and when we reached the office of the British Deputy High Commissioner we stoned it with a feeling of intense hatred.

[20] And this includes not only Callard, Khalid bin Sayeed and Wayne Wilcox, but also, for some strange reason, Gankovsky and Polonskaya. In addition Kamrudin Ahmed in his *Social History of East Pakistan* (op. cit.) is so busy praising Suhrawardy that he does not even mention the Suez crisis(!) or its effect on Pakistani politics (e.g. a split in the Awami League).

Mass demonstrations were called by the radical political parties throughout the country, and in the face of mammoth protests the Suhrawardy government was forced to alter its line; though the change had no practical effect since the United States had also decided to oppose the invasion.[21] Suhrawardy switched his support from the invasion to the idea of the Canal User's Association, which was also supported by the United States. The net result of all this was that Pakistan's reputation sank even lower in the Middle East, and in many Arab countries Pakistani diplomats were asked to stay indoors as their safety could not otherwise be guaranteed. At the same time Arabs were naming their children after the Indian Prime Minister, Nehru, because of his unflinching support for Egypt and his unequivocal denunciation of British, French and Israeli aggression. Pakistan, as far as the Middle East was concerned, deserved no better than to be what she was—a sewage tank of imperialism.

But the Pakistani government did not learn the lessons of Suez. It continued to support imperialistic policies throughout the world, and was hostile to the guerrilla war being waged by the Algerian people against French imperialism. The more servile the government became, the more angry were the people, and when President Iskandar Mirza of Pakistan went to visit President René Coty of France in November 1957 their anger turned to disgust. The *Pakistan Times* once again pictured accurately the mood of the people:

One subject common to the States, over which they preside is the frequent rise and fall of Ministries. They could with mutual advantage, compare notes about the speed with which their Cabinets disappear, and the prolonged negotiations that are often necessary before a new Government can be set up. On the present occasion political instability in France has an edge over the situation in Pakistan; after successfully persuading a new Coalition into power in Pakistan, President Mirza is in a position to give a few tips to President Coty ... [22]

Mirza had also claimed that his projected trip to France was a private one and that he would accompany Coty on a hunting excursion. No

[21] The Soviet "threat" that rockets would rain on London and Paris unless the "aggressor" withdrew aroused pro-Soviet feeling which was somewhat diminished when Russian tanks moved in to crush the Hungarian Revolution at roughly the same time.

[22] *Pakistan Times*, October 31st, 1957; Footnotes section headed "Two Presidents".

one was deceived by this. Even a section of the bureaucracy felt that a show of cordiality was completely unnecessary at this stage, and that if the Pakistan government could not support the Algerian struggle they could at least refrain from helping its enemies.

> When President Mirza wields a French gun standing shoulder to shoulder with the President of France, let him remember that French guns are not used merely to shoot pheasants, that French-men also use their guns to slaughter Algerian men and women — a people whom the people of Pakistan regard as brothers, with whose struggle for freedom we have the deepest and sincerest sympathy.[23]

Relations with India had steadily deteriorated and the reason for this was the thorny problem of Kashmir. Before Partition it had been decided that the inhabitants of predominantly Muslim areas of India would be allowed to decide for themselves whether they wanted to join Pakistan or remain a part of India. Well over 70 per cent of the inhabitants of the state of Kashmir and Jammu were Muslim, but the Maharaja of Kashmir was a Hindu. He refused to allow a plebiscite in Kashmir and finally decided to opt for India. War broke out between India and Pakistan, but as both armies were commanded by British officers it was not allowed to develop and there was a cease-fire on January 1st, 1949. The Indian government stated quite clearly that it was prepared to allow a plebiscite in Kashmir, but when Pakistan joined U.S.-sponsored military alliances the Indian govern-ment made this the excuse to go back on its promise. The attitude of the Indian Communist Party on this question, too, has been marked by a mixture of chauvinism and opportunism.[24]

[23] Ibid.

[24] For a long time the attitude of the C.P.I. was that a Kashmir in Pakistani hands would become a military base against China; however, since the Sino-Indian conflict and the Sino-Soviet dispute this is what Kashmir has become in Indian hands! The disgusting chauvinism displayed by both the Indian Com-munist Parties during the Indo-Pak war in 1965 is unrivalled even in the annals of international Stalinism. The only Indian Party to adopt a principled position on the Kashmir question, i.e. to demand the right of self-determination for the Kashmir people, and the only organization to oppose the chauvinism of the Communist Parties, was the Socialist Workers Party of India which is the Indian Section of the Trotskyist Fourth International. The "Naxalite" tendencies had at that stage not constituted themselves into one organization, though I have no doubt that they would have adopted a similar position as many individuals associated with them did.

Kashmir has always been the main bone of contention between the two countries. The Pakistan government, on its side, must bear complete responsibility for the fact that it has never allowed the Kashmiris living on the Pakistan side of the cease-fire line, in the area somewhat euphemistically designated as Azad (Free) Kashmir, to determine their own political future. (The treatment of the Kashmiri people on both sides of the cease-fire line is a subject which needs full investigation.) Kashmir has also been used cynically to divert attention from the more pressing problems facing the Pakistani and Indian governments at home. However, the problem of the Kashmiri people's right to national self-determination can be solved by them alone, and it is likely that they will have to struggle against both India and Pakistan and, fantastic though it may seem now, perhaps even against the united ruling classes of both India and Pakistan.

The end of the road

The year before the coup d'état in 1958 saw no major political developments. Ministry-making and breaking had by now become the favourite pastime of the Pakistani landlord-politicians. It seemed almost that they were fulfilling a death-wish. These were some of the features of the political game which was being played in Pakistan:

Firstly, the same faces are brought into the lime-light again and again. Secondly, the game does not directly concern the people in whose name it is played. The highest prize is POWER, and on its altar no sacrifice – of principle, decency or loyalty – is considered too great. Those deprived of it are insane with desire to regain it; those whose greasy hands grasp the heady cup are equally determined to ensure that they will hold it in perpetuity. These are the game's basic characteristics. However, variations do occur, depending on the political weather, the economic field conditions and on the personnel of the rival teams – those who are "in" and those who are "out". A great deal naturally depends on the qualities of the captain of the "in"-team, and the loyalty that he can exact from his team and its supporters ... With new selections scheduled for November 1958, for the first time in our history, everybody – would-be captains and players and committee members – is keen to join the "in"-team so that the selectors do not forget him next year.

Furthermore it appears that a large number of players insist on being appointed captain before agreeing to join the next round of the game. It is not possible to satisfy all the aspirants to captaincy without changing the rules; and if this were done there would be more captains than team members.[25]

As readers will have realized, the political bankruptcy of the land-lords and bureaucrats had reduced the country internally to a complete mess, while its external affairs were run entirely by the State Department in Washington. The long-awaited general election was being promised for November 1958, and the radical-democratic forces in the country were insisting that this date be finalized. However, President Iskandar Mirza was not very keen on the idea of a general election. Apart from his natural aversion to encouraging the masses to take part in the country's politics, he was also convinced that he and his creation, the Republican Party, would be routed in any free election in Pakistan. He had learnt from the experience of the international bourgeoisie: when you think you can't win an election, either postpone it or rig it. In Mirza's case it is possible that he would have lost even a rigged election unless he had the backing of the army to pressure the bureaucracy into supporting him.

Meanwhile, away from the cesspool of political intrigue, important developments were taking place both at the centre and in the provinces. The peasant organizations were beginning to elicit an encouraging response from the peasantry in both East and West Pakistan; industrial strikes were on the increase; and Maulana Bhashani had decided to split from the Awami League because of its pro-imperialist policies and had set up the National Awami Party, the first political party since Partition which could claim considerable support in both East and West Pakistan. These developments did not please the bureaucracy or Iskandar Mirza, and they started to move in order to circumvent the general election.

Maulana Bhashani had been involved in the anti-imperialist struggle for a long time before he split with Suhrawardy in the Awami League. At his instigation, and with the support of Mian Iftikharudin and the Azad Party in the West, September 11th, 1953, had been observed throughout Pakistan as "A day for struggle against imperialism". Hundreds of thousands of people had been mobilized at meetings and in demonstrations to attack the government's pro-American foreign policy. So it was not surprising that

[25] *Pakistan Times*, October 17th, 1957.

when Mr Suhrawardy became Prime Minister, and licked the arse of Anglo-American imperialism even more assiduously than his predecessors, the Maulana would not tolerate his presence in the Awami League. In early 1957 Bhashani visited West Pakistan, where he conferred with left-wing leaders, and in collaboration with them decided to call an All-Pakistan Conference of progressive organizations.

The conference was held in Dacca on July 25th and 26th, 1957, and resulted in the creation of a National Awami Party. The composition of the party varied from province to province, but broadly speaking it could be described as the first social-democratic party in Pakistan. Its declared aims were to create an anti-imperialist democratic state, to end feudalism, to speed up measures to industrialize the country and to hold immediate general elections. In some parts of West Pakistan it won supporters not because of its radical stance on imperialism or agrarian reform, but because of its principled and uncompromising stand on the question of regional autonomy for the component parts of West Pakistan and for East Bengal.

The formation of the N.A.P. was greeted with hysterical rage by a large section of the press and by all the right-wing parties. The Awami League, which had been the object of similar vilification some time ago, now joined in the anti-Communist fervour. The Awami League leaders, including H. S. Suhrawardy, had no arguments to rebut the charges levelled against them by Maulana Bhashani and his supporters, and started a campaign of abuse and slander which culminated in their supporters using knives and batons to break up some of the Maulana's meetings. One of the members of the East Pakistan cabinet, Mahmud Ali, resigned in protest at this gangsterism. The government continued to refer to the attempts to break up the N.A.P. convention and its meetings as "popular demonstrations" on the part of the people, when it was crystal clear that the hooliganism was inspired by the men in power. The atmosphere created in East Pakistan by the actions of the Awami League was later to provide the generals with an excuse for taking over.

In September 1957 reports in the press claimed that there was a plot to assassinate Maulana Bhashani. For some time the East Pakistan government refused to comment, and many people took their silence to mean that whether or not the plot existed the government thought it was a good idea. In September the Prime Minister admitted for the first time that perhaps elections could not be held in March 1958. The split in the Awami League, and the formation of the National Awami

6

Party were said to be not completely unconnected with this decision.

Despite the fact that the N.A.P. became the most radical party in Pakistani politics, it was not a revolutionary party in any sense of the term, and while it was right that Communists should work within it for a specific purpose, there was no justification at all for them doing so at the cost of building their own independent organization. Many Communists, foresaking the arena of the class struggle in the factories and in the countryside, became functionaries of the National Awami Party, and in West Pakistan they completely abandoned the task of building an underground revolutionary party. In East Pakistan the underground party continued to exist but some of its best cadres submerged themselves in the N.A.P.; some of them have yet to surface.

While the National Awami Party indulged in a certain amount of political intrigue in West Pakistan with the extreme right-wing Republican Party and the Muslim League, it must be said to its credit that it was the only political party in Pakistan which did not succumb to the lure of office. In both East and West Pakistan the N.A.P. could have made expedient alliances to get a few ministerial posts for its leading members, but though it was prepared to make unprincipled alliances to undo One Unit in West Pakistan, it was not prepared to sink any lower, and in the murky politics of Pakistan this was a unique distinction.

In October 1957 the Suhrawardy government had fallen and a new government had been sworn in. Two months later the new government fell, and in December 1957 the last parliamentary government came into power. It was headed by an old Punjabi landlord, Firoz Khan Noon.

During 1958 the political and economic situations both deteriorated still further. In the countryside "acreage of land under cultivation decreased, the yield of food crops fell and the level of rural production and consumption declined still further. Agricultural output in Pakistan decreased by 4·2 per cent in 1958, while the yield of rice the principal food crop dropped by almost six per cent."[26] The government was forced to increase considerably the prices of essential foodstuffs. The reason for this was the American economic recession, which had increased the strain on the producers of agricultural raw materials, who were the most direct victims of recessions in the West. Countries like Pakistan rely on the export of their raw material for

[26] Gankovsky and Polonskaya, op. cit.

badly-needed foreign exchange, and their dependence on the West in foreign trade makes it virtually impossible for them to extricate themselves from the downturns in the capitalist economy of the United States and Western Europe. Besides the economic recession there was also a crop failure in East Pakistan, and it was necessary for Pakistan to import some food grains from abroad.

But the Pakistani ruling class was not too worried by these trends, and they went ahead calmly to increase the amount of money to be spent for military purposes in the 1958 spring budget, while at the same time reducing the amounts normally allocated for the social services. In February 1958 price control was formally abolished, and the prices of principal consumer goods rocketed sky high. The living costs of the workers rose phenomenally, and according to some estimates the cost of living in different Pakistani towns went up by an average of 8·2 per cent.[27]

Since the end of 1957 the workers had been becoming increasingly active, and to deal with the industrial unrest the Pakistan government tried to curb still more stringently their right to strike. Strikes continued, nevertheless, and in suppressing them the police resorted to violence and intimidation of the worst order. Where the police were not available, the employers had their own hired thugs who performed the same task.

Between 1957 and October 1958 the militancy of the urban proletariat had reached a new height. But it was not restricted to the workers: it also began to affect the peasants. In January 1958 Maulana Bhashani had set up the All-Pakistan Peasant Association. A campaign demanding the abolition of landlordism was initiated throughout the country. Its climax was a march by hundreds of thousands of peasants through the streets of Lahore, the West Pakistani capital, demanding that the eviction of tenants be stopped, that landlordism be ended and that uncultivated land be handed over to landless peasants.

The demonstrations had no effect. On the contrary, many of the peasant leaders were victimized, and landlords threatened that their paid gangsters would "deal" with peasants who took part in any similar demonstration. On May 8th, 1958, an incident took place in Lundo village in the countryside of Sind. The local police made a completely unprovoked attack on the *haris* (peasants) in the village, they seized their harvest, ransacked their homes, assaulted their

[27] *Financial Times*, May 11th, 1959.

women, and arrested seventy of the men. The local landlords made their contribution by burning the houses of a few *haris*.

> The situation which this woeful tale of pillage, arbitrariness and unlawful persecution brings to light did not arise simply as a result of an aberration on the part of a few hotheads among landlords and of a few policemen who became their helpers and abetters. Such occurrences are easily made possible by the pattern of rural relationships (in West Pakistan) ... [28]

Only a month later the newspapers published horrifying tales of the way peasants were treated by feudal landlords in the North West Frontier. One of the accused landlords was the Nawab of Hoti, a provincial cabinet minister. As usual, the government promised inquiries which came to nothing. The result was increased militancy on the part of the poor peasants.

At the same time other strata of society were pressing their demands for better working conditions. In April 1958 over thirty thousand school teachers came out on strike in West Pakistan, and some five thousand of them demonstrated on the streets of Lahore. Over two thousand of these teachers (those employed in Multan) had not received the preceding month's wages. The teachers threatened an indefinite general strike until their demands were met, and the authorities were forced to make some concessions. The government did not seem to be learning the lessons of the increasing militancy. On the morning of June 20th, 1958, workers were trying to occupy a strike-bound factory in Lyallpur after the President of their union had been arrested. Without warning, the police had opened fire. Six workers were killed and twenty-one seriously injured. While the class struggle was beginning to envelop the entire country, its self-appointed legislators showed no signs of understanding the importance of the events taking place in the factories and in the countryside.

It became clearer and clearer that the ruling class was not interested in a general election, and it almost seemed that the bureaucracy was deliberately engineering a situation where "law and order" was seen to deteriorate. Police excesses in 1958 reached massive proportions, and it should be remembered that the police were, in practice, under the control of the bureaucracy.

It seemed as though the politicians, too, were behaving in such fashion as to provoke military and bureaucratic forces to come out

[28] *Pakistan Times*, May 16th, 1958.

in the open and exercise power directly. Incidents in the West Pakistan legislature on March 20th, 1958, where fist-fights broke out, were described thus:

> Some heat and passion inside a legislature is understandable when vital national issues come up for discussion ... However it was not because of some matter of national life and death under discussion in the House that important party leaders ran amuck, members stood on their seats, shouted en masse, packed the verandas and corridors of the Assembly precincts with tough and strong-armed men ... All this commotion occurred not because one party sought to reduce the miseries of the common man and the other tried to add to them ... All this infernal row was over a dozen Ministerial chairs which in the situation prevailing today, are hardly worth the wood they are made of ...
>
> Feudal lords and their retainers, old bureaucrats and their satellites, business sharks and soldiers of fortune, men who have never lost a day's rest or a night's sleep in the cause of freedom, democracy, or people's rights, have little use for rights, conventions and institutions won after centuries of suffering and struggle. They are only interested in the benefit which the trappings and stage-properties of democracy may help them to grab ... [All this] provides an argument against democracy and people's rights to those who would prefer to have even the trappings and stage-properties out of the way ... [29]

The murder of the Chief Minister of West Pakistan, and the murder in the East Pakistan legislature of the Deputy Speaker by angry members, did not improve matters much. Increasing anti-American sentiment among the people, which was forcing even the Pakistan government to admit that it might have to change its foreign policy, also increased fears that a general election would provoke a mass upsurge. President Iskandar Mirza had been engaged in an intrigue with General Ayub for quite some time, and on October 7th, 1958, the army seized power directly.

[29] *Pakistan Times*, March 22nd, 1958.

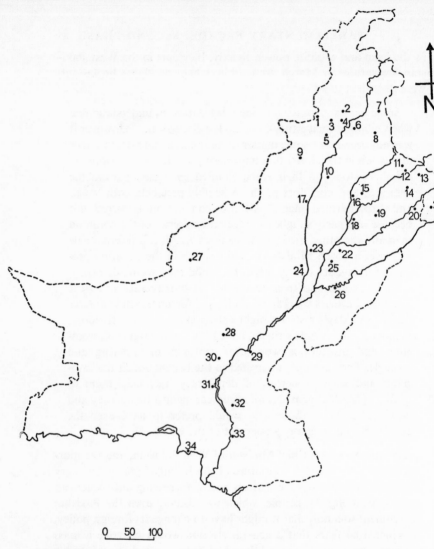

0   50   100

West Pakistan Towns

1. Landi Kotal	13. Sialkot	24. Dera Ghazi Khan
2. Mardan	14. Gujranwala‡	25. Multan
3. Peshawar‡	15. Sargodha	26. Bahawalpur
4. Nowshera‡	16. Sahiwal	27. Quetta
5. Kohat	17. Dera Ismail Khan	28. Kanpur
6. Campbellpur	18. Jhang Maghiana	29. Sukkur
7. Abbottabad	19. Lyallpur	30. Larkana
8. Rawalpindi‡	20. Lahore‡	31. Dadu
9. Bannu	21. Amritsar	32. Nawabshah
10. Mianwali	22. Kabirwala	33. Hyderabad‡
11. Lala Musa	23. Kot Adu	34. Karachi‡
12. Gujrat		

KEY: All the towns marked on these pages were affected by the struggle. Deaths occurred in the towns marked with a double dagger.

CHAPTER THREE

Military-Bureaucratic Dictatorship I, 1958-62

> "We must understand that democracy cannot work in a hot climate. To have democracy we must have a cold climate like Britain." General Ayub Khan (after becoming Chief Martial Law Administrator)

Martial Law

The main reason for the army's coup d'état on October 8th, 1958, was the bureaucracy's overriding urge to prevent Pakistan's first-ever general election from taking place in March 1959. The prospect of the forthcoming election had increased the growing restlessness of the masses, and this had tempted the leaders of the opposition parties into making a number of sweeping promises of radical reform. The collapse of the Baghdad Pact following the liberation of Iraq from the rule of a corrupt and feudal monarchy had increased anti-American and anti-British feeling. Any elected government of Pakistan would have had to make concessions to this manifestation of public opinion, and a new government would have been forced to withdraw from the military alliances. An elected government would also have had more confidence to combat the influence of the bureaucracy, and to establish civilian control over the army.

As far as the Pakistani civil service, the army and the C.I.A. were concerned an elected government was something Pakistan could do without at this particular stage. The President of Pakistan in 1958 was a hardened old civil servant, trained by the British, who had first hired him, in the fine art of political intrigue and in the appreciation of the nuances of political power. Mirza had perfected his talents after independence, and in recent years his position as Defence Secretary, the bureaucrat in charge of relations with the army, had given him an opportunity to establish contact with the army and its Commander-in-Chief, General Ayub.

When the army and the civil service decided on a military take-over they were, in fact, formalizing a situation which had existed almost

87

since the Partition of the sub-continent. The United States involvement in the coup could not be proved, though Ayub's brother was later to allege that the C.I.A. was definitely involved. Despite the lack of evidence it is quite a logical conclusion. The State Department virtually controlled every facet of policy-making in Pakistan and without foreign aid the very existence of feudalism and capitalism in Pakistan would be threatened. United States ambassadors to Pakistan were in the habit of behaving like proconsuls and their arrogance and condescension succeeded in annoying a significant section of the Pakistani bureaucracy.

The coup d'état was thus inflicted on the people of Pakistan by a military-bureaucratic complex with the connivance of the Central Intelligence Agency. The *New York Times*, commenting editorially on the new regime in Pakistan, stated somewhat blandly:

> As a matter of principle we deplore the suspension of constitutional government and the substitution for it of rule by martial law. For that reason we shall watch with some anxiety the present crisis wherein the cabinet and parliament have been dismissed and the army under orders from the President has taken over ... At the same time it is necessary to recognize the purposes for which such drastic action has been taken. In Pakistan both President Mirza and the army's head General Ayub Khan have stated clearly that what they propose and wish to do is to establish in due course a fine, honest, and democratic government. There is no reason to doubt their sincerity.[1]

But others, particularly progressive Pakistanis, were in no doubt as to the intentions of the army and the civil service. The power of the civil service had increased vastly because of the lack of any strong political party, and because of the general instability of the political situation, which was manipulated by the civil service itself. A leading Pakistani socialist wrote that:

> In Pakistan the army and the bureaucracy had played a dominant and decisive role; the "seizure" of power in 1958 by General Ayub Khan in the name of the army was just a dramatic movement in that continuing domination. The army came to the fore during crises; but the bureaucracy actively dominated the

---

[1] *New York Times*, October 12th, 1958.

AYUB'S FRIENDS

(*top*) With Lyndon Johnson in Washington (Z. A. Bhutto, then Foreign Minister, is in the centre).

(*centre*) With Kosygin and late Indian Prime-Minister Shastri at Tashkent, after signing the declaration.

(*bottom*) With Chairman Mao in Peking.

BENGALI LEADERS

(*above*) Maulana Abdul Hamid Khan Bhashani, eighty-six-year-old peasant leader, and leader of the pro-Peking faction of the National Awami Party. He started his political career as a terrorist while he was still in his teens, and he told me that he had killed over a dozen British civil servants. Since then he has been working in the countryside, where he has a strong base. Though he is completely non-theoretical and semi-religious, he supports the idea of a peasant revolution in Pakistan. He has visited Peking, Moscow and Havana and has met both Mao and Fidel.

(*left*) Sheikh Mujibur Rehman, leader of the Awami League and the Bengali bourgeoisie. He is denounced by left-wing students as the Bengali Chiang Kai-shek, but is popular with some of the petit-bourgeoisie and an ardent Bengali nationalist. He was imprisoned intermittently during the years of the Ayub regime.

(*top right*) The revolutionary student leader Mahbubullah addresses a meeting of workers, students and peasants, estimated at over a million strong, at the racecourse in Dacca.

(*right*) One of the few peaceful and unprovoked marches of the upsurge. Bengali women march in solidarity with dead and injured students in Dacca. Their bare feet are a sign of both protest and mourning.

(*above*) A demonstrator is attacked by a Dacca policeman.

(*left*) Bhashani defies the military curfew and harangues the soldiers. By his side is a West Pakistan colleague, Arif Iftikhar.

(*facing page*) Bhutto being greeted at Lahore airport after his release from prison.

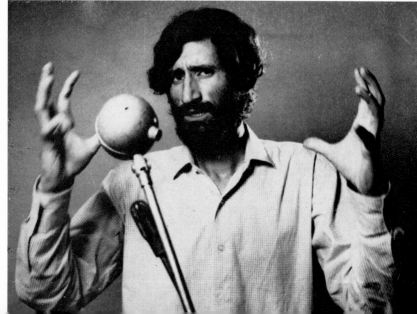

(*top left*) A massive demonstration of workers in Lahore.

(*left*) Raja Anwar, the Rawalpindi student leader, addressing a press conference. His initiatives resulted in the Rawalpindi upsurge taking a political direction in November 1968. Because of his known left-wing views, Anwar's role was grossly underestimated by the government-controlled press.

(*above*) Tariq Ali addressing a workers' demonstration in Lyallpur, where the Saigol family (one of the twenty families which control the country's economy) has its industrial stronghold.

(*following page*) A secret anti-communist memorandum issued by the Education Department in West Pakistan soon after Ayub assumed power.

Copy of Memo No.25988-G., dated 10.8.1959 sent by the Director of Education, Lahore Region, Lahore to the Registrar, University of the Panjab, Lahore for information.

S E C R E T

SUBJECT:-CONTROL OF COMMUNIST LITERATURE.

.000000000000000_

Instances have come to the notice of Government of Pakistan where communist missions particularly that of Russia are making intensive efforts for disseminating communist literature through their contacts. This is, therefore the time to prevent the publicity and wide circulation of such undersirable publications, magazines etc. In view of the foregoin position the Government have, after discussing the issue, come to the conclusion that it has become essential at this st.ge to take stringent measures possible to

(a) stop the infiltration of communist literature in to the country; an
(b) prohibit its publication and circulation within the country.

In this connection this Department has been directed to undertake a survey of books etc in university and college/school libraries to ensur that all objectionable materials already with these institutions are withdrawn and substituted with good literature.

It is, therefore, requested that statistics showing the extent of undesirable literature particularly that relating to communist trends & themes that has found its way into Colleges and Libraries and needs replacement in the matter may please be supplied along with your comments, in triplicate, to this Directorate immediately.

UNIVERSITY OF THE PANJAB.

No. 9110 /Ec   Dated 22.9.1959.
          Copy of the above is forwarded to the Librarian, Panjab University Library, Principals of affiliated Colleges exoluding Government Colleges, Heads of the University Teaching Departments and Conveners of the Boards of Studies for necessary compliance in regard to Library Books and the Books recommended, suggested or prescribed for stud for the various Examinations. Your, reply may kindly be sent to the undersigned in sealed cover by the 30th of September, 1959 at the latest.

                                        Yours obediently,

                                   Assistant Registrar(General),
                                        for Registrar.

political scene then and in normal times. In the first decade after independence the façade of parliamentary government obscured the role of the bureaucracy and did its bidding. However, when radical political parties posed a challenge to its authority the bureaucracy put an end to the constitutional apparatus of government and assumed power directly ... [2]

In October 1958 the army and the bureaucracy were fulfilling their traditional role in capitalist and feudal societies: they were taking precautions against a revolutionary movement threatening the hallowed institutions of private property. The middle-class in West Pakistan had failed to build a solid bourgeois-democratic party which could successfully maintain political stability and at the same time attempt to sidetrack and divert revolutionary upsurges. This failure was a boon to the army and the civil service, who were well organized, well paid and in the case of the army well armed, making them the two strongest "political parties" in Pakistan. When the British ruled India the civil servants and the army were directly under their control, but on their withdrawal from the political scene, and in the absence of strong indigenous class forces in Pakistan, the army and the bureaucracy tended to dominate the situation. Unlike India, where the Congress Party was to a large extent the party of the native bourgeoisie, in Pakistan the Muslim League could not fulfil that role. Its narrow, feudal base made its existence as a political party something of an anomaly even in Pakistan. When the League collapsed, there was no party that could take its place. The bourgeoisie had no option but to deal directly with the bureaucracy, which in its turn became the defender of capitalist interests in Pakistan.

As governments changed rapidly and ministers were replaced with monotonous regularity, the civil service became responsible for granting import and export licences, government loans and route permits for private bus companies, and by this distribution of patronage it acquired great political influence. Many bureaucrats were thus assured of financial security, and sometimes they even turned their talents to accumulating profits more directly and joining the ranks of the bourgeoisie. The bureaucracy also had direct links with the feudal landlords in the countryside through the *lambardars*,

[2] Hamza Alavi, "Army and Bureaucracy in Pakistan", *International Socialist Journal*, Year 3, No. 14 (March–April, 1966). The journal has now ceased publication.

whose formal function was to collect land revenue and who was in most cases the local landlord appointed directly by the government (i.e. the bureaucracy).

Thus the bureaucracy maintained links with both the landlords and the bourgeoisie. The latter were extremely hesitant to support any movement which was likely to challenge the power of the bureaucracy. Opposition to the bureaucrats was therefore restricted to the petit-bourgeoisie. Small businessmen often showed signs of a general discontent, but their position was too vulnerable for them to attempt a direct confrontation with the bureaucracy. The trade associations through which they could perhaps have articulated their demands were effectively silenced some years after the coup when the associations were amalgamated in the federal framework of the Chambers of Commerce dominated by the big bourgeoisie.

The confusion which existed in virtually every sphere of administrative activity after Partition left the bureaucrats in an extremely strong position. The Muslim politicians were inexperienced; the Muslim bureaucrats were not. Ministers had no option but to leave the real business to the civil servants while they immersed themselves in the struggle to cling to political power. In the article quoted above, Hamza Alavi stressed the cohesiveness of the Civil Service of Pakistan (C.S.P.) and argued that:

> The supremacy of the bureaucracy was facilitated by the fact that the top bureaucracy is a tightly-knit cohesive group with caste-like characteristics. Five hundred men of the civil service of Pakistan now stand at the top of an administrative machinery of over 500,000. Within this small group there is an inner elite — the survivors of the eighty-two members of the former Indian Civil Service who came to Pakistan. Their distinctiveness was underlined by the special constitutional guarantees of their status and terms and conditions of service — virtual guarantee of permanence in service. The C.S.P. is a closed group. The process of recruitment and subsequent training is controlled by the bureaucracy through the Public Service Commission whose "autonomy" is jealously guarded.[3]

The Pakistani civil servant is a caricature of the British civil servant in India. He has his own special clubs, his own private and

[3] Ibid.

closed circle and he even attempts to cultivate the mannerisms of his superiors, who learnt them from the British. But he has not been able to mimic successfully the paternalism of the British as the colour of his skin is no different from that of the people he has been chosen to rule over. This means he has to maintain his sense of superiority in other ways, which tends to make him even more oppressive. The net result is that civil servants form one of the most despised and hated sections of the population. But their complacent attitudes and their training have made them impervious to the feelings of the people who, when they complain, are obviously being manipulated by Communists, Indian agents, anti-Islamic elements in our society ...

The Pakistan army, despite similarities to the bureaucracy, has one important difference. While the upper crust of the army remains true to the "glorious traditions" handed down by the British, the lower stratum consists of rank-and-file soldiers for whom the army is merely a means of employment. In most cases they are peasants in uniform, who, instead of seeking employment in the cities, have turned to the army, where average wages and conditions are far superior. Instead of becoming proletarianized they have become militarized.

Until the turn of the century the British army in India had been officered exclusively by whites; the natives were considered useful only as cannon-fodder. During the First World War however, the necessities of the battlefield dictated British policies and a few Indians were made officers. Recruitment was very selective, and only old-established landed families were encouraged to send their young men into the army. But the colour of their skin was brown, and a breach had been made. The mood of post-war nationalism in 1918–19, and the fact that the British army in India was short of officers, allowed the British to solve their officer problem as well as appease the demands of moderate nationalism. Moreover, the native officers would be useful in "combating subversion and terrorism in India itself".

The recruitment policy concentrated on the politically apathetic and backward areas of India, which meant virtually restricting recruitment to the countryside; those with an urban background were more susceptible to nationalist politics. Sir George MacMunn wrote about this aspect quite openly in his appalling book *The Martial Races of India*:

The staunch old Indian yeoman who came into the Indian commissioned ranks via the rank and file, or the young Indian landowner made the Indian officer as we know him ... The clever young men of the Universities were quite unfitted for military work ... the army officers had long realized that the Indian intelligentsia would never make officers.[4]

To rationalize this policy the myth of "martial races" was invented, and the Sikhs, the Gurkhas and Muslims from the Jhelum and Campbellpur areas in the Punjab were recruited to do British imperialism's dirty work both inside and outside India. After Partition the Pakistan army continued along the same lines, and as a result the Bengalis of East Pakistan were virtually excluded from the army, as they had been in the days of the raj: Bengal had always been a strong nationalist base in India. The same racial myths were effectively propagated throughout West Pakistan: the Bengalis were short and ugly; they were not fighting people; they were cowards at heart; and many other crude and semi-fascist generalizations. Bengalis with whom I discussed the matter were not amused. They pointed out that their physical characteristics differed from the Vietnamese only in that the average Vietnamese was shorter than the average Bengali.

Many of the Indian officers recognized that they were being used to fight against the interests of their own people. In most cases they tried to rationalize this contradiction by citing the doctrine of professionalism, which had been instilled into them by the British to preserve them from politics and the native politicians: the army was supposed to be above politics. Writing on the role of Muslim Indian officers in the service of the British a Pakistani general maintained that: "They fought and died not as hirelings of a mercenary army, but as loyal soldiers conscious of their worth and proud of the splendid part they were playing in defending *their own country, their own culture, and faith.*"[5]

But historical realities cannot be distorted by pompous phrases. The Indian officers who served in the British army were essentially mercenaries, and the treatment they received from the British was much worse than the treatment white mercenaries in Africa today receive at the hands of their black employers. These officers were *not*

[4] Quoted in R. P. Dutt, *India Today* (London, 1940).
[5] Major-General Fazle Muqeem Khan, *Story of the Pakistan Army* (Karachi, 1963).

"defending their own country": they were defending British interests throughout the world. Their country was being ruled by the British and by serving in the army they were perpetuating that rule. It is as simple as that. The British used Indian troops for quelling uprisings in China, Malaya, Burma and Iran. In 1945, when Ho Chi Minh's armies had established control in the main cities of Vietnam, Indian troops commanded by General Gracey re-established control on behalf of the French. By no stretch of the imagination can this be construed as Indian officers "defending their own country, their own culture". From this background came the Indian officers who were to form the core of the future Pakistani and Indian armies.

When it was decided to Indianize the army the British arranged for a number of Indians to be trained at Sandhurst every year. Ayub Khan was one of those who was sent. He was, as he proudly recalls, "the first foreign cadet to be promoted Corporal and given two stripes".[6] What the young Ayub did in the racist atmosphere of Sandhurst to be the first *coloured* cadet to become a Corporal we will never find out, unless of course some of his contemporaries in the Indian army decide to write their memoirs.

The massacres which occurred during Partition and the migration of eight million Muslim refugees from India to Pakistan left a deep mark on some officers, and many Muslim officers had to leave their families behind as well as their property. Many of them saw the massacres but were powerless to prevent them. Others did defend the refugees from attack. The conflict with India on Kashmir further affected the army, and

> Therefore from Partition the army was deeply involved in the political conflict with India which has dominated Pakistan's foreign policy. This conflict has provided the army with its central creed and purpose. Patriotism in Pakistan has taken an essentially negative form which uses the Indian conflict as a foil. Otherwise people see themselves as Bengalis, Punjabis, Sindhis, Pathans or Baluchis with their different linguistic and cultural roots; our people are Muslims, a category which transcends national patriotism. The search for an identity is a major problem in Pakistan.[7]

In the early 'fifties, and particularly after the British General

[6] Mohammed Ayub Khan, *Friends Not Masters — A Political Autobiography* (Oxford, 1967).
[7] Hamza Alavi, op. cit.

Gracey was no longer Commander-in-Chief of the Pakistan army, there was a distinct and clear-cut trend towards establishing closer links with the United States. Under the first Pakistani Commander-in-Chief, General Ayub Khan, this trend was transformed into a pattern, and it later became an established principle that the United States and not Britain controlled the development of the Pakistan army. In February 1954 an American military mission was received in Rawalpindi by army chiefs, and in October U.S.M.A.A.G. (United States Military Assistance Advisory Group) was set up at the army G.H.Q. in Rawalpindi. It was no secret that the Pakistan army dealt directly with the Pentagon and that the civilian government had little idea of what went on.

The economic-military-political relationship with the United States meant that Pakistan had been "admitted to the free world", like South Vietnam and South Korea and Thailand. In other words, Pakistan's domestic and foreign policies became completely subservient to American interests. The Pakistani government was not so much a dictatorship of the native bourgeoisie as a client government of the United States. United States influence in the army became all-powerful; officers were bribed with U.S.-sponsored study tours in America and special training courses, and individual American officers were attached to Pakistani army units and headquarters. It was in these circumstances that the army assumed political power on October 7th, 1958, and declared Martial Law. Its leader, General Ayub, became Chief Martial Law administrator.

Ayub was not completely unprepared for this eventuality. In fact it could be said that he had been actively concerned in planning the take-over with the President Iskandar Mirza for a number of years. In 1957 Ayub had been due to retire. The politicians had been quite eager that he should do so, but they were overruled by Iskandar Mirza who was personally responsible for an extension of Ayub's term as Commander-in-Chief. Meantime Ayub had initiated discussions in the army with a group of "like-minded" officers – and unfortunately for the army there were quite a few of them in existence – on how the country should be run. It is possible, though unlikely, that Ayub would have continued to share his power with Mirza. However, the President, unable to resist any opportunity for intrigue, questioned Ayub's authority, giving Ayub an excuse to remove him. In the brief period of twenty days Ayub became undisputed ruler of Pakistan.

Martial Law administrators were appointed and made responsible for running both East and West Pakistan. They were backed to the hilt by the Pakistani Civil Service, who in reality carried out the actual administration of the country. The C.S.P.'s support could be relied on all the more confidently because the military government was threatening to investigate the financial resources of some civil servants.

In the first flush of power Ayub promised many reforms, and commissions were set up to prepare reports for the military government. There were, for example, reports on Land Reform, on Education, on Pay and Services, on Food and Agriculture, Medical Reforms, Sports and Culture, and on Marriage and Family Law. The most important of them all was the report on Land Reform, and it is worth considering the whole question of land reform, and the report itself, in some detail.

Land Reform

The prompt establishment of a Land Reform Commission by the new regime was hailed by many Pakistanis who were looking for any excuse to welcome their new rulers; and even people who were less favourable towards the regime saw in the commission a glimmer of hope, as it might mean that there was a "Nasserite" element in the army.

The report, which was used to a large extent as a propaganda gimmick to illustrate the "progressive" nature of Ayub's government, turned out to be simply an old ruling-class trick: a few theoretical reforms whose main function was in practice to preserve the status quo. The Ayub regime decreed an ownership ceiling of 500 acres of irrigated and 1,000 acres of non-irrigated land. However, exemptions were provided, such as an extra 150 acres for orchards or for lands being used for cattle-farming. Landlords who had gifted some of their land to their heirs or other dependents to avoid paying tax or because they had been warned of the impending reforms were not seriously affected. Certainly the landlords themselves praised the land reforms in glowing terms. Mir Ghulam Ali Talpur, a former Cabinet Minister and a big landlord of Sind, declared that the reforms were extremely generous to the landed gentry and the reason for this was " ... because of the big heart of the President". Arbab Noor Mohammed Khan, a leading landowner of the North West Frontier, was even more blatant: "Had these reforms been delayed longer a violent revolution might have taken place destroying the present goodwill between tenants and landlords."

The major aims of the land reforms were to create the impression that the new regime was a reforming government, and that it was fighting the landlords. In fact nothing was farther from the truth. The principle underlying the reforms was not equality for the peasants but equality for the landlords. While the very large landowners were a bit irritated by the reforms they did not affect the average landlord at all. More important, the basic problem of the Pakistani country-side was left completely untouched. The main cause of the backward-ness of the agrarian system, the separation of ownership and cultivation, remained exactly the same. Admittedly, it was stated that some of the excess land taken from some landlords would be available for sale and that the existing tenants would be given the first option, but in most cases the tenants lacked funds to buy the land, and moneylending in Pakistan is controlled by the landlords.

But there was something even more fundamentally wrong with the land reforms. The problem in Pakistan was not simply that of dividing the big estates and giving them to the peasantry; the peasants tilled most of the land already. The answer was to make them owner-cultivators; to give them legal rights of ownership over the land which they and their forefathers had been tilling for decades. It was ridiculous to impose a ceiling of five hundred acres and leave it at that. The ceiling should have been restricted to the number of acres the landlord tilled himself, and ownership should have been made conditional on self-cultivation. This is what was required if the government was seriously intent on land reforms. Ayub's land reform merely boosted the existing system of land tenure. Small wonder that the peasant leaders used to laugh when the regime's friendly "intellectuals" used to talk about the advantages of land reform.

At the time of the "reforms" 6,000 landowners representing 0·10 per cent of the total number of persons engaged in agriculture owned 7·5 million acres of land in estates of 500 acres and over. 2·2 million persons owned less than five acres, and another 2·5 million peasants owned no land at all and were either agricultural workers or tenants. In spite of this concentration, the fragmentation of land into small cultivation units is common because the landlords rent out the land to peasants on the basis of share-cropping. In the Punjab, for instance, the peasant used to hand over 50 per cent of the produce to the landlord. A law bringing the percentage down to 40 per cent was ignored.

Landlordism was introduced to India by the British. Lord Cornwallis's "permanent settlement" scheme had two main purposes: First, to create a "vast body of rich landed proprietors deeply interested in the continuance of British Dominion and having complete command over the mass of the people" (Lord Bentinck). Secondly, to use the new landlords to collect land revenue for the British administration. The existing cultivators of the land were thus reduced to produce-sharing tenants and forced to live in conditions of even harsher poverty. This situation still exists in large parts of West Pakistan today. The land reforms of the Ayub government were completely irrelevant to the needs of the peasantry.

Of course, few socialists expected Ayub to solve the agrarian question. Experience has shown us that the agrarian problem can be solved only by a workers' and peasants' government acting on the theories of scientific socialism. What is striking about the Ayub reform is that it was so blatantly a preservation of the status quo that even its propaganda effects were limited as far as the Pakistani people were concerned, though it is possible that it had the desired effects on the dispensers of aid in Washington, Bonn and London.

The Pakistani landlord still lives in a medieval world of his own construction, ruling "his" tenants with an iron hand. The power of the feudal landlords has increased since Partition. The main reason for this is that the Hindu and Sikh moneylenders, who were the main group of moneylenders, migrated to India. They had been oppressive and grasping it is true, but they did offer an independent source of cash to the peasant. Now this function, like many others, is performed by the landlord.[8]

Soon after Partition there had been a great deal of talk about land reform and as the *Pakistan Times* pointed out, "Even a conservative body like the Muslim League Land Reform Committee recommended an upper limit of 150 acres of irrigated land."[9] The plight of the *haris* of Sind forced the Sind government to set up a commission to investigate their problems. The *Hari* Committee, as it was called, was

[8] Much of this information has been quite shamelessly taken from the only worthwhile study made of Ayub's Land Reform, namely, a special number of *Pakistan Today* on this subject. The magazine was brought out by Pakistani progressives living in London and was in the years of Martial Law the only glimmer of hope for some of us in West Pakistan. The journal is now, alas, defunct.

[9] *Pakistan Times*, January 26th, 1959.

composed of Sir Roger Thomas, a landlord and a government official. Thomas produced a report designed to whitewash the landlords and paint a rosy picture of the Sind countryside. The Sind authorities had, however, made a mistake in their choice of the third member of the committee, a supposedly pliant government official. He produced in 1948–9 a dissenting report which was first suppressed by the government and later released under strong pressure from sections of the press. The report has come to be known as the Masud Report, after the name of the official, who himself became known as *Hari* Masud. The picture painted by Masud is on nearly all points at odds with the Thomas report:

They [the *haris*] are human beings and, as such, rational animals, and though they drudge like common beasts of burden, they enjoy no privileges of rationality nor any rights of human beings. Such are the *haris* of Sind ...

When I came to Sind I was shocked to see the miserable conditions of the *haris* ... they are no better than serfs. They live in the most primitive conditions without any conception of social, political or economic rights. They have only one interest in life —food—with which to keep body and soul together. No other problem attracts them because the fundamental problem of living remains unsolved for them.

The *haris* have no organized life, nor has the consciousness of organized living developed in them yet. They live scattered, far from one another, in small hamlets consisting of thatched mud houses ... Most of the *haris* share huts with cattle ... The *hari* who has cultivated a piece of land for several generations does not know how long he will be allowed to stay on it. Fear reigns supreme ... fear of imprisonment, fear of losing his land, wife or life. The *zamindar* (landlord) might at any time get annoyed with him and oust him. He may have to leave his crop half ripe. His cattle might also be snatched away and he might be beaten out of the village. The *zamindar* might at any time send for the *hari* for purposes of forced labour and force him to work on the construction of his house, the sinking of a well or some other *minor* work. The *hari* might be asked to come with his plough and bullocks to cultivate the private field of the *zamindar* or to spend a few days on a shoot with him, or to render some domestic service. He dare not refuse ...

The elections bring in their wake big calamities for the poor *hari*. The rival candidates pull him in opposite directions but he is interested in none of them. His *zamindar* who has received a large amount of money ... calls the *hari* and tells him to vote for the candidate of the *zamindar*'s choice ... If the rival candidate wins there are fresh miseries in store ... He is troubled and harassed ...

The *hari* behaves like a helpless slave when he has to face the *zamindar*. It is not an unusual sight to see how numerous *haris* come and touch the feet of a *zamindar*. As soon as the *zamindar* appears on the fields the *hari* and his children go and bow before him till they touch his feet, then rise up to kiss his hand. This they do not out of respect but to make him feel that they are his humble creatures who prostrate themselves before him and live at his mercy ...

Islam gives him the ideal of the greatness of God and submission to no one except Him. But when his Islam is put to the test in the fields where the *zamindar* has taken hold of all the resources of the earth in the name of Islam and can at any moment starve the poor *hari* to death, the great ideals of Islam vanish from the *hari*'s mind. He forgets the greatness of God and bows in abject submission to the *zamindar*. The *hari* has lived under oppression and tyranny for several generations. He feels that this is perhaps his destiny and the local religious "leaders", the *pirs* and the *mullahs* console the *hari* with the doctrine of "fate".

Let us now look at the *zamindar*. He is a feudal lord and maintains a legion of servants, owns fine horses, cows and buffaloes. He possesses a large number of firearms and his shooting expenses every year run into thousands of rupees. Extravagance in food and dress, gross and vulgar sexual excesses, garish ostentations are the things on which he chooses to devote his income. He has feudal rivalries with the neighbouring landlords and has therefore to maintain a show of power. This he does by commanding a gang of thieves and robbers ... Another way of spreading fear is to have in his confidence the police officials, particularly the sub-inspector in charge of the local police station ...

As long as the *hari* lives in the position of a tenant-at-will he cannot press his rights by any law regulating his relationship with the *zamindar*. His poverty deters him from taking recourse to the extensive processes of law ... Tenancy laws passed in various parts of the sub-continent have been successfully evaded by landlords ...

I cannot but conclude that in order to effect a real and vital improvement in the condition of the great masses of Sind not only as regards physical well-being but also socially, intellectually and morally we must radically change our system of land tenure. It is only when the cultivator of the soil is its actual owner and the produce of his labour upon the land is his own that the maximum of food is produced by it, the maximum of human enjoyment is derived from the cultivation and the cultivator is as a rule healthy and contented.

Ten years after this report, General Ayub's land reform completely ignored the very problem *Hari* Masud underlined.

Political Repression

The class nature of the new military dictatorship had never been in doubt, and soon the vicious anti-socialist bias of the regime became obvious to everyone. In East Pakistan many socialists were imprisoned, including the popular peasant leader Maulana Bhashani. In West Pakistan some left-wing poets and intellectuals had been arrested, and a secret memorandum prohibiting the circulation of Communist literature, reproduced facing page 89, was sent out by the Ministry of Education. The most powerful left-wing force in the country was the chain of newspapers mentioned earlier, Progressive Papers Limited. Despite the fact that the newspapers had been extremely careful since Martial Law, and had not attacked the regime outright, there was no doubt that their continued existence was a major irritant to the new regime. The day after the imposition of Martial Law, when press censorship was in force, every single newspaper except the *Pakistan Times* had printed editorials pronouncing Ayub a saviour. The *Times* had an editorial on soil erosion.

The owner of Progressive Papers Limited, Mian Iftikharudin, had once been a powerful figure in West Pakistani politics, and the only voice in the Pakistani parliament to attack feudalism and United States imperialism. His newspapers had influenced large numbers of students towards radical views, and during the Suez war it had been the *Pakistan Times* which, because of its uncompromising attack on British imperialism and the complicity of the Pakistan government, had been responsible for mass demonstrations in the cities of West Pakistan. Clearly, the *Pakistan Times* and *Imroze*, the largest and most influential English and Urdu newspapers in the country, could not be relied upon to give support to the military dictatorship.

An army officer who considered himself a whizz-kid of the new regime was Brigadier F. R. Khan. He was assigned to the Home Ministry which dealt with "Communist subversion" and similar activities. The Brigadier had also read Goebbels and realized the value of propaganda. He advised the Central government to take over Progressive Papers Limited, and two ministers were duly appointed to handle the physical side of the take-over, General K. M. Sheikh and Mr Zulfikar Ali Bhutto. The intellectual justification was provided by the "brains" of the regime, Manzur Qadir. Formerly a successful criminal lawyer, Qadir had accepted a cabinet post in Ayub's regime and restricted his legal practice to the prosecution of political "criminals". Each and every iniquity of the regime was justified by Manzur Qadir's sophistry.

The take-over of Progressive Papers Limited required an excuse. This was provided by the combined talents of Brigadier F. R. Khan and Mian Anwar Ali, who was the boss of the "Intelligence services" of the regime. A case was manufactured by Anwar Ali, embroidered by F. R. Khan, intellectualized by Manzur Qadir and accepted by the Ayub cabinet. The dirty Communists would be ousted and the regime would acquire a chain of propaganda newspapers. The charge levelled against Mian Iftikharudin was not new; similar charges have been used by semi-fascist governments against their opponents throughout the world: the newspapers were being financed with money from foreign countries. Which foreign countries? Russia and China, of course.

On April 16th, 1959, a special ordinance was passed by the Martial Law regime which empowered the government to change the management of newspapers which "in the opinion of the government, published or contained matters likely to endanger the defence, external affairs or security of Pakistan". On April 17th, the government took over Progressive Papers Limited. A press note issued by the government stated:

The Central government were satisfied on the basis of information from *very reliable sources* that the previous management of the Progressive Papers Limited was in the hands of persons some of whom had contact with certain foreign sources from whom they received guidance and financial assistance directly or by indirect methods ... There was an objectionable innuendo in their writings which, even if it was not discernible in any single article, was, in its cumulative influence on the mind of its readers, meant to engender subversion ... [10]

A civil servant was appointed administrator of the newspapers and from that date onwards the newspapers became the faithful and slavish voices of the government. A Mr Qudratullah Shahab, who had served as secretary to three heads of states and was a "respected" civil servant, wrote an editorial entitled "The New Leaf" which appeared in the *Pakistan Times* on April 19th, 1959. Written hurriedly and incoherently, the editorial claimed that "Distant orbits and alien horizons–far from the territorial and ideological boundaries of Pakistan–exercised a progressively increasing charm on the tone and policies of this newspaper which gradually began to look like a stranger in the house ... " The Editor of the *Pakistan Times*, Mazhar Ali Khan, resigned in protest, and a few months later the Editor of *Imroze*, Ahmed Nadeem Qasmi, followed suit. The charge that Moscow gold was financing the newspapers was never proved, despite the energetic efforts of Mian Iftikharudin to bring the matter up before a court of law; the dictatorship was not even prepared to trust its own laws.

Every single national newspaper in the country supported the government action and celebrated the fact that Progressive Papers had been taken away from the radicals. These same editors claimed at international press conferences that there was complete freedom of the press in Pakistan. That is the extent to which they had prostituted themselves. Many erstwhile progressives in the *Pakistan Times* and *Imroze* suddenly discovered unsuspected merits in the Ayub regime and began writing articles in praise of it. Some of these writers had once been members of the Communist Party and had suffered prison sentences. They were obviously determined to forget the past and concentrate on the present.

When Martial Law was lifted in 1962 there was for a short period a certain amount of freedom for the press. Zuhair Siddiqui, who had seen the take-over of the *Pakistan Times* from close quarters, wrote about it in a column for the *Civil and Military Gazette* which he

[10] *Pakistan Times*, May 1st, 1969. Italics mine.

edited before it was forced to close down under new pressure from the post-Martial-Law Ayub government. Under the pen-name of Rambler, Siddiqui wrote an article headed "Strangers in the House":

On the seventh day of June last year [1962], the newspapers announced the death of Mian Iftikharudin—feudal lord turned leftist, noted political leader, and expropriated newspaper magnate. The news was belated. Mian Iftikharudin had died not on June 6th, 1962, but three years earlier on April 18th, 1959. On that day the chain of newspapers founded by him had turned "a new leaf"—a leaf that was to prove the opening of the darkest and most lamentable chapter of their life ... For more than a decade he had devoted most of his time and prodigious energies, and a great deal of his money, to the newspapers he had brought into existence. And with the help of a dedicated band of journalists he had succeeded in making each of those periodicals a leader in its own field.

On the 18th of April, 1959, by one of the most iniquitous edicts in our political history, the whole chain of newspapers was suddenly taken over by the government. In the small hours of the morning, security men in plain clothes were planted at various places on the premises ... when the staff arrived it was flabbergasted and appalled to find a host of strangers in occupation of the house ... The staff was shocked and bewildered. For nearly three hours they had to wait in the corridors while the strangers strutted about the house. By midday they were in complete control, the Editor of the most important chain of newspapers having walked out in protest ... The next morning the issue of the paper that carried the news of his resignation also carried in its editorial columns a bundle of falsehoods and gibberish and bad English ... In The New Leaf—the editorial in which an unknown hack sought to dub Mian as a foreign agent—the *Pakistan Times* was described as "a stranger in the house". The phrase could be used aptly for both the newspaper and the man who built it—although in a sense very different from that in which the writer of The New Leaf had used the words. Iftikharudin began to look like a stranger in our political world soon after Partition. And as the war of each against all became more and more fierce, he looked more and more outlandish ... He pleaded for civil liberties when the powers that be were learning to deal with their opponents and critics through arbitrary and repressive laws bequeathed by the British raj ...

The newspapers too, therefore looked like strangers in a newspaper world dominated by unprincipled men, by witch-hunters, by purveyors of hatred and fanaticism and by time-servers ... The history of the Press in Pakistan will certainly record that the "strangers in the house" sought for a whole decade to make the house worth living in and raised the prestige of our press in the world ... [11]

It is not surprising that the bourgeois chroniclers of Pakistani history under Ayub either fail to deal with the press laws which his regime initiated, or when they mention them fail to see the significance of the seizure of the *Pakistan Times*. The newspaper *was* the Left in West Pakistan. An attack on it was a direct attack on the progressive movement in West Pakistan. Many leftists deliberately refused to acknowledge this fact and some even collaborated with the regime, at times quite openly. For example, they helped to re-organize the government's cultural façade. Instead of building or trying to build a movement to oppose Ayub Khan, the left-wing in West Pakistan either collaborated with the regime or opted out of politics; they did not even attempt to set up an underground propaganda organization to explain the political situation to the people. Once the government had confiscated Progressive Papers Limited the Left became completely disorientated and disheartened, instead of learning the lessons of the take-over.

As the months progressed and the basic human rights of the people continued to be denied, an undercurrent of unrest began to make itself felt. Many left-wingers had been imprisoned, Maulana Bhashani among them. He had been arrested on October 12th, 1958, and was to spend the next few years as a guest of the Central government. Others were not treated so well. A Communist militant from Karachi, Hasan Nasir, was arrested and brought to the Lahore Fort. Here he was cruelly tortured, by men who had been taught their skills by the British and who now used them on behalf of the new tyrants. Hasan Nasir eventually died under torture, the first victim of the Ayub dictatorship. His body was secretly burnt to

[11] *Civil and Military Gazette*, Lahore, June 6th, 1963. The paper was suppressed a few months later.

ashes. When there was a public outcry and a demand for an inquiry the authorities said that he had committed suicide. The body they produced as his had decomposed and was unrecognizable. Hasan Nasir's mother, who came from India to identify it, said that it was not the body of her son. She comforted Nasir's associates by telling them that he had died in a good cause and that his death would be avenged by the Pakistani people some day.

The student community in both East and West Pakistan was beginning to flex its muscles. The murder of Patrice Lumumba in 1961 gave many students the opportunity they had been waiting for, and demonstrations took place in Karachi and Lahore. They were the first mass protest rallies since the imposition of Martial Law and it was a punishable offence to participate as all demonstrations had been banned. In Lahore "the processionists, chanting anti-United Nations and anti-American slogans visited the American Consulate General ... in a strongly worded resolution they described the murder of Mr Lumumba as 'one of the most coldblooded, inexcusable and uncalled-for crimes in recent history'!"[12]

The next day the provincial government repeated the ban on all meetings and demonstrations and stressed that Martial Law was still in force: "The District Magistrate said that the ban had been imposed as more demonstrations were feared in view of the situation in the Congo."[13]

As a participant in the demonstration I can verify that the Lahore students were not blind to the situation at home, and many anti-Ayub and anti-Martial-Law slogans were shouted – an offence punishable by death. The next day we defied the ban again, and were attacked and tear-gassed by the police. Though the demonstrations were contained, many students had come into contact with the repressive state for the first time since October 1958 and it was a heartening experience. In Karachi some students were killed and many injured in anti-U.S. and U.N. demonstrations. The spirit of revolt was spreading. In the next few months, as Ayub was preparing to impose a constitution on the Pakistani people, the unrest increased.

[12] *Civil and Military Gazette*, Lahore, February 21st, 1961.
[13] Ibid.

As his Governor in West Pakistan Ayub had appointed the Nawab of Kalabagh. Kalabagh was an old feudal landlord who thought and behaved like a medieval robber baron. He regarded West Pakistan as his estate and the people as his tenants. It is not possible here to recount all the crimes for which this man was responsible; that would require a book on its own. Suffice it to say that Kalabagh's rule in West Pakistan was harsh and oppressive. In dealing with the political opponents of the military dictatorship he used brute force or, where this was not possible, economic pressure. The nawab was not only opposed to the principle of one man, one vote; he was also opposed to education, and was often heard to remark that there wasn't a single school in his village: he was not going to educate people who would only grow up and cut his throat. If the trade unions had defended their class interests as single-mindedly as Kalabagh defended his, the Ayub regime would have crumbled long before it did.

In May 1961 Kalabagh's administration refused permission to the students of the University at Lahore to observe a Day of Protest in solidarity with the Algerian struggle against French imperialism as the "Pakistan government was on friendly terms with France". But there was trouble at the university — trouble which rapidly increased.

In early 1962 the Cabinet Minister Z. A. Bhutto came to address the students of Lahore at Punjab University on the subject of Kashmir. Those of us who had managed to get into the small hall where the meeting was held were determined to protest against the political situation nearer home. As a result Mr Bhutto could not make himself heard amidst shouts of anti-Ayub and anti-dictatorship slogans. It was pointed out that while we were all in favour of a plebiscite in Kashmir we were at the moment more interested in a plebiscite at home. At one stage Mr Bhutto decided to end the political "discussion" by telling a persistent heckler, "I am a young man too. Come out and we'll see who's stronger." The heckler refused to take this up and continued to heckle. In the end Mr Bhutto was forced to leave after having answered unsatisfactorily questions dealing with the political situation in Pakistan.

The importance of this incident lies in the fact that it was the first time that a Cabinet Minister representing the military dictatorship had been attacked in public. When Manzur Qadir, another Minister, went to East Pakistan to defend the Ayub Constitution the students of Dacca University nearly killed him. The anger and bitterness which had been repressed for a long time was coming to the surface. When the constitution was finally published, copies of it were burnt by students in East Pakistan.

On October 27th, 1959, to commemorate the coup d'état's first anniversary, a system of local councils had been announced by which, according to Ayub Khan, "every village and every inhabitant in every village in our country would become an equal partner with the Administration in conducting the affairs of the state." This system, later formalized in Ayub's constitution, was known as "basic democracy", and was a five-tier system of "elected" councils. The intention behind it was to consolidate the power of the bureaucracy. The system enabled the bureaucracy to tighten its control at the village level, co-ordinate its surveillance and establish links with the landed gentry. It also increased the power of the landed gentry by strengthening their ties with the bureaucracy.

The units in "basic democracy" were to be the village councils and town committees, which were to be elected on the basis of adult franchise. A population of 100 million people was to elect 80,000 basic democrats, who would then become an electoral college for the country as a whole. Superimposed on the basic councils was a hierarchy of councils whose members were all nominated by the bureaucracy. The basic democrats were in fact to be basic bureaucrats, and were to be encouraged to assist in the administrative functions of the established bureaucracy and the police. They were also designed to make redundant the old politicians.

Those politicians who could not be trusted had been dealt with by Ayub under the E.B.D.O. (Election Bodies Disqualifying Order), by which politicians were charged with corruption and banned from taking part in politics till 1966. Many politicians contested these charges and proved their innocence; but Ayub's regime was both prosecutor and judge, and the system was too heavily rigged for the innocent to be acquitted. So the game of discrediting the politicians continued while at the same time the ground was being prepared to hold fake elections under the new constitution. As the "basic democrats" had duly "elected" Ayub as God's representative on earth, the new elections would only vote for members of a new parliament. The latter's powers were virtually non-existent; it was a parliament which had been castrated before birth. The election was fought in reality by the bureaucracy, which saw to it that Ayub's ciphers were elected as a majority, though there were some opposition members. In the summer of 1962 the new National Assembly met in Rawalpindi. Martial Law faded away.

The feudal nature of the "elected" parliament was emphasized when the West Pakistan provincial assembly united to prevent a discussion on the ejection of five thousand tenants from state lands in the various districts of the Punjab region. And when some politicians began to attack the system they were severely reprimanded by Mr Z. A. Bhutto: "It was unjustifiable on the part of the politicians to shift their guilt to the bureaucrats, the feudal landlords and the bourgeoisie."[16] Mr Bhutto did not elaborate as to who was in fact responsible for the system of property relations which dominated the political and economic life of Pakistan.

The Leader of the Opposition was Sardar Bahadur Khan, an old Muslim Leaguer. He also happened to be Ayub's brother. In the first few months of the new Parliament Ayub felt confident enough to allow one or two other flowers to bloom as well. The opposition took advantage of this and started an effective propaganda campaign inside the Assembly. Opposition members from East Pakistan were particularly hostile. Masihur Rehman said in Parliament that there were over 1,500 political prisoners in Pakistan and demanded their release. On June 28th, 1962, Sardar Bahadur spoke in the National Assembly on the situation in Baluchistan, where a strong anti-One-Unit and pro-autonomy movement had been developing since 1954. At times it had even taken the form of tribal guerrilla warfare. Bahadur revealed that the government had organized concentration camps and large-scale political victimization in that area. The parliamentary reporter wrote in the *Civil and Military Gazette*: "A hushed house heard Sardar Bahadur Khan, disclose startling details of a concentration camp being run in Quetta and of the prisoners being hung by their feet half-naked."[14]

And for the first time also there was public criticism of the wealth which Ayub's sons had been amassing. At a press conference in July Sardar Bahadur attacked his brother again:

We feel betrayed. Never before was corruption so rife, the administration so weak and the people so demoralized as at present ... We are governed not by a popular or representative government. A ruthless minority presides over our destiny. Under no conditions are we prepared to pull the chestnuts out

[14] *Civil and Military Gazette*, Lahore, June 29th, 1962.

of the fire for them. The answer to the grave political situation
lies in the return of power to the people and the restoration of
their inherent rights.[15]

He also claimed:

> that if he had known that he would have to pass the "fag end of
> his life in these political conditions" he would have revised his
> stand on the establishment of Pakistan. He also said that the
> land reforms had been more in the interests of the landed
> aristocracy than of the tenants.[16]

Sardar Bahadur Khan did not last as opposition leader for too
long; fraternal pressure succeeded in gagging him. But the breaking
of the silence inflicted on the nation by Martial Law acted as an
important psychological spur. In early July in East Pakistan the
students were out on the streets attacking the Ayub dictatorship in
no uncertain terms. There were episodes of police brutality in Chittagong, East Pakistan's largest port, and students decided that July
19th, 1962, was to be observed as a Protest Day. They called for
strikes, meetings and demonstrations to prove once again that
students can take up the challenge thrown by "fascist, reactionary
and anti-people's forces."[17]

In Dacca and other cities of East Pakistan there were massive
student demonstrations on July 19th. The students demanded the
release of all political prisoners, including Suhrawardy and Bhashani,
and the freedom of speech and press. Encouraged by these protests,
the National Awami Party, only a few days later, issued a call for a
united front to work towards "achieving a full democratization of
the constitution".[18] In August the railway workers in Lahore held
protest rallies and their General Secretary went on a five-day hunger
strike. The government was forced to accept some of their demands.
It must be remembered, of course, that only the press which was free
from government control could report all these happenings,[19] and
even their scope was reduced when further press laws were instituted.

[15] Ibid., July 23rd, 1962.
[16] Ibid., April 27th, 1963.
[17] *Civil and Military Gazette*, Lahore, July 15th, 1962.
[18] Ibid., July 17th, 1962.
[19] This includes some of the Urdu and Bengali newspapers. Also the *Civil and Military Gazette* in Lahore and the *Pakistan Observer* in Dacca. The non-government newspaper *Dawn* was at times more servile than the newspapers actually under government control.

The Information Minister, Fazlul Quader Chowdhuri, declared that: "As Information Minister it is my duty to see that the press in Pakistan is completely free from Communist elements and people who want to achieve this aim will get substantial help from the government."[20] The *Pakistan Times*, by now the leading voice of the dictatorship, unleashed a barrage of crude propaganda against Communists in an editorial headlined "Norms of Patriotism":

> Patriotism is to a country what air is to a man. One cannot live without it. Like democracy patriotism is a modern concept ... But the most implacable enemy of this dear land is the Communist. By religion he is opposed to the genesis of Pakistan ... What are we doing to frustrate their designs? Of course their party is banned and they are small in number. But the ban does not worry them; they are used to working underground. As for the smallness of their number, by creed they are a minority. Lenin proudly named his faction Bolshevik, the minority ... When the President calls upon patriots to come forward and serve the nation he also accepts the duty of eradicating this land of its enemies. Of them all the Communists are the bitterest.[21]

The ludicrous definition of Bolshevik and the semi-literate style should not lead one to underestimate the strength of anti-Communist feeling which existed in the different branches of the government and was encouraged by the government itself. A Bureau of National Reconstruction was set up under the inspiration of Brigadier F. R. Khan. It was meant to be a propaganda bureau for the dictatorship, but though the bureau wasted a large amount of government money, it never got off the ground. F. R. Khan was dismissed from government service, and that may have been one of the reasons why the bureau could not function as a Goebbels-type organization.

Meanwhile, student unrest was on the increase in Pakistan. One of the many commissions set up by the government had been a Commission on National Education. A report was prepared in 1960, and in 1962 the government was about to implement it when the students, piqued at not being consulted, decided to obstruct it. The report itself was a conglomeration of clichés, utopian and in places insidious, and its effect would have been to make it even more difficult for the

[20] *Civil and Military Gazette*, Lahore, August 31st, 1962.
[21] *Pakistan Times*, Lahore, August 19th, 1962.

masses of poor people in Pakistan to attain an education. The report concentrated on higher education – this in a country where the main problem was primary and secondary education. It recommended increasing the degree course by one year, which in practice would have prevented many students from completing their degrees because of lack of funds. Besides, many students felt that an extra year at university would be wasted; the quality of teaching was unlikely to improve unless the pay scale of university lecturers was increased, and the libraries and other facilities were so inadequate that students could not work usefully on their own.[22]

Another important factor contributing to student unrest was that the provincial governments had unilaterally imposed the hated University Ordinances in both West and East Pakistan. These Ordinances forbade students to take part in politics, and those who disobeyed risked having their degrees rescinded. (This was actually done at Dacca University.) The system of direct elections on the University level was also to be taken away though at a later stage. In West Pakistan the government imposed a variety of restraints, threatening to prosecute male and female students who were seen talking together after classes had finished, and forbidding the performance of plays with a "mixed cast".

On September 12th, 1962, the students of Dacca formed massive processions to protest against the recommendations of the Education Commission, and called for a general strike for September 17th. Despite repeated police charges, the students held their ground. Over forty students were injured in the clashes and the army was called in to occupy parts of the city. Two government vehicles had been destroyed, and a private Mercedes Benz belonging to the provincial Minister for Communications was burnt. The students' call for a general strike was answered by the proletariat of Dacca and the rest of the province, and in the industrial areas of Tejgaon and Postogola the workers demonstrated in large numbers in support of the students. The next day there were demonstrations in solidarity with the East Pakistani students in Lahore and Karachi, and also in some

[22] In general, student unrest in East Pakistan reflected the situation of the province, which was grim, both politically and economically. There were serious floods in the last week of August 1962, and the relief was not very effective. Ayub visited the flood-ravaged province and pronounced his verdict: "I have never seen so much water in my life." (*Civil and Military Gazette*, Lahore, September 2nd, 1962.) Many East Pakistanis undoubtedly wished that he had drowned himself in it.

cities in West Pakistan, though here they were confined to the students. Meanwhile the strikes and demonstrations continued in East Pakistan, and in Dacca a fourteen-year-old schoolboy died from wounds inflicted on his head by a policeman's *lathi* (baton).

The students in Dacca formulated broad political demands articulating not only their own needs but also those of the masses, but in West Pakistan the demands were restricted to education. They were:

1. That the three-year degree course be ended;
2. There should be a drastic cut in tuition fees;
3. Teachers' salaries should be increased;
4. Student Unions should be allowed to function on democratic principles.

The Dacca students demanded that the entire report be scrapped, and called for mass demonstrations till this was done. In Karachi, twelve student leaders were expelled from the city. They travelled all over the province, and colleges which had been completely apathetic came out on the streets after a visit by the magnificent twelve.

On September 30th, 1962, the government gave in and withdrew the three-year degree course and accepted various other student demands. The then Education Minister, who had declared that concessions would be made over his dead body (to which we had replied, "So be it"), was, unfortunately, still alive. Student power had triumphed and the bureaucracy appeared somewhat demoralized. Maulana Bhashani was released on November 3rd, 1962. As if they had not had enough on their hands another commission report was produced – the Pay and Services Commission Report, which recommended drastic changes in the bureaucratic structure. The report was quietly shelved and the Finance Minister, Abdul Qadir, admitted that: "So far as organizational changes in cadres, structures, interchange ability of services was concerned these recommendations were so radical that grave risks were involved in their adoption in full."[23] The risk involved was no minor one: a serious revolt of the bureaucracy was threatened.

Foreign policy

At the first meeting of the Ayub cabinet after the imposition of Martial Law, the new President is reported to have made his views on foreign policy quite clear, telling his ministers that "There is only

[23] *Civil and Military Gazette*, Lahore, October 27th, 1962.

one embassy as far as I am concerned and that is the American Embassy."[24] There is no reason to doubt this story. It was Ayub, as Commander-in-Chief of the Pakistan army, who was largely responsible for negotiating the military aid programme during 1953–4. This inglorious deal has been described proudly by a sycophant who wrote a biography of Ayub.[25] The author also tells us that as the United States was mistrustful of Pakistani politicians they preferred to deal directly with the army and have it on their side.

Ayub's foreign policy was straightforwardly pro-American, and in this differed in no way from previous governments. The aim of the United States in the sub-continent in 1959 was to win India away from "neutralism", and they were also anxious for Pakistan and India to have a united defence system against People's China. Pakistan's relations with the Soviet Union at this time were not friendly. They were to be exacerbated further by the U 2 incident, when Peshawar, in north-west Pakistan, was used as a base for the U 2 planes.

In April 1959, soon after he had crushed the socialists at home, the general turned his attention to foreign affairs. His success in taking over Progressive Papers possibly made him think that the same methods could be used in the field of foreign affairs. He suggested to the Indian Prime Minister, Jawaharlal Nehru, that India and Pakistan should get together and work out ways and means of defending the sub-continent. Nehru rebuffed him. In September Ayub approached Nehru once more, obviously on the advice of his friends and masters in the United States. Nehru retorted, "Joint defence against whom?" In November, Ayub told a British correspondent that "A Russian-Chinese drive to the Indian Ocean is a major aim in the Communist drive for world domination". Even when the Indian ruling class had decided on a confrontation with China, and border conflicts were taking place, Ayub wrote to Nehru to assure him of Pakistan's natural interest in the "peace and stability of the region" and of her desire for peaceful relations with India. This was the green light which enabled the Indians to move their troops from the frontier with Pakistan and transfer them to the Sino-Indian border. But even in these circumstances the social-democratic, old Harrovian Nehru viewed the semi-literate, Sandhurst-trained Ayub with

[24] A former Cabinet Minister told me this in a private conversation.
[25] Colonel M. Ahmed, *My Chief* (London, 1963). The book makes amusing reading and also contains some interesting facts.

contempt. It was an antipathy he could never overcome, and the very idea of an alliance with a military dictator was distasteful to him. Besides why deal with the monkey when the organ-grinder – the United States – was prepared to help?

Despite Nehru's rebuff there was a great deal of sympathy for India in her border dispute with China. The military-bureaucratic nexus was violently anti-Communist. As a result of the Sino-Indian border conflict New Delhi and Washington moved closer to each other. Britain and the United States rushed military aid to India, and in the haste to deface India's neutral façade, Pakistan was forgotten. As far as the United States was concerned, of course, a base in India to combat the spread of Chinese Communism was infinitely preferable to a base in Pakistan. Ideally, both countries should make common cause, but if for some reason they could not, then the United States had its own priorities clear and would let nothing stand in its way.

In 1962 President Kennedy appealed for better relations between India and Pakistan. Ayub's long-winded reply is extremely interesting, as it sets down in writing the contradictions of his regime. On the one hand he pleads with the United States, and on the other tries a little gentle blackmail; at the same time he assails Indian foreign policy and explains to the American President where he thinks India has gone wrong:

> Why has such a situation developed on this sub-continent and around India? We believe that this is the direct outcome of distorted and fallacious thinking on the part of Mr Nehru and his associates and a consequence of a baseless foreign policy that he has been following ... It has been based on the following factors:
> (a) bending over backwards to appease Communism;
> (b) hoist the white flag of neutralism to appease Communism and get other wavering nations to join India in order to be able to create a world nuisance-value for themselves;
> (c) intimidate and threaten Pakistan in order to politically isolate it and economically weaken it; and
> (d) abuse the West, and especially the U.S.A. in season and out of season.
> The events have proved that all that is happening to Mr Nehru is the direct consequence of this warped thinking.[26]

[26] Mohammed Ayub Khan, op. cit., pp. 141–3.

The naivety and imbecility of the approach indicate that Ayub himself was responsible for drafting the letter. His more intelligent civil servants would not have allowed a reply couched in such language to be sent to the American President. Ayub was grovelling in the dust like a spaniel pleading with his master and whining to prove that he was more loyal than the spaniel next door.

When it became quite clear that the United States could not be appeased, the Pakistan government started sorting out its relations with China. A delegation had been sent to Peking, where the demarcation of the Pakistan-China border was successfully negotiated. The Chinese gave 750 square miles to Pakistan and the Pakistani government agreed to accept Chinese control over the rest of the disputed territory. It should be added that this territory had never been under the control of either the Pakistan government or their British predecessors.[27]

All this did not please the United States, but for the time being they were busy wooing India and they could not be bothered with Ayub's jealous flirtations with China. They knew full well that at the slightest command Ayub would rush straight back to the United States, and later events proved how well they knew their clients.

[27] See Alistair Lamb, *The China-India Border* (Oxford, 1964), pp. 105–14. The book has been banned by the Indian government.

CHAPTER FOUR

Military-Bureaucratic Dictatorship II, 1963-8

> "For too long Pakistan has become a land of great silence; a silence born of fear, of apathy, of cynicism, of ignorance; a silence so oppressive that often truth finds expression only in uncertain whispers." *Civil and Military Gazette*, March 10th, 1963

Ayub raj

The second part of Ayub's decade can be divided into two periods. The first, from 1963 to 1965, when the regime was consolidating its new civilian dictatorship and not letting anything stand in its way, ended when the repressive apparatus of the state machine had fought and won the "election" of 1965 for Ayub—although, as we shall see, not without some spirited opposition. The second phase was a time of blind complacency on the part of the bureaucracy which was to be shattered by the spontaneous action of the Pakistani students and workers in November 1968.

A number of unexpected developments had occurred after the end of Martial Law, and two particularly important decisions were made as a result. First, the ban on political parties was lifted, a move which must have been opposed by Mr Manzur Qadir who had "made" the constitution for Ayub and Ayub alone; no one else was supposed to disturb the tranquillity of the regime, or Manzur Qadir's capacity for self-deception. Secondly, and worse, Ayub Khan decided to set up his own political party.

The latter turned out to be a collection of hangers-on and the thugs of Pakistan's political underworld, an apt combination, which symbolized well the rule of the oligarchy. Ayub's party became known as the Convention Muslim League, as it was set up after a convention of Muslim Leaguers. The "real" Muslim League was henceforth known as the Council Muslim League, and it included most of the politicians associated with League politics both before and after Partition. In fact even these could have been won over. Most of them would have been only too pleased to compromise, and indeed some of them had indicated their willingness to do so, but

Ayub's pet ministers saw the re-emergence of the old politicians as a threat to their own positions. And let it be said that these positions were based in most cases not on any real support but on their subservience to the Boss. From the point of view of the Left the split was unfortunate as it meant that the spurned Muslim Leaguers could play an opposition role instead of being tainted politically by their association with Ayub raj.[1]

The end of Martial Law and the transitional period during which it was being replaced by bureaucratic law marked an important phase for the non-government-controlled press in Pakistan. It gave these journals a brief opportunity to criticize the Ayub regime fairly harshly, though it should be added that this was always done within the confines of a bourgeois-democratic framework. In Karachi a liberal weekly, *Outlook*, had been established. Its circulation was very small but it was a powerful irritant to the government. Gradually the bureaucratic laws began to deal with the limited amount of freedom which existed. On March 28th, 1963, the government promulgated a new Press Ordinance which banned the publication of any news items relating to strikes or industrial unrest. The dictatorship was also determined to clear the path completely for the "election" of the Boss and barbs like *Outlook* were removed.[2]

In September 1963 the government issued yet another ordinance: no Assembly proceedings "not authorized by the Speaker or court proceedings not authorized by the Chief Justice or the presiding authority shall be published".[3] The ordinance further insisted that all newspapers should publish in full all the press notes or handouts distributed by the Central or provincial governments.[4] Some of the journalists attending the press conference where the "Minister for Law", West Pakistan, announced the new ordinance walked out in protest. The next day the *Civil and Military Gazette* ceased publication. In its last phase this newspaper had broken decisively with its pro-imperialist and pro-government past.

[1] It could be argued that the eight years in which Z. A. Bhutto was associated with the dictatorship did not seem to harm his credibility. However, the reasons for this rest also in the fact that Bhutto was capable at the crucial stage of displaying a certain amount of personal courage—a quality most other politicians lacked. The point is dealt with in full in a later chapter.

[2] This was done by putting pressure on the printer of *Outlook*, and though the journal lasted until 1964 its last few months were spent in court cases.

[3] *Civil and Military Gazette*, Lahore, September 3rd, 1963.

[4] Ibid. When a journalist asked, "Even if the language is incorrect?" the Minister replied, "Yes".

The repression of East Pakistani students continued. A new Governor, Monem Khan, had been appointed and it was thought that given his past as a local bully he was the best person to deal with the students. He started his job by dismissing the Vice-Chancellor of Dacca University, Dr Mahmud Hussain. Hussain was an old-fashioned liberal academic who resented the efforts of authority to turn him into a policeman and force him to use harsh measures against the students. The Governor claimed that Dr Hussain had failed to maintain proper order in Dacca University. His successors were able to do no better and the strikes and demonstrations continued.

When the students demanded an end to illiteracy and more government spending on education, the Minister for Education of Pakistan made some odd remarks. According to a newspaper columnist in Lahore:

> The Minister also tried to justify illiteracy by remarking that the Holy Prophet was illiterate. When some members of the opposition laughed derisively the Minister hastily retreated and said that the government was determined to check illiteracy, but that its resources were limited ...[5]

The resources remained limited, as the Pakistan army and the Civil Service of Pakistan allocated more money out of the country's budget to themselves than ever before. This resulted in a substantial rise in the pay scales of the civil and military services while for the workers and certain sections of the petit-bourgeoisie there was a wage freeze. And "the extra expenditure incurred in the shape of pay increases alone will be roughly equal to the total yearly outlay on the development of health and education services for upwards of ninety million people."[6] At the same time as the government was busy giving itself money, an expensive folly was being erected near Rawalpindi. It was to be the new capital of Pakistan and on the suggestion of Mr Manzur Qadir (who had once been an agnostic) was to be called Islamabad.

During the four and a half years of Martial Law the dissatisfaction of the peasantry with the government's land disposal policy had reached boiling point. The military government had maintained that

[5] Ibid., July 14th, 1963.
[6] *Outlook*, (May 2nd, 1964) p. 3.

its basic aims were to bring the maximum areas of land under cultivation in the shortest possible time. The lands available to the
government for disposal fell under five different categories:

1. Lands owned by the state, formerly known as Crown lands.
2. Land which had become available as a result of the "land reform"
   in the province.
3. Evacuee land which had been vacant since its non-Muslim owners
   migrated to India and which had not been allotted to new
   claimants.
4. Land in the Sukkur Barrage region which had remained uncultivated despite the fact that the Barrage had been in existence for
   thirty years.
5. Land which had become cultivable as a result of the completion
   of the Ghulam Mohammed and Gudu Barrages.

No one could disagree that these lands should be cultivated as soon
as possible, but of course there were different ways of achieving this.
The technique chosen by the Ayub regime was to strengthen the
existing feudal and semi-feudal character of the West Pakistani
countryside. The government sold the land to the men of property;
in many cases members of the bureaucracy who either belonged to
the feudal class or wanted to belong to it were given preference. The
two most popular methods of sale were by open auction and by the
reservation of land for government employees and ex-employees,
both civil and military. This frequently resulted in landlords buying
more land under new names, or in the big business interests extending their grip on the countryside. Since bureaucrats and army officers
own large tracts of land it is quite clear that it is foolish to look to the
army to promulgate ordinances to change the nature of feudal society;
it is asking the army to go against its own class interests.

In many cases the auctioned land, which had been barren at one
stage, had been leased out to peasants under the "Grow More Food"
campaign, and they had been promised that if they cultivated it
they would be given preference at the time of disposal. The peasants
worked like slaves on the land only to be thwarted at the bitter
end.

100,000 acres of the tenant developed land in West Pakistan
is now being put to auction, threatening 200,000 tenants with
ejection, 25,000 being in the Lyallpur district alone. The pro-
fessed objective of the land reform was to distribute land

amongst the tillers. Here also the purpose is being distorted in implementation. We do not have statistics for the whole of West Pakistan but the figures relating to Sind show that out of 832,000 acres of resumed land, only 235,000 have been allotted to *haris* ... Frankly the logic of reserving lands for government officials is incomprehensible to an ordinary citizen. The reservation of land for civil and military officials has opened the way to corruption ... Most of the officials are engaged all the time either in the manipulation for obtaining these lands or in developing them if they have succeeded in obtaining them, through abuse of their official position. Moreover the management of these newly-acquired lands creates other social problems. If these official landlords cultivate the lands themselves, they will find less time to attend to their official duties. This will also swell the ranks of the farm workers, who are more exploited than the landless peasants. And if they leave these lands to be cultivated by tenants, they aggravate the abuses of absentee landlordism to dilute the effects for which the land reforms are enacted. There have been widespread complaints of corruption and abuse of power in the allotment of these reserve lands. Six months ago in Lyallpur the Revenue Minister promised to inquire into the allegation that big government officials had managed to get big plots of land in open violation of the rules, but the promise was needless to say unfulfilled. The abuse of power and corruption is not restricted to the distribution of the reserved lands, the greed for land is having its bad effects over a much wider area. The disposal of evacuee agricultural land is a great scandal. Claimants of ordinary means are not allotted any lands, years are spent by claimants in making the rounds of different offices but the lands remain illusive. If statistics are collected on how much the former evacuee land is now being owned by revenue officials and their relations, they might make quite a startling study.[7]

In the summer of 1963 the outlines of the Third Five Year Plan were presented by the Deputy Chairman of the Pakistan Planning Commission to the National Economic Council. Presenting the report he told the council that "the plan will be a crucial one in our political history as it will determine the pattern of our social and economic life for decades to come."

[7] *Civil and Military Gazette*, Lahore, April 13th, 1963.

The results of this [economic] policy are obvious today. The resources are getting concentrated into a few hands with greater speed than their development. The disinvestment policy of the state is a great contributory factor to this economic phenomenon. *While the National Income is rising, the well-being of the people is not improving, rather it shows a downward curve. According to the 1962 U.N. Statistical Yearbook, average Pakistanis consumed less calories in 1960–61, than they did ten years earlier. In the latest year for which figures were available to the U.N., Pakistan had net food supplies per capita of 1,970 calories per day. Ten years earlier in 1949–50, food supplies were 2,010 calories per day* ... Hence the Real Income that is the welfare of the common man has not increased with the increase in National Income ... Increases in per capita income are taken as indicative of the advancement of the community's well-being, but such averages are completely deceptive ... The concept of per capita income is useful only in comparing the productivity of two national economies, it does not portray a real picture in an economy and cannot be taken as a correct measure of determining the depth of welfare ... [8]

In fact the decline in food consumption coupled with an average increase in per capita income simply shows how the economic condition of a mass of the people can deteriorate in an otherwise expanding and "healthy" economy. The only correct way of reckoning living standards is by determining income according to groups, but naturally the government of Pakistan was not interested in accuracy. The needs of propaganda were the paramount consideration. In an economic situation going from bad to worse, the regime's Finance Minister, Mohammed Shoaib, did not endear himself to the people when he announced that the system of private enterprise and a free market economy "are the only ways of life and is the only way in which we can progress". Nor did Shoaib's "concern" at the growing concentration of wealth deceive anyone; the Ayub regime had used state power to establish industries and had then turned them over to private hands. And since the government's avowed creed was a free market economy, it was no accident that it sanctioned new enterprises to be set up by wealthy industrialists or by bureaucrats in high positions who were able to secure investment sanctions, licences and

[8] Ibid., June 8th, 1963. Italics mine.

accommodation from banking institutions under government control. The marriage between big business and the bureaucracy had been consummated long before. During Ayub's decade the two partners seemed to have indulged in an orgy of copulation without any regard for the techniques of birth-control.

In this atmosphere the opposition parties did not make much headway, mainly because they were not properly organized, but also because public meetings held by opposition leaders like H. S. Suhrawardy were broken up by gangsters hired by the regime. Tactics which Mr Suhrawardy himself had used against Maulana Bhashani's National Awami Party were now used against him. At the end of 1963 the radical parties still had not had any effect on the political consciousness of the people. Ayub's opportunist "anti-American stance" had been partially successful in disorientating elements on the left. The middle-class opposition to the military regime was left without a leader on the death of Suhrawardy in December 1963; no other bourgeois leader could effectively take his place. At this stage the National Awami Party could have played an important role by giving a clear anti-Ayub lead to the people. In West Pakistan, admittedly, little could be done because most of its leaders and party workers were in Ayub's jails; but quite apart from this, the lack of a proper organization made the party completely ineffective. There was even some doubt as to the real policy of the N.A.P. leadership.

> ... The role of the National Awami Party leadership seems to fit in more on the government side than on the opposition side and yet it happens to be sitting in the opposition in the National Assembly and the provincial legislatures. Maulana Bhashani tried to woo the President at Rawalpindi in September. Then he visited China with the blessings of the government. On his return, in Chittagong he said what would become a loyal pro-government spokesman. Maybe he is still courting the President and trying to persuade him to release political prisoners. That he is apparently not willing to do. The mystery is that the Maulana still seems to be hopeful. Or maybe he is afraid of weakening the President's posture in relation to the American lobby in Pakistan.[9]

While it is possible that this report was exaggerated, there can be no doubt that the Maulana's statements on his return from Peking were extremely ambiguous.

[9] *Outlook*, (December 28th, 1963), p. 4.

The death of Suhrawardy had also been the virtual death of the National Democratic Front (N.D.F.) which he had led. It had included a sprinkling of "leaders" from pre-Martial-Law political parties, but as they had few followers, and depended on the press to publicize their activities, the curbs on the press almost caused them to disappear from the political scene. In fact the only group which was working in an organized way to oppose Ayub was the Jamaat-i-Islami, a semi-fascist party. It was fairly efficiently run, and was quite obviously being used by the Central Intelligence Agency as a pressure group to influence Ayub. In January 1964 the Jamaat-i-Islami was banned and its Führer, Maulana Maududi, arrested. The government claimed that the party was being financed by subsidies from foreign countries, and had been for the last sixteen years. This was probably true, but the government never actually presented any evidence to prove its point. The reason for that, too, is simple. The Pakistan government itself had been kept going by subsidies from the same foreign Powers as were supplying money to the Jamaat-i-Islami. On those charges the people should have decided to ban the Pakistan government for accepting money from foreign powers whose interests were directly opposed to the interests of the Pakistani peasants and workers.

Political repression in both West and East Pakistan was efficiently carried out by the two thugs who were Ayub's pro-consuls in the respective provinces. The Nawab of Kalabagh in the West and Monem Khan in the East had earned the approval of their master, and both were given a free hand in distributing political and financial patronages as long as they did not conflict with similar tasks being performed by the Central government.

The formation of Ayub's own party had encouraged the dregs of Pakistani politics to clamber on to the government bandwagon. These were the old opportunists in a new guise; some had been bribed with government licences, others had been threatened, but the majority had decided to join the party of the future. The "consolidation" of the Convention Muslim League was carried out, but not without some difficulty as rival factions vied with each other to win the support of the Boss and hence become office-holders of the new, dynamic, organization. The stage was being prepared for the presidential election in 1965.

To combat the opposition, the government had increased its repression in the universities, set up a National Press Trust to co-ordinate its propaganda, and ventured into the cultural sphere to see how the nation's writers could be used. A Writers' Guild was set up under the direction of Qudratullah Shahab to co-ordinate this side of the propaganda war. A leading capitalist, Adamjee, was encouraged to award yearly prizes to "deserving writers" as a further inducement to them to write what the government wanted to hear. Many progressive writers flocked to the guild and a few of them were to receive Adamjee awards. On the occasion of the presentation of the first of these awards, the Secretary of the Writers' Guild told President Ayub, who had kindly consented to present them:

> It is you, the greatest component of this era, the central power of all this activity, who promised freedom of expression to writers in the days when they suffered from nothing but doubts about their destiny. Under you we have enjoyed complete freedom of expression, and we are proud of the fact that we have not misused it.[10]

If anyone vomited after this speech it was not reported in the national press. The intellectuals, with a few honourable exceptions, had offered themselves for sale and the regime had decided to buy them with the money of one of the richest men in Paksitan. Even a liberal intellectual would have baulked at this; our progressives, many of whom had been either members of or close to the Communist Party, showed no signs of discomfort.

By the middle of 1964 Ayub's government was applying the finishing touches to its pre-election schemes. East Pakistani newspapers had been prohibited from publishing any news concerning student unrest and, characteristically, were ordered not to publish news of the ban.

On July 1st the West Pakistan Education Minister, Yasin Wattoo, announced that educational institutions not under direct government control should be asked to ban their teachers from taking part in politics (lecturers in government colleges were automatically debarred from politics as they are "government servants"). The regime was making doubly sure that they would not have to face articulate opposition. A letter sent by the Ministry of Education to all principals of colleges and schools read thus:

[10] *Outlook*, vol. 2, no. 28 (May 16th, 1964), p. 3.

... in regard to educational institutions receiving financial assistance from the government, a condition of grant should be that the institution concerned will frame rules and regulations on their own initiative to ensure that the employees whether serving on whole-time or part-time basis will not offer themselves as candidates in any election ...

In a country with a population of over a hundred million there is a literacy rate of below twenty per cent of which about three per cent are women and owing to the existing circumstances they count for little. Of the remaining seventeen per cent about seven per cent are disqualified from politics because they are government employees and that includes journalists and teachers (in government service). The teachers and students comprise the largest single body of "literate" people in the country. They are banned from politics.[11]

Any display of independence on the part of the workers was also to be violently suppressed. During a strike at a jute mill, workers were intimidated and killed, with the silent consent of the government, by thugs in the pay of the mill owners. This only strengthened the workers' resolve, and finally the Governor of East Pakistan, Monem Khan, intervened. Their leaders were arrested and in prison they were made to sign a statement calling for a return to work. The workers refused, and in desperation the Governor accepted the demand of a pay increase of Rs. 16 per month. The workers' wages were thus raised from Rs. 65 to Rs. 81 a month (from £5 to just over £6 on the official exchange rate, but at the black market rate the figures are much lower). Their victory was a great blow to the government.

The workers have shown that even if their leadership fails them, they will continue the struggle. The traditional tactics of winning over labour leaders and then to floor a labour movement, proved abortive for once ... members of the whole working-class extended their support — material and moral — to the striking mill-workers. This demonstration of unity was so strong that all attempts to alienate the non-Bengali workers from the strike produced no result. And in the mill areas, which has more than once been disturbed by organized communalism, the workers now appear to identify themselves as members of the working-class alone ... [12]

[11] *Black Dwarf*, January 10th, 1969.
[12] Sirajul Hosain Khan, *Outlook* (August 15th, 1964).

The General's election

Since the beginning of 1964 the opposition parties had been attempting to set up some sort of a united front to oppose Ayub. It was not an easy task, as all the normal channels, such as the press and radio, were virtually closed to them. The only real alternative was for a revolutionary underground organization to start a policy of selective sabotage. A leading politician agreed that it was difficult to think of a way of opposing Ayub, "apart, of course, from a revolutionary movement for which our types were not equipped."[13] However, before the October/November 1964 elections for the basic democrats, who in turn would elect the President, the opposition parties got together and formed a Combined Opposition Party (C.O.P.) to contest the election.

The C.O.P., an unholy alliance of neo-fascists, liberals and radicals, consisted of four and a half political parties: the Council Muslim League; the National Awami Party; the Awami League; the Jamaat-i-Islami[14] and the Nizam-i-Islam Party. The latter represented a few people in both parts of the country and was important only because it had an ex-bureaucrat-cum-Prime Minister, Chowdhury Mohammed Ali, in its ranks. But the C.O.P. could not have a joint slate of candidates for the basic democrat elections and in parts of the country C.O.P. candidates ran against each other.

When the C.O.P. was set up in August 1964 the leaders of the parties glossed over their differences, instead of admitting them openly and stating their own policies as well as campaigning for the removal of Ayub. Consequently their nine-point programme was a watered-down scheme limited to demands for a "democratization of the constitution"; it made no reference at all to foreign policy. The National Awami Party, to take one example, was so over-eager to make concessions in the interests of unity that it concurred in the neo-fascist Jamaat-i-Islami Party's demand that the Family Laws Ordinance be amended and brought into line with the teachings of Islam. (The Family Laws Ordinance was probably the only progressive reform initiated by the Ayub regime in so far as it recognized the inequality of women in Pakistan society and moved in the direction of protecting them by changing the existing marriage and divorce laws.) It was completely unprincipled of the radicals to agree to this

[13] Mian Mumtaz Daultana, leader of the Muslim League, in the course of an interview with the author in Lahore, July, 1969.

[14] The ban on the Jamaat had been lifted in October 1964.

proposal for the sake of unity. The C.O.P. platform had a strong right-wing bias throughout the campaign. Nevertheless, their demand of one person, one vote, was undoubtedly popular with the masses and the Ayub dictatorship was extremely unpopular. The fact that the campaign failed stressed the need for a principled revolutionary platform.

The greatest success of the C.O.P. was that it persuaded Miss Fatima Jinnah to contest the presidential election as their candidate against Ayub. Miss Jinnah, the sister of the "founder of the nation', Mohammed Ali Jinnah, commanded immense respect from the people, and the effect of her campaign was overwhelming. She was called the "mother of the nation", and everywhere she went, tramping the countryside and making speeches against Ayub, millions of people turned out to greet her. She attacked the repressive policies of the government, and called for the political freedoms which she said had been too long denied the Pakistani people. She exposed the corrupt nature of the regime, pointing out that Ayub's sons were amassing fortunes. For many, this frail, silver-haired old lady became a symbol against oppression; her fragility seemed almost to embody the hopelessness of the situation. The C.O.P. claimed that 63,000 out of the 80,000 basic democrats would vote for Miss Jinnah; but they had not bargained for the repressive forces which the Ayub regime commanded.

Miss Jinnah's decision to accept the C.O.P. offer, and her extraordinary success, surprised and shocked Ayub and his courtiers. Ayub had been so confident of his power that his party, the Convention Muslim League, did not even take part in the election. Their own support was largely bought — even the people who greeted Ayub at airports and railway stations were paid, a fact which the weekly *Outlook* exposed before it was banned.

> The Karachi Convention Muslim League collected a sum of Rs. 50,000 to be utilized for [Ayub's] reception arrangements ... Truckloads of workers were brought out from industrial areas on payment of Rs. 1 per head. They proved to be the money's worth, but some of them had to trudge back home. Unless one is extra-vigilant, transport arrangements on such occasions turn out to be one-way affairs.
>
> In the case of some children it became a cruel joke. Children from some of the down-town schools were taken to the Karachi

airport. They clapped and cheered. The reception over, some of them were left behind ... In certain cases worried parents had, in the meantime, reported to the police that their children were missing ... [15]

At one stage Ayub was sufficiently shaken to threaten a re-imposition of Martial Law to save the country from "chaos". But of course it was the basic democrats, and not the people, who were going to vote, and the government was quite capable of withstanding the demands of the people and of making sure of the basic democrats: some were simply bought with money or with government licences; others were threatened, and in some cases the local police arrested basic democrats the day before the election and took them in police vans to the polling booths where they were forced to vote for Ayub.

The combined efforts of the bureaucracy and the police won the election for Ayub. Considering the difficulties, it is surprising that over thirty per cent of the basic democrats withstood the pressures of the dictatorship and voted for Miss Jinnah. A sense of betrayal, of shock, numbed many people, and they began to realize that they could never succeed against Ayub under the rules which he had laid down. A further blow to the weakened morale of the opposition was the unsubstantiated rumour that a section of the National Awami Party had asked its basic democrats to vote for Ayub. Maulana Bhashani denies this vigorously, though there is no doubt that "illness" prevented him from campaigning effectively for Miss Jinnah.[16]

The Jinnah election campaign had proved one fact quite conclusively: it had demonstrated in action how deeply the Ayub government was despised. One might have thought that the toadies who surrounded Ayub would have learnt the lessons of the campaign. But they did not. While some government party workers "conceded that they had won the election but lost the people", in the main the government remained complacent. Ayub himself was to write that

The nation had given a clear and final verdict on the Constitution. Never before in the country had general elections been

---

[15] *Outlook*, Karachi (August 1st, 1964), p. 5.

[16] Khalid bin Sayeed, *The Political System of Pakistan* (Oxford University Press, Pakistan Branch, 1967); "Maulana Bhashani, leader of the National Awami Party, who had considerable influence in the Rajshahi division, did not campaign actively for Miss Jinnah, probably because he did not want to upset Ayub's foreign policy which was veering steadily towards increasing friendship with China."

held. The interest and response of the people was most gratify-
ing. The country had chosen stability against chaos, security
against disintegration, progress against stagnation ... I thanked
the people who had supported me and also those who had
differed with me: they too had served the cause of democracy. I
wanted the moment of vindication to become a symbol of lasting unity. No trace of malice or of regret should inhibit anyone
from rejoicing in the glory of the people ... [17]

Unfortunately Ayub did not give this advice to his son, Captain
Gohar Ayub. Intoxicated with his father's "victory", he led
hundreds of hired mercenaries into those areas in Karachi which
had voted against Ayub and indulged in an orgy of senseless
brutality. Ironically, most of these areas were inhabited by Muslim
refugees who had left India to come to the land which was to be their
"paradise". Houses were burnt, girls were raped and Gohar Ayub
and his gangsters opened fire on unarmed people, killing some and
wounding many others. Neither the police nor the bureaucracy felt
it their duty to intervene.

This episode was censored in the press but news travelled by word
of mouth throughout the country, and the people were enraged. No
organization existed to focus their indignation and give a lead. The
C.O.P. still existed in theory, but in practice it had disintegrated, and
a feeling of impotent frustration swept the country. It is important
to bear this in mind when we discuss the 1968 uprising.

The opposition leaders tried to regroup, and met in Lahore in
March 1965. Sheikh Mujibur Rehman proposed his six-point plan
for the autonomy of East Pakistan.[18] This completely disorientated

[17] Mohammed Ayub Khan, *Friends Not Masters — A Political Autobiography*
(Oxford, 1967), pp. 240–41.
[18] The six points were: (1) A federal system of government, parliamentary
in nature and based on adult franchise. (2) Federal government shall deal with
only Defence and Foreign Affairs. All other subjects shall be dealt with by the
federating state. (3a) Two separate but freely convertible currencies for the two
parts of the country; or (b) one currency for the whole country. In this case effective constitutional measures to be taken to prevent flight of capital from East to
West Pakistan. (4) Power of taxation and revenue collection shall be vested in the
federating units and not at the centre. (5) Separate accounts for foreign exchange
earnings of the two parts of the country under control of respective governments.
(6) The setting up of a militia or para-military force for East Pakistan. These six
points clearly reveal the class nature of Sheikh Mujibur Rehman's Party, the
Awami League. It was quite blatantly the party of the deprived East Pakistan
bourgeoisie. The latter was demanding an equal share of the capitalist cake.

9

the West Pakistani leaders, and some of them claimed that the six points had been drafted by the regime's pet civil servant, Altaf Gauhar, simply in order to sabotage the opposition parties. Discussions started on a compromise formula, but the rigid position adopted by some West Pakistani leaders left no room for a compromise and the conference ended in chaos. (The conference was held in the Gulberg area of Lahore, which is where the bourgeoisie lives, and the complete isolation of Gulberg from the working-class slums of Lahore symbolized the gulf between the "leaders" and the masses.)

While the political parties and their leaders seemed to be in disarray, the mood of the masses was still militant. They felt that they had been cheated by the elections and were quite prepared to resume the anti-Ayub struggle when the beginning of the Indo-Pakistan war disrupted all internal politics in September 1965. For a time chauvinism gripped the country, and Ayub gained support, but the direction and conclusion of the war resulted in another upsurge of feeling against Ayub throughout West Pakistan. The Tashkent Agreement was seen as a "betrayal", and there was a somewhat quixotic attempt to oppose it by the Muslim League. But again there was no organized movement, and the leaders of the anti-Tashkent agitation were imprisoned. They had hoped that mass revolt would follow their arrests, but, in the words of the Muslim League leader Mian Mumtaz Daultana, "Not a dog barked, not a bird twittered." Daultana was at this time barred from taking part in politics and he claims that he advised the League against the campaign.

Foreign policy

The "progressive" nature of Pakistan's foreign policy from 1962 to 1968 was used by many Leftists as an excuse to refrain from opposition to the Ayub regime. Their action had far-reaching effects on the direction of the upsurge in 1968-9. As described in the last chapter, Ayub tried his best to reach agreement with India soon after he came to power. He wrote in the American journal *Foreign Affairs* in July 1960:

> As a student of war and strategy, I can see quite clearly the inexorable push of the North in the direction of the warm waters of the Indian Ocean. This push is bound to increase if India and

Pakistan go on squabbling with each other ... If, on the other hand, we resolve our problems and disengage our armed forces from facing inwards as they do today, and face them outwards, I feel we shall have a good chance of preventing a recurrence of the history of the past, which was that whenever this sub-continent was divided someone or other invited the outsider to step in.[19]

Behind this simpleton's view of history can be plainly detected a bid for a combined military alliance against Chinese Communism. The United States wanted Pakistan to patch up its relations with India, and this the Ayub regime obediently tried to do. However, the Indian government, for reasons of its own, was not interested. Pakistan turned back to the United States, but by this time they were cultivating India themselves. Trained over the years in the art of political prostitution, Pakistan looked for other customers.

The Chinese were quite prepared to establish friendly relations with Pakistan, and there had in fact been a gradual improvement in relations between the two countries since 1962. In February 1964 the Prime Minister, Chou En-lai, visited Pakistan for three days. Here he announced quite unequivocally China's support of the people of Kashmir and of their right to act as they wished – a major change in Chinese policy. The discussions between the Chinese leader and the Pakistani dictator were most amicable.

The United States was not pleased with these developments, as Pakistan was fully aware, and as a sop to American sensibilities Pakistan remained loyal to the U.S. position in Vietnam. In May 1965 the Pakistan Foreign Minister, Mr Bhutto, signed a communiqué issued by the SEATO Council meeting in London. It was obviously a piece of American propaganda prepared by the United States State Department, and it accused Ho Chi Minh's government of invading the South as an aggressor. The tenor of the communiqué ran counter to the views of the Pakistani people, who had demonstrated their opposition to American policy by wrecking the U.S.I.S. library in Dacca the day after the United States started bombing North Vietnam.

The economy of Pakistan was linked to United States aid and to the world capitalist system as a whole, and if the United States had wanted, it could have ended Pakistan's flirtation with China without

[19] *Foreign Affairs*, vol. 38, no. 4 (July 1960).

much difficulty. There were, however, benefits for the United States in Pakistan's friendly relations with China. The fact that Pakistani airlines were allowed free access to China and the facilities afforded Pakistani "academics" to visit China were utilized by American Intelligence for their own purposes.

But Pakistan's relations with China were soon overshadowed by the outbreak in September 1965 of war between Pakistan and India. Very little material has been published on the war which is not propaganda by one side or the other, so it is impossible to analyse the specific causes. In general, however, we have already seen that the government was completely isolated from the people following the 1965 election. The political situation in the country had deteriorated to such an extent, and the contradictions of the regime were such that it could not bring off the economic miracle that was needed to restore confidence, so there had to be a major diversion.

It was decided to focus attention once again on the people of Kashmir. Pakistani-trained infiltrators were sent across the cease-fire line, and it was hoped that they would be able to take advantage of the prevalent unrest in Indian-held Kashmir to precipitate an armed conflict. It seems quite clear that the Pakistan Military Command reckoned that the war would be confided to the Kashmir area. Clashes took place between Pakistani infiltrators and Indian troops and the Pakistan army went in to engage the Indian army in direct combat. The Pakistani forces were regarded with sympathy in Kashmir, but the general uprising they had hoped for, and which could have been decisive, did not materialize. The Indian troops suffered serious reverses in Kashmir, launched an attack across the international border near Lahore, and then began to cross the Pakistan border in order to divert Pakistani forces from Kashmir. The resulting clashes ended in a stalemate, though both sides claimed a victory.

If the war had continued for another few weeks both countries would have faced severe economic crisis, which would have led to mass upheavals. Ayub, who had not expected a limited intervention to result in an all-out war, understood the risk he ran. He was in an extremely nervous state throughout the war, and was in constant touch with the United States Embassy.

During the course of the fighting itself, he appealed to President Johnson for his intervention and said that the President should tell both India and Pakistan, which depended on large

United States aid programmes, that the United States "will not stand for this conflict" and that the two countries should arrange a purposeful and permanent cease-fire.[20]

At the same time he appealed to the Chinese for support, and they responded immediately. The threat of Chinese action forced the United States and Soviet Union to intervene and stop the war, and was also largely responsible for the Indian ruling class's decision not to attack vulnerable East Pakistan.[21] It was this which brought home to many East Pakistanis for the first time the dangers of their geographical situation, and further increased their political consciousness.

The cease-fire resulted eventually in a meeting of Indian and Pakistani leaders under Russian direction in Tashkent, and the Tashkent Agreement was signed on January 10th, 1966. (It was perhaps paradoxical that the Soviet Union should have mediated between two bourgeois states and prevailed on them to accept the status quo.) Taking into account later Russian moves in the same region, the Tashkent Agreement can be seen quite clearly as an effort to bring India and Pakistan together in order to contain China and lessen Chinese influence in Pakistan. American and Russian interests coalesced at this point, and American monopoly capitalists found themselves applauding the actions of the Soviet bureaucracy. *Peking Review* of February 4th, 1966, stated its view without equivocation: "The course taken by the Soviet leaders in the Vietnam, Indo-Pakistan, and Japan questions completely conforms with the requirements of imperialism, and especially with the latter's policy of encircling China!"

As might have been expected, the plight of the Kashmiri people was completely forgotten at Tashkent, and Pakistan's ill-timed intervention in Kashmir has, if anything, put the Kashmiri struggle a few years back.[22] However, it had one positive effect: it convinced

[20] Khalid bin Sayeed, op. cit.

[21] In a conversation with the author in August 1969, Mr Bhutto told him that the Chinese had made it clear to the United States at Warsaw that the Chinese would not sit back and see East Pakistan occupied. The threat was effective.

[22] The condition of the people of Kashmir in both Azad (Free) Kashmir — controlled by West Pakistan bureaucrats — and occupied Kashmir — controlled by the Indian army — is grim. The Pakistani ruling class would not take kindly to the idea of a genuine war of national liberation by the Kashmiris as it would undoubtedly involve Azad Kashmir and would wipe out the bureaucrats who have made the area into a happy-hunting-ground.

many young Kashmiris that they should not look to the Pakistani ruling class for national liberation but should fight for themselves and on their own and, still more important, on both sides of the cease-fire line. The Tashkent Agreement should have made this abundantly clear to those who had any doubts left. The *Sunday Telegraph* published reports of a secret Protocol in which the Pakistan government promised to abandon the cause of Kashmir, but this has been denied and no real evidence has been presented by the *Telegraph*.

As China was the only major Power which had supported Pakistan's side of the argument it was natural that its popularity in Pakistan should sharply increase. Whenever Chou En-lai appeared on newsreels in local cinemas there was loud and prolonged applause. On the other hand, when Ayub's face was seen, there were catcalls and volleys of down-to-earth Punjabi abuse. The Chinese government, unfortunately, continued to go far beyond its diplomatic requirements. After Ayub's fake election victory he had received a congratulatory message from the Chinese Prime Minister claiming that his success showed quite clearly that Ayub had the support of the people. Again, when Marshal Chen Yi visited Lahore after the war in 1965 he stated that basic democracies had something in common with people's communes. These uncalled-for statements did the Chinese leadership nothing but harm in radical circles in Pakistan. Perhaps they were really meant for pro-Chinese Pakistanis; if so they had the desired effect, for the pro-Chinese groups waxed lyrical in their support of Ayub. They had earlier proclaimed the Indo-Pak war as a "people's war"! They used Ayub's foreign policy to argue against any opposition to him, thus forgetting that for Marxists, "Foreign policy is everywhere and always a continuation of domestic policy, for it is conducted by the same ruling class and pursues the same historic goals."[23]

There is a long history of conflict of interest between an anti-imperialist workers' state and forces working for social revolution. The state interests of the Soviet Union had dictated that it sign the treaty of Brest-Litovsk with the German monarchy: at the same time, Lenin and Trotsky had not compromised in any way by watering down their support of the German revolutionary socialists. On the contrary, Lenin had declared that the German revolution was of paramount importance for the development of the Russian revolu-

[23] Leon Trotsky, *The Revolution Betrayed* (New York, 1969), p. 186.

tion. After Lenin's death, the expulsion of Trotsky and the bureau-
cratization of the Russian Communist Party, Stalin's policies
reversed this course and the state interests of the Soviet Union overruled the need for a European revolution. The subsequent betrayals
by the European Stalinist parties and the evolution of these parties is
well known.

As there is no present-day Chinese equivalent of the Comintern it
is not easy to speak of "wrong advice", "betrayals" and so on, but
the policy of the Chinese government in relation to the dictatorship
in Pakistan has been one of class collaboration on an international
scale. Only a lunatic would argue that the Chinese were wrong to
develop friendly relations with Pakistan and try and break the
imperialist encirclement of China, but at the same time it would be
irresponsible of socialists not to criticize certain aspects of this policy,
which led the Chinese into making statements directly opposed to
the interests of the Pakistani workers, peasants and students. Some
Chinese spokesmen even pandered to the delusions of the Pakistani
ruling class that Pakistan had existed for centuries; it seemed to suit
them to forget that the very idea of Pakistan was hardly thirty years
old. The Vice-President of the China-Pakistan Friendship Association, for example, wrote in an article in Peking on the occasion of the
tenth anniversary of Republic Day:

> Pakistan is a country with an *ancient* culture and a glorious
> tradition of anti-colonialist struggles. In order to win inde-
> pendence and freedom the Pakistani people carried out a *pro-
> tracted, hard and heroic struggle*. After the independence of
> Pakistan, the Pakistani people under the leadership of President
> Ayub Khan have scored in the last few years delightful achieve-
> ments ... From ancient times a profound traditional friendship
> has existed between the Chinese and Pakistani people ... The
> relation of friendly co-operation between China and Pakistan
> are established on the reliable basis of the five principles of peace-
> ful co-existence and the Bandung spirit ... On the great festival
> of the tenth anniversary of the founding of the Islamic Republic
> of Pakistan we heartily wish the *Pakistan government* and people
> new and greater successes in the cause of a developing national
> economy, consolidating national independence and safeguarding
> state sovereignty.[24]

[24] Chang Chieh, Vice-President, China-Pakistan Friendship Association:
Dawn, Karachi, March 23rd, 1966. Italics mine.

One can ignore the historical distortions which even the Pakistani establishment historians would find difficulty in accepting. But the whole question of a "national economy" and "national independence" implies somehow that these things are unrelated to the world-wide system of capitalist and imperialist relationships; it ignores the fact that Pakistan is a member of CENTO and SEATO and that Pakistan is completely dependent on the financial support of the United States; that the only way of breaking these relationships is by a social revolution similar to that of the Chinese people under the leadership of Mao and Chu Teh. The Chinese should have raised the question of a revolutionary party which would bring about a socialist revolution in Pakistan and would thus be a source of strength to the development of the Chinese revolution and a hammer blow against United States imperialism.

It could be argued that the writer of the article quoted above is an insignificant functionary, so let us ignore him and turn for a moment to the Chinese Foreign Minister, Marshal Chen Yi, who in a speech in Lahore *after* the signing of the Tashkent Agreement said that:

> Under the leadership of President Mohammed Ayub Khan, the Pakistani people united as one and filled with a common hatred towards the enemy, triumphed over the enemy ... and finally repulsed the aggressor in safeguarding the independence and sovereignty of their country ... [25]

Marshal Chen Yi did not elaborate on whether the poverty-stricken Indian peasant was the enemy of his Pakistani counterpart, or whether it was the Indian and Pakistani ruling class who were united in opposition to the peasants and workers in both countries. He said nothing about the collaboration of the Pakistani and Indian ruling class at Tashkent. Nor did he refer to the fact that for the Kashmiri people the war had been a defeat. That task was left to the leader of a visiting forty-eight-member acrobatic troupe from China who gave support to the right of self-determination for the Kashmiri people.[26]

While the acrobatic troupe was still performing, a Chinese labour delegation arrived in Pakistan as the guests of the Pakistan Confederation of Labour, a government-sponsored body which acted in the interests of the employers and had been created to prevent the

[25] *Pakistan Times*, Lahore, March 30th, 1966.
[26] Ibid., October 17th, 1966. Mr Kuo Po-Chung, leader of the acrobatic troupe, made a statement supporting self-determination for Kashmir.

growth of independent trade unions. If they had wanted to the delegation of Chinese trade unionists could have raised the question of why trade unionism had been curbed by the government. They could have drawn attention to the appalling working conditions of a large majority of the urban proletariat, and they could have reported to the Chinese workers that Pakistani workers lived in semi-feudal societies. The very least the Chinese delegation could have done was to have refrained from making tactless statements. But even this was too much to hope for. Speaking in Lyallpur, a stronghold of the Saigol family, the leader of the delegation, Mr Wang Chieh, was reported as saying that:

> Pakistan had made impressive progress during a short span of time and its achievements in various fields of national economy promised a bright future for the people. He added that a strong and prosperous Pakistan would play an important role in stabilizing peace in Asia. The Chinese trade union leader said that during his tour of West Pakistan he noted that workers were imbibed [*sic*] with a spirit of self-reliance and were determined to strengthen the economy of their country.[27]

In two years' time the Pakistani workers were to demonstrate how deeply they were 'imbibed with a spirit of self-reliance".

These speeches by various Chinese spokesmen went far beyond mere friendly relations. They were doing something the Russians had long been doing and for which Mao had repeatedly attacked them. At the same time as Chinese delegations were praising Ayub in Pakistan, the *People's Daily* was busy denouncing the Indian ruling class and calling for armed struggle to overthrow the Indian bourgeoisie. The organ of the Chinese Communist Party omitted to explain how it was correct to support at the same moment a revolution in India and a military dictator in Pakistan.[28]

Despite China's friendship, the military regime was moving back to a position of complete subservience to the United States. Ayub had

---

[27] *Pakistan Times*, October 31st, 1966.
[28] On March 24th, 1967, *People's Daily* of Peking wrote: "The Indian people have a glorious revolutionary tradition. The great armed uprising of the Telegana peasants of 1949–51 struck terror in the hearts of the Indian ruling class. Today the country is convulsing to struggle against hunger and starvation ... a new revolutionary storm is about to rise in India." One agrees completely with this analysis, but, comrades, what about Pakistan?

visited Washington immediately after the conclusion of the Indo-Pakistan war and had "explained Pakistan's position" to the American President – which means, stripped of diplomatic euphemisms, that he was apologizing to his master for his quarrel with another of America's stooges.

As a result of American pressure Ayub had also decided to sack his ebullient Foreign Minister, Z. A. Bhutto, who had displeased the Americans by some of his anti-American rhetoric at Afro-Asian gatherings. Though Bhutto was undoubtedly a radical compared to everyone else in the Ayub administration, he was by no means blindly anti-American, and had occasionally stressed the importance of friendship with the United States in his public statements. After his talks with Dean Rusk in April 1966 a journalist had asked him if the talks had brought Pakistan and America closer. Bhutto had replied, "We have always been close, perhaps in the final analysis we have gone even closer to the United States, by going closer to others."[29]

The removal of Bhutto coincided with the resumption of American aid to Pakistan, and the Pakistan government tried its best to cool down its relations with China. Some formalities still had to be maintained, however, as the people of Pakistan were pro-Chinese, and the Chinese themselves were still behaving in an extremely friendly fashion towards Ayub. A delegation from Pakistan, led by Khwaja Shahabuddin, Ayub's Minister for Information, arrived in Peking to take part in National Day celebrations in October 1967.

> According to Radio Peking, thousands of revolutionaries and Red Guards carrying placards and portraits of Chairman Mao Tse tung and President Ayub gathered at the airport to give the Minister a warm welcome. The Information Minister told newsmen at Dacca airport before his departure that he carried with him a copy of *Friends Not Masters* which he will present to Chairman Mao.[30]

Neither the Chinese press nor the radio reported how the Chairman received the book or what he thought of it.

A Chinese Trade delegation came to Pakistan on a return visit on October 29th, 1967. Its leader, Mr Chia-Shih, distinguished himself by the following remarks when in reply to an address of welcome at a lunch arranged by the Chamber of Commerce and Industry he said:

[29] *Morning News*, Karachi, April 25th, 1966.
[30] *Dawn*, Karachi, September 29th, 1967.

Under the inspiring leadership of President Ayub, Pakistan has made a remarkable progress in the industrial and agricultural sectors and the day is not far off when Pakistan will achieve complete economic independence.[31]

Mr Shih did not explain himself further, but taken at face value his statement is a complete revision of Marx and Lenin and Mao! He is saying that it is possible to build an *independent* economy — in direct contradiction to the theories of scientific socialism, as even a cursory reading would have shown Mr Shih. But he committed an even worse crime by ignoring the teachings of Mao, who had written quite clearly in his text *On the People's Democratic Dictatorship*:

> Sitting on the fence will not do; nor is there a third road. We oppose illusion about a third road. Not only in China but throughout the world, all the people without exception, must lean on imperialism or socialism. Neutrality is merely a camouflage; a third road does not exist.

Delegations came and went, but it became clear that Pakistan was tied as firmly as ever to the United States, and that there was no possibility of Ayub or the army initiating any shift of loyalty. A complete change of foreign policy could come about only if the regime changed its existing social structure, and to this its own class interests were the strongest impediment. Pakistan remained a member of CENTO and SEATO, and while professing friendship for the anti-Zionist cause it continued to develop its military-political contacts with Iran's regime, which was close to Zionism and was despised by the Palestinian guerrillas and even by some of the Middle East governments.

The "Left" and the Ayub regime

It is not easy to generalize about the role of the Left. In the first place the situation is not the same in both parts of the country, and also the term "Left" is necessarily used here in a very broad sense and includes radical and progressive elements *in Pakistani politics*. In the early stages of the Ayub raj the Left was virtually unanimous in its opposition to the regime. But as time went on it became clear that some left-wing groups found themselves incapable of organizing themselves, while others who were organized found it difficult to

[31] *Pakistan Times*, October 29th, 1967.

oppose the military government. To many of them Ayub's foreign policy eventually seemed like an easy way out.

The attitude of the regime was utterly straightforward: we have already recounted the murder of Hasan Nasir.[32] Maulana Bhashani had been arrested as soon as he returned to Pakistan from Egypt, where he had been the guest of President Nasser. In East Pakistan hundreds of people had been arrested, prominent among them many Communist Party cadres and in West Pakistan the government jailed left-wing intellectuals and trade-union leaders (although after the withdrawal of Martial Law many of the prisoners in West Pakistan were released).

Soon after Maulana Bhashani was released from prison in 1963, he agreed to go as the leader of a government delegation to the October celebrations in Peking. There he had discussions with the Chinese leaders, including Mao Tse tung and Chou En-lai. According to the Pakistan Ambassador to China at that time, General Raza, who was present during the Maulana's discussions with Chou, the latter said in no uncertain terms that the Chinese would welcome a rapprochement between the National Awami Party and the Ayub regime. According to Raza, the Maulana agreed. Whatever the truth of that story, there is no doubt that the attitude of Bhashani's party to the Ayub regime was discussed in Peking. When I was in East Pakistan in June 1969 I asked the Maulana during the course of a tape-recorded conversation:

"When you went to China what did Mao discuss with you when you met him?"

The Maulana's reply was quite unequivocal, and does seem to confirm General Raza's impression:

"Mao said to me that at the present time China's relationship with Pakistan was extremely fragile and that the United States, Russia and India would do their utmost to break this relationship. He said, "You are our friends, and if at the present moment you continue your struggle against the Ayub government it will only strengthen the hand of Russia, America and India. It is against our principles to interfere with your work, but we would advise you to proceed slowly and carefully. Give us a chance to deepen our friendship with your government ... "

[32] See p. 104–5. In addition many left-wing students who were arrested in 1962 were tortured into submission. (One of the methods used was to strip the students naked and make them lie down on a large slab of ice.)

It was no coincidence that after the Maulana's return from Peking a section of the National Awami Party adopted an ambivalent attitude towards the Ayub regime and toned down its opposition. In April 1964 *Outlook* printed an interview with a "Communist" – understandably, he preferred to remain anonymous – who claimed that Ayub's regime was more progressive than previous regimes had been. Among the theories he propounded in the interview were the following:

> Our new rising bourgeoisie is bound to come into conflict with the American and European bourgeoisies which dominate the world markets. The pressure of economic necessity will force the Habibullahs and the Valikas and the Saigols [leading industrialists] and all the rest to seek trade with the socialist bloc and this will break the stranglehold of the imperialist West on our economy. This is the direction in which we are moving and I will be damned if I condemn Ayub Khan for this opening to the Left.

In answer to another question our "Communist" replied: "If only class consciousness was there among the people, basic democracies could become training schools for soviets." And he ended by saying that at the next election he would vote for Ayub Khan, giving as his main reason the "development of friendship with China".[33] Four months later, in the same journal, another "Communist" took up the arguments of the first "Communist", and criticized some of his views, particularly on the question of basic democracies:

> Let us take this comrade's observation that basic democracies could become training schools for soviets! This is a most puerile hope! The basic democracies are specially made to order for the perpetuation of the bureaucratic-bourgeois rule in this country ... It is as laughable to say that basic democracies can be transformed into soviets as to suggest that Falangists or Blackshirts can be transformed into Bolsheviks ... We must be absolutely clear about the class composition of those running this country.

He, too, crumbled later in the interview, agreeing that as "President Ayub Khan is at loggerheads with imperialism" he must be supported. He advocated giving critical support to the regime.[34] Both

[33] "Dialogue with a Communist", *Outlook*, Karachi (April 25th, 1964).
[34] "A Communist Comments", ibid. (August 8th, 1964).

these "Communists" considered themselves "pro-Chinese", and their views were representative of a large section of the pro-Chinese Left in West Pakistan.

The increasing rift between the Soviet Union and China was also reflected in the National Awami Party, though somewhat artificially. Moscow Communists who had influence in the N.A.P. had virtually liquidated themselves politically and they were indistinguishable from ordinary liberal democrats. They seemed to regard the establishment of parliamentary democracy as an end in itself, and in order to achieve it were prepared to make all sorts of shabby compromises with other parties who shared their goal. On the international scale they believed in "peaceful coexistence" and were strongly pro-Russian. The pro-Chinese wing, on the other hand, while toeing the line on international affairs (they regularly passed resolutions and distributed leaflets on the war in Vietnam, for example), were of dubious respectability on the question of the Ayub regime; their deeds suggested that they found Ayub preferable to a parliamentary government based on adult franchise.

So while one can criticize the pro-Moscow wing of the N.A.P. for its liberal illusions, the attitude of the so-called pro-Peking N.A.P. deserves equal condemnation. Of course, many pro-Peking members of the N.A.P. could argue that, while some of them had suffered imprisonment in the pre-Ayub days, they had for some time been allowed to do political work by the government, and for them that was the acid test. In fact, during the last five years of the Ayub raj they had not engaged in any radical activities. Since they spent 99 per cent of their time attacking the bourgeois politicians and ignoring Ayub there was no reason why the regime should arrest them.

In East Pakistan the underground Communist Party had not taken advantage of the opportunity to form an official party when the ban had been lifted in 1954. Many party leaders had refused to come out into the open, and confined their activities to the National Awami Party and parliamentarism. As a result they became isolated from the masses, and this question was being discussed within the party when Martial Law was imposed in 1958. The impact of parliamentary politics had been such that the party did not make an outcry against Martial Law. Not even a cyclostyled leaflet was issued.

There were already the seeds of a division, as one group maintained that the organization of the party should be consolidated, while another argued that C.P. organization could not be isolated from parliamentary activities – a somewhat ludicrous position, as no parliament existed and even the bourgeois parties had been banned. The Sino-Indian border conflict increased the division inside the party and pro-Moscow and pro-Peking lines developed.

In 1964 two members of the Central Committee submitted a brief document which partly explained the trend in the international Communist movement and supported the Peking thesis. The Central Committee agreed to circulate the document with its reply, and the resulting discussion was interrupted by the Indo-Pakistan War of 1965. The party line was that India was the aggressor, and that there should be an immediate cease-fire. A difference of opinion existed on the latter point, some of the comrades maintaining that if it was a war of aggression the Indians should be asked to withdraw. The party supported the Tashkent Declaration, but the pro-Chinese group maintained that Pakistan should have continued to fight. Both sides of the argument were to a certain extent influenced by chauvinism. Some leading members had, as we have seen, described the conflict as a "people's war". Among them was Anwar Zahid, Maulana Bhashani's secretary and Editor of the N.A.P. weekly, *Janata*. Zahid printed an article declaring the war to be a people's war, and was strongly criticized for this within the party; but after Tashkent, *Janata*, loyal as ever, supported the Tashkent Declaration. In a later editorial Zahid wrote that there were only two anti-imperialist voices in Pakistan – Ayub and Bhashani. It should be mentioned that Zahid was later expelled from the underground party.

The faction-fighting continued unabated and there was a sharp division in May 1966. A reception committee had been set up to welcome Liu Shao-Ch'i on his arrival in Dacca. Liu had not yet been denounced as an imperialist agent, and was still the President of China. The pro-Moscow group withdrew from the reception committee on the grounds that it would amount to a reception for Ayub, who was accompanying Liu. (One of those who withdrew was Professor Mozaffar Ahmed.) In the end the Chinese themselves asked for the reception to be cancelled, on the grounds that Liu's reception at Lahore had been so stupendous that security precautions had become impossible. The real reason may well have been that the decision to downgrade Liu had already been taken in Peking.

In December 1966 a split in the underground party finally took place. It was a "peaceful" rift, and both sides refrained from crude denunciations. Only the trade-union and peasant committees remained united. Of the eleven members of the Central Committee, nine sided with Moscow, and most of the old members and party organizers remained loyal to the old Stalinist tradition of obedience to Moscow, while most of the new, young members sided with Peking. Both groups now concentrated their activities on the National Awami Party, and it was inevitable that the N.A.P. would also split sooner or later.

For the pro-Peking group it was an incorrect decision. Not that they should have abandoned the National Awami Party; but their main priority should have been to set up an independent organization and devote all their energies to strengthening it in the countryside and in the factories: a party whose class nature was never in doubt, which could articulate the demands of the workers, peasants and students without any hesitation and with the full knowledge that it was beyond the influence of the press and the bourgeois parties. Only some of the pro-Chinese cadres were capable of doing this effectively, as the pro-Russian groups believed that Pakistan was not yet ready for a socialist revolution and that therefore all the left-wing forces should unite and work for a bourgeois-democratic revolution. The Mensheviks used this theory to dissuade the Bolsheviks from seizing state power, and Lenin and Trotsky had combated it vigorously; the same theory was later used by Stalin to justify his alliance with Chiang Kai-shek in China and his betrayal of the Spanish Civil War.[35]

So at a time when popular discontent against the Ayub government was accumulating, neither the pro-Moscow nor the pro-Peking groups were aware of the undercurrent. The former was busy cementing its alliances with "like-minded" forces equally isolated from the reality of the Pakistani political situation. The latter was entangled with the N.A.P. (Bhashani's group), and its attitude towards the Ayub regime had lost them the respect of large numbers of people.

[35] This fact is not mentioned only as a polemic. Stalinist policy in Spain should be studied by all Asian revolutionaries as the betrayals of the Stalinists which led from a belief in the revisionist theory of "revolution by stages" finally resulted in a fascist counter-revolution. It is therefore important for all revolutionaries, particularly in the Tricontinent, to study and learn from these lessons. In this connection an excellent book is Felix Morrow's, *Revolution and Counter-Revolution in Spain*, which has been published in England by New Park Publications Ltd, and is available in limited quantities from Pioneer Book Service, 182 Pentonville Road, London N.1.

In West Pakistan in the first half of 1967 there had been a successful railway strike. The right to strike had never been recognized by the Ayub regime; workers were forced to seek redress through the conciliation machinery established by the government and industrial courts, and in most cases, of course, the workers lost. The official railway workers union was completely subservient to the "national interest" and financed by the government. The unofficial union was controlled by the "pro-Peking" section of the National Awami Party and was led by Mirza Ibrahim. They were opposed to any strike action, mainly because of their lack of organization outside Lahore, but also because a national strike would only aid imperialism, in view of the "anti-imperialists nature of the Ayub regime".

The economic situation had deteriorated very sharply after the Indo-Pakistan war, and the price of sugar and flour had risen phenomenally. Strict rationing had been imposed, and workers, peasants and some of the petit-bourgeois had to queue for hours to buy food; many were forced to miss a day's work in order to collect their weekly rations. For large numbers of railway workers the situation was intolerable. Often those who worked on trains could not afford to miss even one day, as it meant that they would not be able to catch their train and would lose two or even three days' work. The railway workers appealed to the authorities to set up special ration shops. The government refused point-blank.

Completely spontaneously, independent workers' committees were set up; the call for a strike went out by word of mouth, and a few almost illegible leaflets were circulated. The strike action was a complete success, and for two whole days not a single railway carriage moved on the tracks in West Pakistan. Veteran trade unionists observed that this was the first complete strike of railway workers in the history of Indo-Pakistani trade unionism.

The government summoned Mirza Ibrahim, assuming automatically that his union was involved in the strike. Nothing was further from the truth, but despite the loyalty of a section of the National Awami Party, the ideologues of the regime still could not trust them completely. Mirza Ibrahim was asked to call the strike off and was promised that if he succeeded the unofficial union would be recognized by the government. C. R. Aslam, the President of the Punjab and Bahawalpur pro-Peking N.A.P., denies that Mirza agreed to this deal, but certain incontrovertible facts point the other way. Mirza Ibrahim called a meeting of railway workers in Lahore and took with him to the meeting the Provincial Minister for Labour, Ahmed Saeed Kirmani (the same gentleman who had "defeated" Mirza Ibrahim in the 1950 elections in Lahore when Ibrahim was in prison). Two of the "arguments" they used to get the men back to work were that the strike was being financed by the C.I.A. and that it was "preventing grain from reaching the peasants". Kirmani was universally despised as the most fawning of the sycophants in Ayub's circle, and when the workers were asked to listen to him they could contain themselves no longer and both Kirmani and Mirza were spat on and abused.

When it became clear that Mirza Ibrahim's union could not end the strike, the government accused them of not trying hard enough, and arrested Mirza and other leaders of the pro-Peking N.A.P. The government itself used every form of intimidation in its attempt to end the strike. There were mass dismissals, arrests without trial, and at Hyderabad, when strikers lay on the tracks to prevent black-legs from driving trains, one train was driven over them, killing one and injuring many others. Eventually, the strike ended, but only after the government had conceded some demands.

> The amazing thing about the strike was the level of organiza-
> tion and the spirit of solidarity displayed by the workers. The
> leadership of the strike was localized and restricted in the main
> to young workers. The coffee house intellectuals hadn't even
> heard their names before and certainly have not since. The
> unions, both official and "unofficial" and their structures were
> completely bypassed![36]

In fact, although the spontaneous militancy of the young workers had been a source of great strength since it had taken the government completely unawares, it was also a weakness in that there was little effective co-ordination with other sections of the working class. The 1967 railway strike was extremely significant politically. It showed that young workers were prepared to combat the Ayub regime. It also revealed the depth of feeling against the dictatorship. Yet despite this the pro-Peking elements within the West Pakistan N.A.P. persisted in their ludicrous defence of the "anti-imperialist" face of the government.

The emergence of Mr Z. A. Bhutto as a "radical" force in Paki-stani politics can be attributed in part to the inadequacy of the

[36] *Black Dwarf*, January 10th, 1969.

National Awami Party. Ever since he had been dismissed Bhutto had been skulking in the background, sometimes talking to the leaders of the Muslim League, at other times to the National Awami Party. He finally decided that he wanted to set up his own party. The People's Party was formed in December 1967, despite the slanders of the press and the obstacles set in its path by the government. The fact that by this stage Mr Bhutto was attacking the Ayub regime in public attracted a certain amount of support to the People's Party. Many radicals who had been disgusted by the attitude of the pro-Peking N.A.P. because of its pro-Ayub stance were so pleased by Bhutto's outspoken opposition that they began to idolize him. To the students, too, Bhutto appeared as the redeemer who was going to strike the dictator down. There can be no doubt that Bhutto played a leading role in the anti-Ayub movement at a time when no other political leader was prepared to speak up in public against the dictatorship. All socialists should have supported Bhutto's war of attrition against Ayub, even if they could not agree with the programme of the People's Party. Bhutto had served the regime faithfully for several years and now considered this to be his biggest crime. However, his intimate knowledge of the workings of the government meant that he was in a good position to expose it; for example, he told the founding conference of his party how this supposedly anti-imperialist government,

> had instructed the press not to write a single word that might offend the aggressors in Vietnam. What a shameful directive! Have we become so timid and degenerate as to remain completely silent about the terrible destruction wrought in an Asian country? Our press has been directed not to publish photographs of war scenes released by international agencies and published all over the world, including the United States and Western Europe ... This is the measure of our independence and the strength of the government which boasts so much about its stability and achievements![37]

The government had been persecuting Bhutto throughout 1967; charges of corruption had been levelled against him but they were so ridiculous that they resulted in general merriment. In a situation where Ayub's own family had prospered by graft, corruption and tyranny, it did not behove the government to accuse Bhutto of petty

[37] *Foundation and Policy* (Lahore, 1967).

acts of corruption. Although Bhutto deserved support in his courageous stand against the Ayub dictatorship, it was also necessary that his party programme should be subjected to a severe critique by socialists. Even Bhutto underestimated the strength of the masses. In an interview in London published in autumn 1968[38] he seemed to think that Ayub would remain in power indefinitely.

Bhutto was and always had been a social-democrat at heart, and the manifesto of his party was a mixture of idealism and liberal capitalism. While talking about nationalizing the key sectors of industry it also spoke in terms of: "The private sector will play its own useful role in the kind of *mixed economy* envisaged, but will not be able to create monopolistic reserves. It must flourish under conditions proper to free enterprise, namely those of competition ... "[39]

However, the details of his party programme are not to our purpose now. The traditional Left at this time seemed paralysed by its own past. In West Pakistan, and to a limited extent even in East Pakistan, the Left had devoted most of its energies to the Stalinist tradition of organizing Friendship Associations with China, Russia, Poland, Czechoslovakia, East Germany and so on. Arranging tea parties for visiting delegations became a substitute for any meaningful political activity. There were petty intrigues between factions for the posts of President and Secretary in these organizations, and quite often there were rows over sums of money which had disappeared, no one knew quite how. These were the people responsible for providing some sort of leadership during the November uprising of 1968; no wonder that in West Pakistan it floundered miserably and allowed itself to be outflanked by the Right.

The decade of development

The bureaucracy spent 1967 preparing for 1968, the tenth year of Ayub's rule. Ayub had been becoming more and more unpopular since the Tashkent Agreement and the repression which had followed it. The widows of those killed in the war led a procession in Lahore. Chanting "Give us back our husbands," they marched to the Governor's House where they returned their husbands' medals. The police had opened fire and four demonstrators had been wounded. Perhaps becoming unsure of his strength, Ayub had dismissed his Governor

[38] Interview with Z. A. Bhutto by Aziz Kurtha, *Pakistan Left Review*, London.
[39] *Foundation and Policy*, op. cit. Italics mine.

in West Pakistan, the Nawab of Kalabagh, partly because of an inter-bureaucratic struggle, but also because Ayub feared Kalabagh's increasing power. In his place the Commander-in-Chief of the army, General Musa, had been appointed Governor. Musa was not only weak but also a fool, and proved to be completely incapable of handling the province. In January 1967 even Ayub's oldest admirers seemed to be losing faith in him. *Life* magazine reported:

> In Karachi, Pakistan's commercial centre, it had been known in certain circles that Ayub's family and his cabinet had been getting rich with the aid of government loans and licences. Now his government is unabashedly accused of corruption. The son of Altaf Hussain, Pakistan's Industry Minister, has been given a major share in a steel-rolling mill. Ghulam Faruque, Ayub's canny Commerce Minister had acquired large stockholdings in companies he had helped promote as Chairman of the Pakistan Industrial Development Corporation and so on.
>
> Ayub himself is a large landowner, with citrus orchards near Rawalpindi and sugar lands in Sind. Near the site of the latter the Army Welfare Association erected a sugar mill and has been buying the President's output. Gohar Ayub, the President's stocky, mustachioed son, has become a millionaire. With the help of government financing, Gohar led a syndicate which bought out General Motors shares of an assembly plant in Karachi. He has since extended his holdings and was recently granted exclusive rights for the distribution of Toyota cars in Pakistan ... Nearly 1,000 political prisoners are crammed into Pakistan's jails ... [40]

For most people in Pakistan this was common knowledge. It was well known that since his retirement from the army in 1961 Ayub's eldest son had applied himself with notable success to amassing wealth. Ayub is reported to have remarked that he had had no idea of his son's talent for business! By 1965 the total capital of the Ayub family had been unofficially assessed at about Rs. 25 crores (or Rs. 250 million), and this did not include money in foreign bank accounts.[41]

In 1967 Ayub authorized the writing of his memoirs. *Friends Not Masters* was in fact ghosted under the supervision of Ayub's Information Secretary, Altaf Gauhar. The book is a semi-literate

[40] Quoted in the *Times of India*, January 29th, 1967, p. 7.
[41] Figure quoted in *Link*, New Delhi, May 19th, 1968, p. 33.

mixture of the paternalistic and bourgeois ideas implanted in Ayub's head during his Sandhurst days, and the Pakistani press was hysterical in its praise. It should have made the Pakistani intelligentsia weep with shame: but the large majority welcomed the book as a masterpiece. Ayub himself said, "You should study this book, understand and act upon it ... it contains material which is for the good of the people."[42] Quotations from it were displayed in schools, colleges, offices and other institutions, and a few sycophants actually succeeded in having the book included in school and university courses. No doubt Ayub hoped to deepen understanding of the student problem with such comments as these:

> Most of the newly-emerging countries adopted the western system of government because they did not have time to work out a system of their own. As a result, governments have been functioning in a state of tension with the people ... In new countries, such as ours, traditions of responsibility are not sufficiently developed; irresponsibility comes easy, since it often goes unpunished.

And here is his method of dealing with students' over-abundant energy:

> Organized physical training, for example, in our schools and colleges could take the place of more complicated and expensive games. One instructor on a platform with a loud-speaker can take a very large body of students at one time, and just half a day should build up their bodies and minds, and take the devil out of them.[43]

The book is littered with such gems. It is beneath contempt, and if it had been written by a British Viceroy he would no doubt have been recalled to London. It's few ideas reflect all too accurately the meagreness and superficiality of the views of the Pakistani ruling class; in fact we can recommend it to sociologists as a study of the effect on them of British ideology.

Friends Not Masters received favourable reviews in most of the British press and it was left to *Private Eye* to debunk them (which it did to such good effect that cyclostyled copies of this *Private Eye*

[42] *Dawn*, Karachi, August 21st, 1967.
[43] Mohammed Ayub Khan, *Friends Not Masters — A Political Autobiography* (Oxford, 1967), p. 101.

article were shown conspiratorially to each other by young Pakistani civil servants and journalists.)

The liberal British press has taken the publication of Ayub Khan's "political autobiography" as yet another occasion to present the Sandhurst-trained Field Marshal as a veritable apostle of common sense and liberalism in Asia.

Ayub avoids mentioning various significant facts which might tarnish his liberal reputation in England built assiduously over the years by *The Grauniad, The Observer* and Kingsley Martin.

He does not tell us, for instance, about the Pir (a Muslim Guru) of Dewal Sharif, a complete fraud who has virtually hypnotized Ayub into believing that he (the Pir) is in direct communication with God. Before making important decisions Ayub always consults his Pir who gives him God's sanction and on one occasion told Ayub: "Every word you utter is put in your mouth by God — You are his servant and whatever you do is done on God's instructions" — a comment which rather perplexed Oxford-educated Professor Tanvir Ahmed Khan, an English don, who writes most of Ayub's speeches.

Both the Pir and Ayub have prospered over the years. The Pir's influence has reached such heights that a telephone call from him to Ayub's secretary works wonders. Businessmen in quest of import licences are known to visit the Pir in large numbers with packets of Rs. 15,000 (about £1,200) as "gifts for God" — they usually get their import licences. The Pir reassures Ayub that God has willed that Ayub's family should prosper.

Result: (i) Ayub's eldest son, Captain Gohar Ayub is a Member of Parliament and has taken over three large industries from businessmen opposed to the regime.

(ii) Ayub's second and thickest son, Shaukat Ayub, is a director of thirty-two firms.

(iii) Ayub's youngest son, Tahir Ayub, is reputedly trying to buy Crockford's via a Pakistani businessman called Fancy, in case "things go wrong back home".

(iv) Ayub has bought a farm in Sardinia for "better days".

(v) Ayub has a large bank-balance in Geneva, acquired via a Jewish arms-dealer who sells arms to the Pakistani government at double his usual price and puts the balance into Ayub's bank account.

(vi) Ayub's daughter Nasim, who married into the Swat Royal Family guarantees that her husband and his cousins can grow opium in Swat State and smuggle it into Afghanistan.

(vii) Ayub is trying to hasten the economic development of the district surrounding his village, Hazara, at the expense of the rest of the province. For instance the Chinese are building a machine-tool factory in Hazara whose effect will be to bolster the reputation of the Ayub family in Hazara (vive la Thoughts of Chairman Mao).

(viii) Ayub's supporters have doubled toll-taxes in Hazara and use force and terror to blackmail farmers into selling them wheat at half its usual price; this wheat is then sold to poor peasants at three times its usual price and God (or the Pir) protect the poor peasant who refuses to buy.[44]

However, if Ayub's fallacies and paternalisms had been confined to the memoirs we would not have worried too much. Unfortunately the country was run on the same lines. Dr Mahbubal Haq, the chief economist of the Planning Commission and a former apologist for the regime, made certain disclosures which startled public opinion. There had been an enormous concentration of wealth in Pakistan, and it was now revealed that 66 per cent of the industrial capital was in the hands of twenty families. The same "lucky twenty" also controlled over 80 per cent of the country's banking and 97 per cent of the country's insurance. Of the remaining 34 per cent, more than half was controlled by foreign firms. The development of a viable middle class was therefore retarded, and this greatly worried Dr Haq.

Of considerable interest to the people was the fact that Ayub's family was one of the twenty. The other families were, in order of merit, Dawood, Adamjee, Latif, Saigol, Mian Bashir, Valika, Bany, Bimjhee, Dinshaw, Dada, A. Jalil, Fancy, Naseer Sheikh, Allawala, Munir Bashir, Marker, Mohammed Yahya (no relation to General Yahya), Haji Habib (1) and Haji Habib (2). The twenty-first family was the Ispahanis.

Ever since October 1958 the propaganda network of the regime had painted Pakistan in glowing economic terms. The scores of advisers and "academics" loaned by the United States to Pakistan had helped considerably by giving an over-optimistic bill of health

---

[44] *Private Eye*, September 29th, 1967.

to the dictatorship and implying that its economic successes should be noted by other "third world" countries and its example followed. Nothing could have been further from the truth. We saw earlier that there had been a rise in the average per capita income, and we pointed out the deception involved in these figures. Similarly, the industrial progress of Pakistan has not resulted in a growth of real wages for the Pakistani working class; in fact, their wages have gone down. In addition to this there is even greater inequality between the wages of the urban petit-bourgeoisie and the working class. "34·5 per cent of the urban income was earned in the top 10 per cent of the urban tax paying population whereas only 23·5 per cent of urban incomes was earned by 50 per cent of the urban population."[45]

Dr Rehman Sobhan, whose figures are quoted above, gave in the same article a breakdown of income: an average working class *family* in East Pakistan had an income of Rs. 78 per month, which worked out to an average income per head of just under Rs. 17 per month (just over £1). The figure in West Pakistan was marginally better, and the monthly income per head of workers was Rs. 17·4. If these figures are compared to the profits being made by big business we see that the surplus value being extracted by Pakistani capitalists is among the highest in the world. The increasing poverty of the urban proletariat has gone hand in hand with the growth of rural inequality. In West Pakistan the entire development strategy of the government, aided and abetted by advisers from the United States and the World Bank, is involved in promoting the interests of the landlords and big farmers.

This strategy is predicated on the needs to channelize the fertilizers, insecticide and high yielding seeds to those farmers who can afford to invest in tube wells, which provide the guaranteed water supply necessary to make this package work. In the last eight years about 45,000 tube wells have been privately installed. Given the high costs of investment and installation it follows that only the landlords or rich farmers can afford to invest in them. Estimates reckon that 77 per cent of these tube-wells have gone to holdings of 25 acres or more. Since only 8 per cent of the farmers in West Pakistan have holdings of this dimension the class basis of the tube-well revolution is apparent.[46]

[45] Rehman Sobhan, *Pakistan Left Review*, London (Spring, 1969).
[46] Ibid.

The tube-wells only succeeded in strengthening the landlord's grip on the life of the peasant, for the latter had to depend on him for his water supply. Thus under the Ayub regime the rich prospered and the peasants continued to live in grinding poverty—a condition which, the local *mullah* assured them, was the "will of God".

In March 1968 Ayub suffered a serious stroke and the rumour that he was dead swept the country. This was wishful thinking on the part of his opponents, but Ayub's illness was serious enough to confine him to his bed for several weeks. Certainly the army Commander-in-Chief, General Yahya Khan, was prepared to form a caretaker administration if Ayub was permanently incapacitated, and a great deal of manœuvring and intriguing went on behind the scenes while the Boss was ill. This did not please Ayub when he was recovering, but it did show forcefully that the army was the real power in the land. Ayub's illness also gave usually servile journalists and columnists the opportunity to say that perhaps he should prepare a second line of defence while he could. The "decade of development" ended with 1968, and the next general election was only two years away.

An extra thorn in Ayub's side was the increasing trouble in Baluchistan, where a tribal guerrilla war was being fought between pro- and anti-government tribesmen. The facts that Ayub ruled Baluchistan like a colony, that there were an unspecified number of political prisoners in Baluchi prisons, and that a few years ago the Pakistan air force had been used to bombard a Baluchi meeting, had aggravated the situation. The Baluchis had turned on the Punjabis, whom they saw as symbols of the Ayub raj. The army had been called in and curfews imposed.

It was with the full knowledge of the general state of the country that the bureaucracy was preparing to observe in October 1968 the tenth anniversary of the coup d'état. The fanfare had already started. Radio and television ceaselessly recounted the heroic deeds performed by the Great Man over the last ten years. Among the "facts" celebrated by the propagandists were the country's economic "progress", and the "greater political and cultural freedoms" given to the people. This propaganda had the unexpected effect of increasing the political consciousness of the masses, who could not help but notice the enormous and widening gap between the propaganda of the Ayub government and the harsh reality of their every-day existence. The students, too, faced with the repressive atmosphere in the universities and affected by the general decline of living standards, were equally nauseated by the drivel which the propagandists turned out. As if to give the propaganda a finishing touch all the newspapers produced special supplements on the "Decade of Development". The Karachi newspaper *Dawn*, supposedly not under government control, managed to print Ayub's photograph sixty-nine times in one issue of the newspaper![47] It was blatantly obvious that when the explosion came it would be no ordinary upheaval. In a month it was to engulf the whole of West Pakistan.

---

[47] *Dawn*, October 27th, 1968. Some of the photographs were made more ridiculous by captions such as the following one: "President Ayub receives news about his resounding victory at the Presidential election on phone in 1965!"

CHAPTER FIVE

The Beginning of the End

> "In all critical moments the masses intervene 'spontaneously' — in other words, obeying only their own inferences drawn from political experience, and their, as yet officially unrecognized leaders. Assimilating this or that premise from the talk of agitators, the masses on their own volition translate its conclusions into the language of action." Leon Trotsky, *History of the Russian Revolution*

Rawalpindi and West Pakistan: November – December 1968

Like the May 1968 revolt in France, the November uprising in Pakistan had very small beginnings. Pakistan's Nanterre was a small shopping centre called Landi Kotal about twenty-five miles north of Peshawar in the North West Frontier. It was part of the territory designated as "tribal areas" by the government of Pakistan, and the normal laws of the country do not operate there. There is no restriction on imports being taken into this area, for example, though technically it is forbidden to bring imported goods into Pakistan. Enterprising businessmen took advantage of this and set up a supermarket of luxury goods at Landi Kotal, which soon became a Mecca for bourgeois ladies in search of cheap trousseaus for their daughters, and for large numbers of students who used to buy cheap foreign cigarettes, transistor radios, books, etc. Officially there was a ban on bringing these goods back into Pakistan, but it was never enforced as too many civil servants, army officers and their wives were involved.

In November 1968 about seventy students from Rawalpindi went to Landi Kotal and bought about Rs. 5,000-worth of goods. On the way back the goods were confiscated and charges were brought against them. If a similar incident had occurred some years back it would have ended with the punishment of the students, but by November 1968 feeling ran so high that even this small act of repression triggered off a revolt.

A few other factors contributed to provoke an upsurge at that particular moment. One was Bhutto's tour of West Pakistan: the regime had tried to disrupt it but had failed to stem the growing tide of anti-Ayub manifestations which took the form of mass attendance at Bhutto's meetings. Another was the internal dispute raging in the Polytechnic a few miles outside Rawalpindi. The Polytechnic students had in fact asked Bhutto to stop on his way to Rawalpindi and speak to them, and on November 7th he was on his way there.

Most of the students concerned in the Landi Kotal arrests were from Gordon College in Rawalpindi – ironically, the college was financed by a subsidiary of the State Department of the United States, and there were many American professors on the staff. It was also the college favoured by the sons of bureaucrats, army officers, feudal landlords and the bourgeoisie. Fortunately the majority of students did not belong to any of these categories.

On the night of November 6th a group of students met in one of the college hostels and decided to hold a demonstration the next day. One of the key figures of this group was Raja Anwar, who was also the Vice-President of the Students' Union of Gordon College. The next morning a General Assembly was called and three thousand students gathered. They not only protested against the Landi Kotal repression; student after student assailed the Ayub regime itself, and pointed out that where Ayub and his family had been expropriating the wealth of the nation for the last ten years, the seventy students had only bought Rs. 5,000-worth of goods at Landi Kotal. It was decided by a large majority to take a demonstration out to the office of the local Commissioner (the leading bureaucrat) and to make a protest there. It was also decided that the students should assemble to welcome Bhutto on his arrival at Rawalpindi.

The demonstrators' mood was restless. Every official car with a flag was stopped, the flag was removed and anti-Ayub slogans were shouted at the occupants. The limousine carrying the Chief Election Commissioner, the man who was to help rig the General's next election, was stopped and the bureaucrat's ears were pulled after which he was allowed to proceed on his way. There was no police opposition at this first demonstration, although the students were unprecedentally aggressive. Considering the repressive nature of the dictatorship, it was a striking display of student power.

Rawalpindi, the scene of this first important demonstration,[1] was not only the headquarters of the Pakistan army; Ayub had also made it his capital city, partly because he was reluctant to be far away from

---

[1] In the weeks preceding the Rawalpindi outburst university students in Karachi had been on strike for essentially economistic demands, and schools and universities in Karachi had been closed by the government.

the army, but also because he was engaged in depoliticizing the nation and Karachi's strong political traditions hampered this process. Rawalpindi had no political tradition, and in previous student revolts it had on the whole remained passive. Militants regarded it as a politically dead city, and their view became still more pessimistic when Ayub made it the capital of Pakistan, bringing with him his court of bureaucrats, sycophants, careerists and opportunists, making it even more of an establishment stronghold. However, the effect on the students and other layers was a stimulating one; they could no longer ignore the iniquities of the dictatorship, for they now took place before their very eyes. Gradually the students became more politically aware, but the extent of their militancy on November 7th, 1968, took the entire country by surprise. Rawalpindi had suddenly come back to life, and had done so in such a way that even the censored press of the dictatorship could not quite conceal the fact.

The local bureaucracy was quite unprepared for the demonstration. As the Gordon College students marched towards the offices of the civil secretariat, the Commissioner fled and asked the Deputy Commissioner to deal with the students. The Deputy Commissioner found himself in a quandary. He had sent all the available police to the Polytechnic to deal with Mr Bhutto's arrival, so he came out himself to speak to the students; but they wanted, as they put it, someone "of higher authority". The Deputy Commissioner then informed them that he had come alone to meet them whereas he could have brought a whole posse of policemen to deal with them. This so enraged the students not least because they knew it was a lie, that they tore off the Deputy Commissioner's trousers and spanked him. They would continue to demonstrate, they said, until their demands were met, and they were prepared to discuss these demands only with someone who had authority to accept them. After this the students moved towards the Hotel Intercontinental to go and speak to Bhutto.[2] Outside the hotel they were stopped by the police, but a few

---

[2] The Intercontinental Hotels are the Asian equivalent of the Hilton and there are four in Pakistan (Lahore, Rawalpindi, Karachi, Dacca). Many of them would undoubtedly have been either stoned or burnt had it not been for the fact that most of the opposition politicians patronized them. On my second visit to Pakistan I stayed in two of them to feel for myself the unbearably bourgeois atmosphere and the sense of complete isolation from the reality outside. The hotels were built in order to boost tourism in Pakistan, yet their effect has been slight as only extremely rich tourists can afford to stay in them. The government does not particularly want to build cheap hostels as it would encourage bearded students and other subversives to visit the country.

stones strategically lobbed made the police see sense and the students were allowed into the compound of the hotel. Here they waited for Bhutto to arrive. By now they had been marching the whole day, and were tired and hungry. They unceremoniously denuded the vegetable garden of the hotel and fed themselves on radishes, throwing the ends half-affectionately at the police officers stationed near by. Some of the more impatient had got tired of waiting and had joined the Polytechnic students still waiting for Bhutto some miles away.

At the Polytechnic, Bhutto had not been allowed to address the students, and soon after he drove on towards the Intercontinental Hotel they exchanged angry words with the police. Without any physical provocation the police, who were fully armed with rifles, batons and tear-gas bombs, opened fire. One bullet hit Abdul Hamid, a first-year student aged seventeen, who died on the spot. Enraged, the students fought back with bricks and paving stones, and there were casualties on both sides.

Meanwhile, outside the hotel just before Bhutto arrived, the students were forming themselves into a number of straight lines to receive him. The police ordered them to disperse. They refused, and tear-gas bombs were thrown at them and the police made a vicious baton-charge, injuring a number of students. Some students burst into the lobby of the hotel, by now full of tear-gas; others stoned the hotel from the front, while a small commando group led an attack from the back and stoned some American diplomats who were sunbathing near the swimming pool. Eventually the police managed to drive the students away from the precincts of the hotel.

On their way back the students ran in the direction of the bus terminal of the Government Transport Service. The bus drivers, thinking that they were about to be attacked, armed themselves with bricks and pelted the approaching students. A few of the drivers captured some students and beat them up. In a rage the students started burning and stoning G.T.S. buses. This was the only incident where the students fought the workers, and even this arose from a simple misunderstanding, as the bus drivers admitted later; but the result was that throughout the upsurge not a single G.T.S. bus was safe, and during the next few months they were burnt at the slightest provocation.

There was tension in Rawalpindi when the news spread of the police firing at students. Ten years of bitterness and frustration seemed to be summed up by the incidents on November 7th, 1968, and anger gripped the people. The political isolation of the students from the struggles in the outside world, engendered by the reactionary nature of the courses in schools and universities and the censored press, was perhaps responsible for the fact that not a single student leader had realized the symbolic significance of November 7th: it was the anniversary of the Russian Revolution.

Throughout the evening large numbers of people collected in the streets, and an ominous hush stilled the usually noisy city. Steel-helmeted and armed police were stationed on all the main roads, and army units guarded the President's house.

And while the streets of Rawalpindi had tasted blood, the President of Pakistan was rejoicing in the election of President Nixon as "an old friend and admirer".[3]

The next day the government's favourite newspaper, the *Pakistan Times*, had an editorial welcoming Nixon's election, an article on its leader page justifying the ban on foreign periodicals of a "subversive nature", but no mention of the fact that a student had been killed.[4]

After their battles with the police on the first day, in which they had suffered a tactical defeat, the students began to regroup their forces. The first demonstration had involved only the students of the Polytechnic and of Gordon College, but that same evening the Presidents and Secretaries of the students' unions of all the local colleges had been contacted. They met late that night in Raja Anwar's room at Gordon College, in an atmosphere of elation tempered by sadness at the death of a comrade. It was decided that the ban imposed by the government on demonstrations, meetings and assemblies of more than four people would be defied the next morning, and that a funeral procession would take place.

The government had decided to close all the schools and colleges, including the Polytechnic, for "an indefinite period". When this had happened in the past, most students had obeyed and stayed away. This time, however, they decided to defy the government ban and stay on in Rawalpindi.

The next morning over ten thousand students assembled in the compound of the Government College; Gordon College had been sealed off by the police, who fired tear-gas shells into the college and asked the students to disperse, threatening them with serious trouble if they tried to leave the compound and march on the streets.

[3] The *Pakistan Times*, November 8th, 1968.
[4] Ibid.

The students gradually left the college from the back exit, took a devious path back to the city and re-assembled in the city centre. For the first time Ayub's portraits were burnt publicly in Rawalpindi; every shop-front displaying a photograph of the dictator was smashed and within a few hours not a single photograph could be seen in the main centres of the city. Private cars were stopped, and the passengers forced to get out and shout anti-Ayub slogans, or kicked in the arse if they refused. The students were articulating the class hatred a large majority of proletarians in Rawalpindi felt for the owners of property.

When the students marched through the shopping areas of the city they shouted slogans demanding that the prices of sugar and flour be brought down; prices had risen phenomenally over the last few months, and for some days sugar had disappeared from the shops and was being sold on the black market. The students were joined by members of the general public and many unemployed workers, and they clashed with the police at regular intervals—but this time they fought only where the balance of forces was favourable. In their hatred for private property they attacked banks and, in some cases, the more ostentatious of the private houses. As the day went on, growing numbers of workers and petit-bourgeoisie joined them, and by 8 p.m. on the evening of November 8th, 1968, the entire city was involved. Raja Anwar told the author that if there had been a well-disciplined revolutionary organization it could have seized Rawalpindi with the support of the masses. Great symbolic significance was attached to the fact that Rawalpindi was the headquarters of the army as well as the interim capital of Pakistan. The city was completely out of control.

Workers and students paid unexpected visits to leading members of Ayub's Convention Muslim League and forced them to denounce the regime. The civil administration could no longer cope, and the army was called out to control certain key points of the city. Some hours later a dusk-to-dawn curfew was imposed, and as the students were not really organized they did not defy it. The masses dispersed, and the night of November 8th passed peacefully.

The next day there were no demonstrations, but the police killed two bystanders whom they recognized as having taken part in the previous demonstrations. The two bodies were then dragged through the streets as a deterrent to future demonstrators. According to the *Pakistan Times*, one of those killed was a clerk employed by "some government department", and he had been shot dead as he was "carrying food for his ailing father who was admitted in the Cantonment General Hospital. He was the only son of his parents. The identity of the other victim could not be ascertained".[5]

The same day as people were being killed in the streets, the Central Minister for Information, Khwaja Shahabuddin, said at a meeting that the "people were enjoying full democracy in Pakistan like those of any democratic country in the world".[6] A day later the American President, Lyndon B. Johnson, described Pakistan as "a model of dynamic development under the wise and constructive leadership of President Ayub". The Chinese government was not to be outdone. The Chief of the General Staff of the Chinese People's Liberation Army made a speech at a banquet in honour of the Commander-in-Chief of the Pakistan Army, General Yahya Khan, who was in Peking as the guest of the Chinese government. General Huang Yung-sheng said that as the Pakistan army units in Rawalpindi were helping repress the masses:

Friendship and co-operation between our two countries have been growing constantly over the last few years and there has been increasing friendly contacts between the armed forces of our two countries ... in recent years, the Pakistani people under the leadership of President Ayub Khan, have fought unremittingly to safeguard national independence.[7]

The revolt soon spread to some key educational centres of West Pakistan. The death of the seventeen-year-old student provoked solidarity demonstrations by students in Multan, Karachi, Jhelum, Lahore, Peshawar, Hyderabad and Gujar Khan despite the fact that several student leaders had been arrested under the West Pakistan Maintenance of Public Order Ordinance of 1960. The government had decided to close all colleges, universities and schools in those cities, hoping that the students would stay away and the demonstrations cease. This ruse might have worked several years ago, but now the students were not on their own; as we have seen, they were being

[5] Ibid., November 10th, 1968. What the newspaper did not reveal was that the police had "accidentally" killed a clerk belonging to "some government department". This department was the Intelligence Bureau of the police themselves!
[6] Ibid., November 10th, 1968.
[7] Ibid., November 10th, 1968.

joined by growing numbers of workers and petit-bourgeois. It was already becoming crystal clear that this was no ordinary student revolt, and that the student uprising had struck a chord in the hearts of the workers and the city poor.

The government in Rawalpindi was apparently oblivious of all this. They underestimated the strength of the upsurge and thought that the students could be either crushed into silence or bought with hard cash. These policies had always succeeded in the past, and the authorities saw no reason why they shouldn't succeed in November 1968. They preferred to forget the facts about the "decade of development" they had only recently stopped celebrating; they tended to ignore the food crisis because they were not affected by it; and they overestimated the deterrent power of the army as well as its ability and desire to defend President Ayub and his regime. It did not occur to them that they were in serious danger.

On November 10th, President Ayub was scheduled to speak in Peshawar, the main city in the North West Frontier region where the nationalistic pro-Moscow National Awami Party was fairly strong. Anti-One-Unit feeling had always run high in this region, which also had a tradition of anti-imperialist struggle dating back to the days of the British raj. Some of Ayub's more intelligent advisers suggested that he cancel the Peshawar meeting in view of the recent upheaval, but pro-Ayub politicians from the Frontier region pressed him to come and reassured him that all would be well. The leading voice was Nawabzada Abdul Ghafoor Khan of Hoti; he was the owner of a vast combine of sugar factories. The very sight of him was enough to disrupt a public meeting. But Ayub decided to go ahead. So isolated from reality was he that he was lulled into believing that the demonstrators were simply small groups of politically motivated students and the government had nothing to fear.

When Ayub arrived in Peshawar mass student demonstrations greeted him, and student-police clashes took place all over the city. Ayub's public meeting was packed largely with plain-clothes policemen, members of the Convention Muslim League, local landlords and their tenants who had been forced to attend, in addition to large numbers of hired cheerleaders. Some students had also managed to get past the security barriers. From the very minute Ayub arrived at the meeting-place it was clear that all was not well. Anti-Ayub slogans were shouted, and slogans against the millionaire Ghafoor who was hailed as "sugar thief". After Ghafoor had finished presenting the address of welcome, a young student stood up and fired two shots at Ayub. The result was pandemonium. Ayub hid behind the sofa on the platform while one of his sons threw himself on top of him. The student was arrested and removed from the meeting, but for a long time Ayub stayed crouching behind the sofa. After assurances from his followers that it was over he emerged from his hiding place, and soon after, left the meeting for Government House, shattered and shaken. The student, Hashim Umar Zai, admitted his "guilt", and said that he was sorry he had not succeeded in killing the tyrant who had oppressed the people for so long.

At the same time that Ayub's meeting was ending in fiasco, students and workers were demonstrating in Nowshera against the regime; they ransacked the Nowshera Club, the hideout of civil servants and other privileged sections of the Nowshera community. The police opened fire, killing one student and seriously injuring others, but fighting continued and the army had to be called out. In Charsadda, a suburb of Peshawar, students and workers marched to the Charsadda Sugar Mill, where they burnt some of the files in the manager's office and destroyed the furniture. More and more towns in West Pakistan joined the revolt, and there were riots in Bahawal-nagar, Sargodha and Nawabshah.

Ayub was beginning to realize the seriousness of the situation, but he still thought that it could be contained by repression. His chief worry was that the Punjab area, which had always been loyal, was also being affected; in Bhutto's words, the Punjab had changed from a position of "negative acquiescence to positive animosity". But other representatives of the establishment still seemed to be living in a dream-world; a striking example of surrealism was provided by the Chief Justice of the Pakistan Supreme Court, Fazle Akbar, who attempted to cool the students' political ardour by advising them to "devote a part of their time in the service of the Red Cross".[8] At a time when many students were badly in need of first aid in the streets, this remark had a somewhat bizarre ring to it. The bourgeoisie, too, was happily carrying on in its self-satisfied way in its own isolated corner of Pakistan. Apparently unaware that its very existence was being threatened, the bourgeoisie was attending fashion shows at the Intercontinental Hotel in Lahore where a newspaper which reported violent street demonstrations, also reported:

[8] The *Pakistan Times*, November 11th, 1968.

The mannequins received a big hand from the elegant crowd as they moved up and down the brightly lit catwalk modelling the dresses. Some of the creations which the audience warmly applauded were: "Romantica", "Raja's Ransom", "Sea Nymph" and "Hello Officer" ... The "Eleganza '69" look was defined as a blend of the soft and the severe.[9]

The government had decided on its own political fashions and they were now a blend of the severe and the stupid. Like ruling classes throughout the world, the bureaucratic clique which ruled Pakistan thought that by eliminating some of the "troublemakers" they would be able to solve the "problem". Unable to conceive that the system they represented contained within it the seeds of its own destruction, the ruling class preferred to pin the blame on individuals. Accordingly, the Pakistan government arrested Z. A. Bhutto, Chairman of the People's Party, and Wali Khan, President of the pro-Moscow National Awami Party and some of their supporters, on Wednesday, November 13th. The Governor of West Pakistan, General Musa, explained the arrests in a radio broadcast:

> There is a limit to everything. This morning some ring-leaders of this movement of lawlessness have been arrested. I want to make it clear that if the supporters and companions of these persons try to break the law, severe action will be taken against them. The government will not brook any kind of disorder. So far as the common citizen is concerned, he must rest assured that all this is being done by the government for his sake.[10]

Governor Musa and every provincial and central Cabinet Minister who wanted to endear himself to the Boss launched a vituperative attack on Bhutto, and the only parties, apart from his own, to condemn his arrest were the pro-Moscow N.A.P. in West Pakistan and both groups of the N.A.P. and the Awami League in East Pakistan. The people, however, did not rest assured that the government was organizing this repression for their sake. There were demonstrations in Lahore by students and lawyers; in Multan, students and workers expecting to meet Bhutto stoned the train when they realized that he had been arrested. In the next few days the arrests had serious repercussions throughout West Pakistan, and no one believed the ludicrous propaganda statements issued by the government.

[9] Ibid., November 11th, 1968.
[10] Ibid., November 14th, 1968.

The organs of the British establishment completely misjudged the situation, and thinking that Ayub would survive the "troubles" continued to back him. *The Times* had supported the military dictatorship in Pakistan through thick and thin (of course Nkrumah's Ghana had been a different matter altogether!). An article by one of *The Times*'s "Asia experts", Neville Maxwell, completely ignored the social roots of the explosion in Pakistan:

> Quite apart from the stability (which his opponents of course decry as political suffocation) the Ayub decade has seen a 20 per cent increase in per capita income, an increase in industrial production of something like 50 per cent and a doubling of exports, and food production in West Pakistan has really taken off in the past two years under the impact of the new wheats and booming private installation of tube-wells ... With political disaffection shallow, urban and leaderless in West Pakistan the Government should not find it difficult to put down the present agitations, even if they spring up again on account of Mr Bhutto's arrest.[11]

A pro-Ayub article on its leader page, was not enough; obviously *The Times* also needed a pro-Ayub editorial:

> Certainly it is regrettable that political opposition should be dealt with in this way, even after ten years of politically sterilized good order. The patient might by now have been thought to be capable of risking a slight political injection without any great threat to a regime that has given the country a good measure of order and progress. President Ayub evidently thinks not and is probably right ... The friendship he [Bhutto] most relished when he served as Pakistan's Foreign Minister was that of China ... On this score alone the suppression of Mr Bhutto's activity is beneficial.[12]

The sheer hypocrisy of this editorial, aside from the inaccuracies contained in it, would be difficult to beat. But after all, the newspaper represented the interests of the British ruling class, and to admit that it was justifiable to use violence to overthrow a despot would make it inconsistent to oppose violence at some future stage in Britain itself.

Mr Bhutto certainly did not regard his situation as "beneficial".

[11] Neville Maxwell, "Ayub Khan takes a hard line with political opponents", *The* [London] *Times*, November 14th, 1968.
[12] Ibid.

He had been arrested under the D.P.R. (Defence of Pakistan Regulations) and had been accused of "inciting the masses, particularly students, to violate the law and create disorder by resorting to violence in a manner prejudicial to public safety and the interests of Pakistan". Almost immediately after his arrest, Mr Bhutto filed a writ petition in the West Pakistan High Court challenging his detention. His affidavit included some fascinating information about the methods of the dictatorship, who had first tried to win him back, and then to finish him politically. In his affidavit Bhutto rejected the charge that he had preached violence and claimed that his methods were constitutional. It was the dictatorship that was practising violence. He listed the ways in which he had been victimized by the Ayub regime:

(a) Violent physical attacks on my person.
(b) Efforts to deprive me and my family of our property rights.
(c) Involvement in false cases and interference with the administration of justice in their determination.
(d) Personal harassment by other means.
(e) Interference with my political activities and victimization of my political supporters.
(f) Harassment of my friends, family members and employees.
(g) Maltreatment in jail even during custody of the Court.[13]

Bhutto elaborated these points further, and their truth cannot be doubted by anyone who knows the tactics employed by the ruling class since the days of British imperialism. The Pakistani bureaucrats responsible for victimizing recalcitrant politicians have little imagination. A trip to South Africa and Greece would do our bureaucrats a lot of good as they could learn some new methods of dealing with political opponents.

If the bureaucracy wanted to increase Mr Bhutto's popularity with the students, they went about it in the correct way. As far as the people were concerned, the fact that all Bhutto's attackers were servile mediocrities meant that Bhutto must be right. And there was a certain logic in this conclusion. Whatever differences people had had with Bhutto, no one could deny that in his campaign against Ayub he deserved support — as long as no illusions were created about the People's Party leading the masses towards a socialist Pakistan:

[13] *Affidavit of Bhutto*, in the High Court of West Pakistan, Lahore, in Writ Petition No. 1794 of 1968. Published later as a People's Party document.

Bhutto never claimed to be anything more than a social-democrat of the Scandinavian variety,[14] and people who claim otherwise do both him and socialism a disservice. However, it should be emphasized that Bhutto stood head and shoulders above the majority of the right-wing opposition politicians who joined the anti-Ayub movement when it was already on its way.

Bhutto's arrest resulted in the emergence of another "political leader" in the opposition ranks. Air Marshal Asghar Khan had been a Commander-in-Chief of the Pakistan air force, and his connections with the armed forces increased his appeal to the masses. Asghar had been a loyal supporter of Ayub and had been known as one of the few non-corrupt people in the Ayub administration, but now doubts were cast on his motives, and members of the Ayub faction claimed that he was offended that he had not been made Defence Minister after his retirement in 1965.

The left-wing in West Pakistan, to their credit, had had reservations about the Air Marshal from the very start. His close links with the United States in the past made him suspect, and his refusal to comment on foreign policy heightened their suspicions. Furthermore, he had been allowed to publish several articles criticizing the regime in the government-controlled press, and many people felt that he had been sent into the political arena by the United States, or forces in league with it in Pakistan, to try and wrest the "leadership" of the movement from Bhutto. Asghar Khan himself claimed that he had decided to oppose the Ayub regime actively because "things are so bad today that any self-respecting man cannot remain silent ... We have a very peculiar atmosphere in the country today. Telephones are tapped, opinion is shackled."[15]

Most observers of Pakistani politics agreed that this situation had existed for at least the last ten years, and in some ways went even

[14] In a pamphlet published by his party in June 1968, *Political Situation in Pakistan*, Political Series No. 1, Mr Bhutto states quite clearly what his conception of socialism is: "The socialism applicable to Pakistan would be in conformity of its ideology and remain democratic in nature. There will be no foreign dictation. If there can be a Scandinavian form of socialism, there is no reason why there cannot be a Pakistani form of socialism suitable to our genius ... Islam and the principles of socialism are not mutually repugnant. Islam preaches equality and socialism is the modern technique of attaining it." There must be times when Mr Bhutto regrets that he ever used the word "socialism", because he had been on the defensive about it ever since. However, it cannot be denied that by doing so he has created a tremendous interest in socialist ideas, which neither he nor his party can explain.

[15] *The* [London] *Times*, November 20th, 1968.

further back. However, he was used as a symbol by a rapidly spreading mass movement against the dictatorship. The Air Marshal initially put himself "above" party politics, but was soon forced to identify himself with some of the more right-wing personalities in Pakistan. His subsequent development certainly indicated that the suspicions of the Left had been justified.

Meantime, the intensity of the struggle did not diminish, and the uprising leaped from one town to another. Parts of the countryside were affected—in some village schools the children left their classes and shouted anti-Ayub slogans, and a few of them stoned the buses coming from the cities—but the struggle did not spread in any real sense outside the towns. There were no mass peasant mobilizations in West Pakistan until a couple of months later.

In Rawalpindi the government tried desperately to contain the struggle. To be humiliated before foreign diplomats and journalists was really painful to Ayub. All the careful work done by his propaganda machine abroad was being destroyed by the action of the Pakistani students. Between the first and second waves of the upsurge in Rawalpindi the goverment tried two tactics. First, it tried to frighten the student leaders by arresting them and threatening to implicate them with the attempt on Ayub's life at Peshawar. Some of them were badly beaten in prison, but they refused to concede anything to the government until their demands had been accepted. Then the regime tried a new tactic; it released them and tried to negotiate. The students put forward a list of comprehensive demands linked to education, and the authorities asked for time to consider them. The students agreed on condition that educational institutions were re-opened—they were beginning to feel isolated without the large body of students behind them, and as their only link with them was through student unions they felt that the movement might fade away if the colleges were not re-opened. They gave an undertaking to the government that they would continue to negotiate with them and would not call mass demonstrations. Of course, they planned the exact opposite. The bureaucracy fell into the trap. On November 26th, 1968, all the educational institutions of Rawalpindi were opened. The student leaders immediately summoned general assemblies, discussed the situation and marched out into the streets.

There was a strange paradox in the student movement in Rawalpindi. The students' demands were deliberately limited to the sphere of education, and were reformist in nature. In practice, however, the students had become a strong political force and their slogans and the speeches of some of their leaders (in particular Raja Anwar and Hassamul Haque) were revolutionary. The reasons for this contradiction lie in the attitude of mind cultivated in the students by years of government propaganda: they should not be interested in politics; they should only be concerned with their studies; students who took part in politics were obviously being manipulated by wicked politicians. So instead of stressing their right to engage in political activity, the students, who were still on the defensive during the revolt of November 1968, pandered to the ideology of the ruling class and held back from making revolutionary demands.

However, their actions were more important than their words, and they behaved with exemplary determination and heroism. They regarded the demonstration of November 26th as a propaganda exercise to impress upon the mass of working people that they were fighting the same battle and to ask them to join the struggle. It was also a peaceful demonstration, although immediately it was over the police opened fire and killed a bystander. Its historic significance lay in the fact that the students issued a call for a general strike in Rawalpindi on November 29th, 1968 and asked workers, small shopkeepers and unemployed to march with them.

On the same day there were constant demonstrations and student-police battles throughout the province. In Peshawar, students attacked the U.S.I.S. library,[16] and there were violent demonstrations in Bahawalpur, where the office of Ayub's Muslim League was attacked and burnt, and in Abbotabad, a small summer resort where Ayub spent some of the hotter months every summer. A hundred women marched a hundred miles from Sargodha to Lahore to join a protest against the government. More cities sprang into action; there were demonstrations in Sheikhupura, Sialkot, Gujranwala, Gujrat and Havelian — some of these were small towns of no more than 10,000 inhabitants.

The regime's apologists had boasted that the students' bubble

[16] The *Pakistan Times*, November 28th, 1968. A government handout described the student attack on the U.S.I.S. office and library in Peshawar in the following fashion: "Some hooligans also damaged the U.S.I.S. library and took away books and magazines which they tore and threw on the roadside. Many of these mischief-mongers were chased by the police into the streets and a number of them received injuries. Their exact number could not be ascertained as they managed to run away. The Cantonment Police has registered a case for trespass into the U.S.I.S. Centre."

would burst. If the government still needed convincing that, on the contrary, it was the regime which was disintegrating, it only had to study the demonstration in Rawalpindi on November 29th. The students, it will be remembered, had called for a general strike, and despite false and misleading statements published by government newspapers that the strike had been called off, people refused to be deceived. The press and the government radio had lied to them for so long that they mistrusted them both.

The workers responded to the student call and there was a complete and general strike in Rawalpindi, probably for the first time in the city's history. The entire population, it seemed, had come out on to the streets to link arms with the students. It was the police who decided to start the battle. "In what appeared to be an unnecessary use of force, the police lashed into the gathering crowd of bystanders to clear the streets. Hundreds of demonstrators at once turned and pelted police with a shower of stones and bricks."[17]

Clashes continued for over six hours, and joint student-worker platoons attacked several police stations and set at least two of them on fire. The army was called out to patrol the railway station and some of the main lines. However, once again, the absence of any revolutionary organization precluded a concerted effort at total insurrection.

Large areas of Rawalpindi were out of its control for several hours, but the government continued with its blind policy of attacking the opposition, damagingly exposing the inexperience of the ruling class of Pakistan at this critical juncture in its history. From the revolutionaries' point of view, it was an ideal situation. After the first joint action of students and workers in West Pakistan on November 29th, the revolutionary movement spread like an uncontrollable conflagration to reach East Pakistan, hundreds of miles away. Here the balance of class forces and the nature of the movement were radically changed.

[17] *The* [London] *Times*, November 30th, 1968.

CHAPTER SIX

The Revolt Spreads

> "We are not in the least afraid of ruins. We are going to inherit the earth. There is not the slightest doubt about that. The bourgeoisie may blast and ruin its own world before it leaves the stage of history. We carry a new world, here in our hearts. That world is growing this minute." Buenaventura Durutti, Anarchist leader in the Spanish Civil War

Dacca and East Pakistan: December 1968

The colony of East Bengal, ruled from West Pakistan through bureaucrats and pro-consuls appointed by the Centre since "independence", had been on the boil for a long time. The period of military-bureaucratic dictatorship had heightened the contradictions in East Pakistan. After its overwhelming electoral victory of 1954 the Bengali middle class had been virtually disenfranchised, and the masses had suffered still more from the repression which had been their lot since the birth of Pakistan.

The student movement and the intelligentsia in East Pakistan had always been politically ahead of their counterparts in West Pakistan. The Bengali students had been the first to demonstrate against Martial Law, but in 1962 and 1963 they had stood almost alone and they had been crushed. In 1964 they had been extremely active in Miss Jinnah's election campaign, not because they had any illusions about the old lady's political views, but because she had become a magnet for the forces struggling against the hated dictatorship. As we have seen, her defeat had caused a general feeling of frustration which had affected the students more acutely than anyone else, perhaps because they had suffered most from arrest and torture.

When the student revolt had begun in Rawalpindi, the students in East Pakistan had not taken it seriously. From past experience they knew that the West was not capable of sustaining a mass political opposition to Ayub. Also the censored press was not printing details of the uprising, so in Dacca they had to wait before they were sure of the political situation. Finally, when the Rawalpindi students succeeded in calling a successful general strike in the city, the politically aware in Dacca realized that the struggle was serious and that the dictatorship was worried. The real struggle in Dacca was to begin exactly one month after the uprising in Rawalpindi on November 7th (there had been a few isolated actions declaring solidarity with the movement in West Pakistan, but they were not of a serious nature). No doubt its precise timing was inspired by events in West Pakistan, but the contradictions in East Pakistan itself should not be under-estimated. It is possible that East Pakistan would have exploded on its own, even if West Pakistan had remained passive.

If Dacca is the political barometer for the whole of East Pakistan, the political temperature of Dacca itself is governed by Dacca Univer-sity. The Ayub regime was fully aware of this and at its instigation Monem Khan's administration organized and financed a pro-government student group named the National Student Federation (N.S.F.). The purpose of the group, founded in 1964, was not to defend the "ideas" of the government politically, but to combat physically all opposition to government policies in the University.

The N.S.F. leaders were Monem Khan's favourite thugs; some of them attended the university only in order to terrorize leftist students, and there had been a growing number of violent clashes between the N.S.F. and leftist student groups in the period prior to November 1968. The leader of the N.S.F. faction was a ruffian named, Saeedur Rehman, whose room was decorated with knives, revolvers, rifles, and so on. It is reported that he was saluted by the traffic policeman every morning on his way to the University. His power was recognized even by provincial Cabinet Ministers, and he was responsible only to the Governor, Monem Khan.

For four years Saeedur Rehman and his student gangsters had victimized left-wing students with the full support and collabora-tion of the provincial state machine. By October 1968, the contradic-tions had sharpened beyond the point of endurance and many leftist students were recovering from the injuries inflicted on them. A group of left-wing students met and decided to answer force with force. A revolutionary student commando group consisting of five students was selected to execute the gangster and towards the end of November 1968, Mr Saeedur Rehman was found dead. His death took on a symbolic significance for revolutionary students through-out East Pakistan; as the Marxist student leader Mahbub Ullah put it in a conversation with me: "The progressive students in general heaved a sigh of relief. This act created a certain amount of confidence amongst the students as they realized that they could fight the reactionaries and destroy them. And it also shattered the morale of the reactionary students who realized that the leftists were capable of fighting back."

The political parties which really counted in East Pakistan were the Awami League, Suhrawardy's party, which since his death had been led by his lieutenant, Sheikh Mujibur Rehman, and the National Awami Party, led by Maulana Bhashani. Owing to the Pakistani-China rapport, the pro-Peking section of the N.A.P., headed by Maulana Bhashani, had virtually ceased opposing the government of President Ayub in both East and West Pakistan. The students who supported Maulana Bhashani in Dacca were greatly embarrassed by his change of policy, particularly in the face of Mujibur Rehman's supporters. Mujibur Rehman's six-point programme for provincial autonomy had resulted in his arrest on April 17th, 1966, and he had been released on bail but re-arrested soon afterwards. June 7th had been observed as Protest Day in support of regional autonomy and the six-point programme; and had been a success. The N.A.P. had not participated in this and had lost a certain amount of credibility, as the anti-Ayub fervour of the demonstrations could not be doubted. Twelve people had been killed and over seven hundred arrested during this period, and the reluctance of the N.A.P. to support these demonstrations left the field wide open to the petit-bourgeois nationalists.

In 1968, therefore, it was suspected that the Maulana's N.A.P. would once again be ambivalent in its attitude to the present uprising; it was also noted that the pro-Peking N.A.P. had remained aloof from the struggle in West Pakistan for a whole month. However, Maulana Bhashani's political instinct proved to be more powerful than the ideological bankruptcy of some of the members of his party's political committee. He had grasped the importance of the upsurge and was determined to reassert the political authority of his party.

During the first few days of December a feeling of unrest had been growing among the common people in Dacca. A militant section of the Dacca proletariat—the auto-rickshaw drivers—were being severely harassed by the police, and they had responded with a series of lightning strikes which had spread to the cycle-rickshaw drivers. They had approached Maulana Bhashani and he had agreed to support their demands. Accordingly, the Dacca N.A.P. called a meeting at Paltan Maidan on December 6th, 1968, and it was attended by thousands of workers and students. Bhashani attacked Ayub's regime in the bitterest terms. He demanded provincial autonomy, and said that the rights of the people would never be achieved without a mass movement. The rickshaw workers pleaded with him to call for a general strike in Dacca for the following day, and sensing the mood of the masses the Maulana agreed to do so. Then, under pressure from party leaders, Bhashani changed his mind and tried to limit the strike to the transport workers; but it was too late. Student and worker militants went round the city announcing the call for a general strike. The die had been cast. On the next day, December 7th, 1968, there was a general strike. The revolt had started in East Pakistan.

It had been led by the Dacca proletariat and initiated by the N.A.P. under their pressure. Probably this was the first time that the student movement of Dacca had been bypassed politically by other social layers. In an attempt to try and stop the strike the government had imposed Section 144 (prohibiting an assembly of more than four persons), but it was naive of them to think that it would have any effect. That the bureaucrats could even think that a mere law could forestall the uprising was an accurate indication of their "closeness" to the people.

On December 7th, as the proletarians of Dacca were picketing at street corners, the police and the East Pakistan Rifles opened fire several times; there was no advance warning and in some cases no tear-gas to indicate that bullets were to follow. Twenty-three workers were injured, six of them seriously. The first Bengali to die in the struggle was a twenty-eight-year-old worker, Abdul Majid.

At a mass meeting in Dacca the same afternoon, Maulana Bhashani called for another general strike the following day and led workers and students in a demonstration outside the Government House. The successful action under the leadership of the Bhashani section of the N.A.P. raised a few questions which were articulated by Dacca's liberal, Sunday newspaper, *Holiday*. The newspaper welcomed Bhashani's decision to launch a mass movement but said:

> The proceedings of the opposition parties over the last few months in particular and the past few years in general betrayed a curious negativism [*sic*] which has been hindering a people's

movement in either part of the country. The pro-Bhashani N.A.P. too had fallen into that rut ... Hence, it was only natural that its image before the people would be tarnished. But recent corrective measures taken by the N.A.P. with regard to its action-programme helped restore to some extent its lost prestige. But the lost time in a political movement could hardly be made up.

But can the Maulana who is in his eighties make up for this lost time? Is he capable of inspiring the masses and channelizing the popular wrath into a well-directed and well-organized political movement ... The Maulana, it appears had rediscovered himself at the Paltan Maidan rally. His indictment of the regime was unambiguous; his programme for the people was down-to-earth and his call to wage a relentless struggle against oppression —political and economic—cannot be missed by the countless sufferers ... [1]

Bhashani's call for a province-wide general strike on December 19th, 1968, received a mass response from workers and students throughout the province. Some of the other N.A.P. leaders had once again been slightly reluctant to call a general strike, but they were way behind the people; only Bhashani was able to keep up with the rapidly developing radical consciousness. Within three days there were three successful general strikes in Dacca, two of them extending throughout the province. It became clear to even the most right-wing politician that the days of Ayub's regime were numbered. Some of the rats began to think aloud of deserting the ship.

Ayub himself chose this particular moment to visit Dacca, thus diverting the entire police force and army units in Dacca for his personal protection. He was greeted by angry demonstrators and black flags (a sign of protest in Pakistan) wherever he went—in fact, from the airport to Government House and back.[2] He had come to cheer his soldiers in the National Assembly. This pathetic and grotesque body was meeting in Dacca. Never has a parliament seemed more superfluous, its debates more irrelevant, and the people inside it more isolated, than the National Assembly in Dacca when the masses were demonstrating on the streets of their city. Amongst a host of

[1] *Holiday*, Dacca, December 8th, 1968.

[2] Immediately on his arrival at Dacca, Ayub told reporters that he was happy to be in East Pakistan. "The climate of Rawalpindi is so cold, but God has given such a wonderful climate to this province" (*Pakistan Observer*, December 7th, 1968). For Ayub, East Pakistan was to prove extremely cold, the God-given climate notwithstanding.

other demands, they were asking for a free ballot, and they were being answered by police bullets. It did not even occur to the people to march to the National Assembly and stone it or burn it down; even the most illiterate worker in Dacca knew it for the decrepit body it was. Ayub left Dacca as he had come, skulking like a whipped dog. But he still thought that he could win.

Meanwhile, in Rawalpindi a journalist, Naeem Shahid, had been shot and seriously wounded by one of Ayub's party gangsters, a Mr Sher Bahadur, who had objected to the journalist reporting on the activities of the five hundred thugs Sher Bahadur commanded who had been firing on student demonstrators and workers on strike. The police had not even attempted to charge Sher Bahadur; they were in a dilemma, for he could easily have been acting on the advice of the District Magistrate of Rawalpindi who had encouraged the bourgeoisie to prepare itself for self-defence. In protest, the entire journalist fraternity decided on a national strike, and even the hacks in the government-controlled newspapers reluctantly supported the strike, and the government was powerless to prevent them. On December 11th, 1968, West and East Pakistan were without any newspapers. In East Pakistan journalists organized meetings demanding press freedom and condemning the iniquities of the regime.

The Awami League and the anti-Bhashani N.A.P. realized that they had been upstaged by Maulana Bhashani, and tried to re-assert themselves by calling for a general strike on December 14th. Bhashani endorsed the call, and once again commercial life in the province came to a standstill. From this day on, the struggle in East Pakistan continued under its own momentum. Every single city in East Pakistan was engulfed by a mass of angry workers and students demonstrating their hatred for the regime and the existing system.

For the most part the demonstrations were given their political leadership by the students, but they were given their class character by the presence of thousands of workers and unemployed; of slum-dwellers; of the city poor; beggars and street urchins; pick-pockets; boys who scratched a living by polishing the shoes of the petit-bourgeoisie; vendors of cheap food; in brief, those whom the press and the bourgeoisie designated "hooligans, riff-raff, bad elements". For them Ayub and his acolytes were merely the scum on the top, they were rebelling against a whole society which had determined that they should live in extreme poverty. They could not articulate their demands clearly, but all their pent-up hatred for and bitterness against the system were expressed in street battles against the repressive forces of the bourgeois state. When the police fired on the students, the workers and the city poor did not run back to their hovels as they had done on many occasions in the past; they stayed and fought shoulder to shoulder with the students against the police and the E.P.R.

There is no clear-cut division between the landless peasants and the city demonstrators. Many of the cities of East Pakistan are like small islands in the vast sea of the countryside. The deteriorating conditions in the countryside have forced an increasing number of poor peasants to camp on the outskirts of a city and occasionally to make a limited foray into the city centre to search for food or a job. During the uprising these peasants participated in city demonstrations.

In a conscious attempt to formalize the situation and to involve the large mass of the peasantry, Maulana Bhashani issued a call to the peasants to strike on December 29th, 1968, and to observe a Peasants Demand Day. He argued that the mobilization of the peasants in the country was absolutely vital to sustain the city-based movements,[3] and he asked for mass demonstrations in the countryside to protest against rising prices, exploitation and the indifference of the government to the chronic problem of floods. The participation of the masses of rural proletarians made the upsurge qualitatively different from West Pakistan, where the peasantry had not been mobilized despite the greater degree of oppression.

For some time there had been growing unrest in certain areas of the countryside. The sugar-cane cultivators, in particular, were goaded into expressing the general resentment. The prices they obtained from the sugar-mill owners for the cane were pitifully low. The cane-workers demanded that the fixed price of sugar-cane be raised from Rs. 2 to Rs. 4 per *maund* (i.e. from 2s. 6d. to 5s. for approximately 5½ stone). The peasants had also been forbidden by government order to manufacture *gur*, a form of crude unrefined sugar, for their own use. The government was determined that the mill owners make as much profit as possible from their enterprise and *gur* stood in the way of this. As the peasant could not afford the exorbitant prices demanded for sugar, they continued to manufacture their own. Police seized the implements used to manufacture *gur* and the peasants surrounded the police stations in the area, recaptured their implements and brought them back.

[3] Cf. *Holiday*, December 15th, 1968.

The Maulana had all this in mind when he decided to call for a Peasants Demand Day. Once again his political instincts were proved sound, and large peasant rallies were held all over the country. There were mass arrests in certain areas, and in one village, Hatirdia Bazaar, some fifty miles from Dacca, the police opened fire, killing three peasants and wounding several others, again without any warning whatsoever. The students of the local high school had come out on strike to support the peasants and workers, and when the police tried to isolate and disperse the children they were prevented from doing so by a large mass of peasants and workers.[4]

Enthusiasm for the movement was spreading in the countryside. Maulana Bhashani's age—he was eighty-six—did not prevent him from taking an extremely active part in the peasant upsurge. He toured the rural areas and incited the peasants to militant action which included "gheraoing" the residences of the bureaucrats and forcing them to listen to the demands of the people. (The *gherao* is a technique which was first initiated in West Bengal; it originally consisted of large numbers of workers surrounding a factory on strike and besieging it until their demands were accepted. The method was described as "non-violent violence", and it proved very effective).

The peasants' demands were reformist in character, and the transitional nature of some of them was not stressed. It should have been made clear to the peasants that the agrarian problem could only be solved by a dictatorship of the proletariat, urban and rural; but for this they needed a revolutionary party with a Marxist ideology acting in its own name and in the class interests of the workers and the peasants, and not working within a social-democratic structure. The key problem of the uprising in East Pakistan was the absence of the subjective factor necessary to exploit the situation, which was ripe for socialist revolution.

The only organized force in East Pakistan was the student movement, in the shape of the Student Action Committee (S.A.C.). Briefly, the background of S.A.C. was as follows: after Partition all progressive students had joined the East Pakistan Students' League (E.P.S.L.), but by 1952 some student leaders thought that it was becoming too reactionary. After the struggle over the language movement described in Chapter 2, the E.P.S.L. split, the left-wing group

[4] Cf. *Pakistan Observer*, Dacca, December 31st, 1968.

setting up the East Pakistan Students' Union (E.P.S.U.). Between 1952 and 1964 it grew to become a well-established organization of progressive students. In 1965, after Ayub's "election triumph" against Miss Jinnah, it divided into pro-Peking and pro-Moscow factions, and the two groups differed on a wide range of points. The pro-Moscow faction thought that the pro-Peking tendency had not opposed Ayub sufficiently during the last election because of his policy of friendship with China. This accusation could have been made fairly against the pro-Peking elements in the National Awami Party in both East and West Pakistan, but applied to their counterparts in E.P.S.U. it was simply a slander. Rashed Khan Menon, one of the leading spokesmen of the Maoist faction, had no illusions about the class nature of the Ayub regime. He was also in favour of supporting the opposition, but he maintained correctly that this support must be critical and that the struggle for democracy should be seen as a transitional struggle in the fight for socialism. The differences between the two factions existed because of different analyses on the following points:

1. The struggle for bourgeois democracy. The Left argued that this struggle, while extremely important, must be viewed as part of the struggle for socialism. The Right argued that this was the first stage and that at the moment Pakistan was only ready for bourgeois-democracy; the second stage would come later when the consciousness of the people had been radicalized by participating in the struggle for democracy. The right-wing argument was a typical Menshevik/social-democratic analysis of the situation. It could only lead to right-wing deviations and result in those who held these views being swallowed up by the bourgeois parties.

2. Anti-imperialism and peaceful co-existence. The right wing believed in the theory of peaceful co-existence and did not believe in conducting a struggle against United States imperialism. In practical terms they were opposed to demonstrations against the presence of the Seventh Fleet off Indian shores and posited instead of this the struggle for adult franchise, thus mechanically, like the good social-democrats that they were, separating the one from the other. The left wing argued that the lessons of the election victory of 1954 should not be forgotten; that merely to call for elections without linking this to a comprehensive programme of anti-imperialist and anti-capitalist demands was incorrect. They refused to be a party to this reformism. Some on the right wing regarded the struggle against imperialism

merely as a propaganda fight: ("As L.B.J. isn't in Pakistan, how can we fight him?"). They also refused to recognize the class nature of Indian "democracy" or to subject the Communist governments in India to a severe and critical analysis.

3. The role of E.P.S.U. This was quite simple and straightforward. The Left forces desired to make E.P.S.U. the ideological vanguard and to politicize its entire membership, while the Right preferred the status quo with a self-appointed ideological leadership based in Dacca and a student-union structure. It was elitist economism versus revolutionary vanguardism.

They could not resolve their differences of opinion, and E.P.S.U. decided to split into two factions. The factions were referred to in the bourgeois press as the E.P.S.U. (Motia group) and E.P.S.U. (Menon group); a typical effort to personalize political differences. We shall refer to them as E.P.S.U. (rightists) and E.P.S.U. (leftists), which may be clumsy but is at least an attempt at accuracy. However, the differences of opinion and the split into two organizations did not prevent the E.P.S.U. from uniting for certain specific aims.[5] The E.P.S.L. was by now completely under the control of the Awami League and was firmly committed to the six-point charter put forward by Sheikh Mujibur Rehman. Thus E.P.S.U. (leftists) were forced to struggle against the political position of both the E.P.S.U. (rightists) and the E.P.S.L.

The leftists always put forward demands which stressed the class nature of the struggle in Pakistan and linked it to the international struggle against imperialism, but the other two groups were completely opposed to this, and after three months of discussions they proceeded their separate ways. According to Menon, "Our aim was both to crush Ayub and to fight United States imperialism and we argued that one could not be isolated from the other." Theoretical unity was not to be reached again until the student groups found themselves united in action against the Ayub regime.

In the summer of 1967 there was a great deal of unrest on the question of regional autonomy in Pakistan. The E.P.S.U. (leftists)[6]

---

[5] It is interesting to note that the split in the international Communist movement affected the student movement before it caused the split of the underground C.P. in East Pakistan or the National Awami Party, in which most of the Communists participated.

[6] On July 29th, 1967, their leaders, Rashed Khan Menon, was arrested, and stayed in prison until the upsurge of December 1968 – January 1969 brought about his release in February 1969.

declared that it was not a question of regional autonomy but of national self-determination.

On August 2nd, 1967, the student groups had united to issue a call for a student strike in Dacca which had been 99 per cent successful and had resulted in pitched battles between students and police. The success of this joint effort convinced the student leaders that they should think seriously of pooling their resources in the fight against the dictatorship, and discussions between the different factions were re-started.

At the same time the national question was brought into focus by the decision of the Central government to attack the national movement by a fake "conspiracy" case. Some retired navy officers, Bengalis, had been arrested in December 1967 on charges of conspiring with India, together with some Bengali soldiers. The wife of one of the navy officers, Begum Hasina Kamaludin, was allowed to see her husband after a great deal of difficulty, and afterwards she petitioned the High Court of East Pakistan that he should be transferred to a hospital as he was in danger of death from the tortures which the police had inflicted on him. Kamaludin had been given electric shocks, and his body had been perforated with iron nails and hot pepper sprinkled in the wounds to extract a confession. His refusal had resulted in more tortures, and he had lost consciousness several times. Finally, almost senseless, he had been forced to sign a confession.

On December 16th, 1967, the President had visited East Pakistan and had denounced the Awami League as a party of traitors, and the other opposition parties as "enemies of Pakistan". Three days later some of the Awami League leaders had been arrested. Sheikh Mujibur Rehman was already in jail, and the case against the retired naval officers and some Bengali army men was later widened to include Sheikh Mujibur Rehman and other Awami Leaguers. It became known as the Agarthala case, as the defendants were supposed to have visited Agarthala, across the Indian border, to conspire with the Indian government, though Mujibur Rehman always referred to it as the Islamabad Case as "that is where this conspiracy was hatched". The intentions of the government were threefold; they wanted to discredit the national movement in East Pakistan, to convince the army that Bengalis could not be trusted in the armed forces, and to drive a further wedge between the West and East Pakistani masses. The Agarthala Case unnerved some of the leaders of the

E.P.S.L., who felt isolated, but both factions of the E.P.S.U. gave them complete support and argued that the case was a frame-up to discredit the opposition. The Agarthala Case in fact served to bring the groups closer to each other, and this was the basis of the united front against the Ayub dictatorship which was to have powerful repercussions in East Pakistan in the coming months.

But if the student factions were approaching unity, the same could not be said of the infant trade-union movement in East Pakistan. Workers participated in large numbers in the various uprisings in East Pakistan, but few of the workers belonged to a union. Nevertheless, the trade-union cadres in the factories undoubtedly played a leading role in mobilizing the workers, and in thwarting the industrialists' efforts to prevent the growth of trade unionism and to victimize militant workers after a strike had ended.

The tradition of Indian trade unions in the days of the British raj was an economistic one, and the British government saw to it that the trade unions remained "free from political influences". Of course, this object was not shared by trade-union leaders, but the British attitude was swallowed whole by the "independent" Muslim League government established in Pakistan after Partition. Government and big business financed their own unions and had their own favourite trade-union leaders. Any trade unionists who argued for political involvement on the part of the workers were harassed and dismissed from their jobs.

In 1949 the Central trade-union organization in East Pakistan had been the East Pakistan Federation of Labour, whose President and Secretary were Aftab Ali and Faiz Ahmed respectively. The two parted company on purely personal grounds, and the result was two organizations with exactly the same name, Faiz Ahmed becoming the second President. The Left did not have their own trade-union organization till 1957 when they set up the East Pakistan Workers' Federation with Mohammed Toha as President and Kazi Mohiudin as General Secretary.

In October 1958 one of the first acts of the Martial Law authorities in East Pakistan was to ban the East Pakistan Workers' Federation (E.P.W.F.), seal its office and confiscate all its documents. Many of the trade-union leaders went underground, and after Martial Law was lifted officially in 1962 they surfaced and began again to work openly. In October 1964 the left-wing trade unionists convened the East Pakistan Workers' Convention, which firmly established the political role of trade unionists. From this convention there emerged the East Pakistan Workers' Council, which elected Mahbubul Haq as President and Sirajul Hossain as Secretary. Though the aim of the Council was to unite the entire trade-union movement on the basis of a Fifteen Point Programme it was only to be expected that the right-wing unions would not join.

By May 1966 the Council had taken on the form of a federation which was known, like its banned forerunner, as the East Pakistan Workers' Federation. The three leading trade unions affiliated to E.P.W.F. were the Railway Union, the Water and Power Union and the Tea-Workers Union; the last was the largest member union and consisted of plantation workers on the tea estates of East Pakistan. The reason why these unions affiliated, apart from their political sympathy for the Fifteen Points, was that before the Council had decided to become a federation it had been leading the workers in the struggle against Ayub, and had been able to mobilize mass support and organize a massive general strike in October 1964. The unions wanted to associate themselves with the fight.

In May 1965 the Council had also supported a successful three-day strike by the railway workers which had been crushed by the government as brutally as they were to crush the strike of railway workers in West Pakistan the following year. Six hundred workers had been arrested and 1,400 dismissed from their jobs. This had weakened the council, and created a mood of despondency throughout industry, and the government had seized this moment to promulgate ordinances which restricted trade-union rights still further. This, however, had the opposite effect from what was intended. A United Action Committee was set up by the workers to fight the anti-trade-union laws and in this committee the council was very strong.

In July 1965 a mass labour rally was organized and proved to be the largest-ever workers assembly in East Pakistan. Once again the trade unions were deluged with applications for membership and the government was forced to withdraw the proposed laws. However in October 1965, during the Indo-Pakistan war, a state of emergency was declared. The United Action Committee had little option but to disband, and the employers used the opportunity offered by the war to dismiss and victimize militant trade unionists. Soon after the war the workers defied the state of emergency which was still in force and started agitating for a change in the labour laws, adult franchise and a minimum wage of Rs. 150 (£11) per month. The government responded by using its power to ban all meetings in industrial areas and by preventing individual leaders of the E.P.W.F. from living in industrial areas.

Throughout 1966 the E.P.W.F. continued its work; its most significant success was in organizing the tea gardens. By 1967 the dictatorship was sufficiently worried to make large-scale arrests of workers active in trade unions, among them the General Secretary of the E.P.W.F., Sirajul Hossain, and four of the regional secretaries. Sirajul Hossain was released in December 1967, but the others were in prison until 1968 or 1969. Throughout 1968 localized struggles took place all over East Pakistan, and on the advice of the E.P.W.F. the workers started to apply the *gherao* to win their immediate demands. This was not reported in the controlled press.

When Maulana Bhashani announced the strike of December 7th, 1968, it was the climax of a movement which had started in 1964, and it burst throughout East Pakistan like a river in spate. There was no dam strong enough to stop it. At first little real leadership was given to the movement; the students were scattered because Dacca University had been closed down after the execution of Saeedur Rehman by leftist students, and though they had started to organize themselves towards the end of December 1968, it was not until January 1969 that they were to found the Student Action Committee and make it the most powerful organization in the province.

The December upsurge in East Pakistan brought the masses of both parts of the country together and united them in a common struggle. It was the first time that both wings of the country had acted in unison, and it must have frightened the regime considerably. Ayub tried to concede to the students a few of their university demands, but it was too late. The student movement had penetrated the political structure of the country too deeply for it to be fobbed off. In West Pakistan it had become part and parcel of a much broader movement and had incited other social strata to take action. And the masses had responded willingly, although they did not have any prepared plan for action

They knew that they could no longer tolerate the Ayub regime, and the example of university and school students, some no more than twelve years old, made them feel ashamed of their own passivity. But this was only the beginning of the struggle.

CHAPTER SEVEN

The Fall of the House of Ayub

> "A revolutionary uprising that spreads over a number of days can develop victoriously only in case it ascends step by step, and scores one success after another. A pause in its growth is dangerous; a prolonged marking of time, fatal. But even successes by themselves are not enough; the masses must know about them in time, and have time to understand their value. It is possible to let slip a victory at the very moment when it is within arm's reach. This has happened in history." Leon Trotsky, *History of the Russian Revolution*

East and West Pakistan: The people unite in action January–February 1969

By January 1969 the uprising in West Pakistan had embraced every major city in the province and had not paused for breath since it began on November 7th, 1968. That a spontaneous movement could sustain itself for over two months and show no signs of exhaustion was enough to make even the pessimists think again. The regime and the old right-wing parties decided that this was, after all, not one of those tinpot student revolts which could be crushed by brute force and intimidation. Though the government did not stop the brutality, it had lost its nerve and Ayub was on the run.

Unable to fight for their rights through parliament because of the corruption of the government machinery, the people had decided to take the extra-parliamentary road, and were discovering with the passing of every day that this was the real way to success. The effect of this discovery on the consciousness of the masses was considerable, and their experiences at this time were worth a hundred free elections as far as political education was concerned.

But because there was no revolutionary organization capable of leading the masses to victory and overthrowing not only Ayub but the system he represented, other factors influenced the mass movement. Sometimes it was for the good; usually, though, for ill. We will analyse these factors separately.

Political parties

After the Combined Opposition Parties (C.O.P.) candidate had "lost" to the candidate of the civil service and the army, the C.O.P. disintegrated. The process was helped by the Indo-Pakistan war, during which the opposition backed the Ayub regime quite uncritically, and after the failure of the anti-Tashkent movement the leaders of the opposition parties floundered. They did not have any idea of what they wanted to do.

Some of them negotiated with the government, but broke off the negotiations when the prizes offered did not match their expectations. In 1967 the right-wing parties met and decided to form a united opposition. Accordingly, they set up the Pakistan Democratic Movement (P.D.M.), but in the process they lost Sheikh Mujibur Rehman when they refused to accept his six-points for regional autonomy. A small section of the Awami League, led by Nawabzada Nasrullah, split with Mujibur on this question and joined the P.D.M., but they had virtually no support in East Pakistan, and in West Pakistan the Awami League had at the best of times been very weak. The following parties united under the banner of the P.D.M.: Council Muslim League, Jamaat-i-Islami, Nizam-i-Islam, Awami League (anti-six-points) and the N.D.F. (National Democratic Front).

The strongest of these were the first two. The Council Muslim League had a strong feudal base in the Punjab area of West Pakistan, and the Jamaat had a powerful, subsidized propaganda network and also a very limited amount of support amongst the petit-bourgeoisie. Of the others the Nizam-i-Islam had a former Prime Minister and a Member of the National Assembly to its credit; the Awami League had Nawabzada Nasrullah and his fez plus a hookah which travelled with him; while the N.D.F. was a sorry collection of politicians who had backed Suhrawardy's effort to oppose the Ayub regime, but who were now, after Suhrawardy's death, merely a group of discredited, partyless men.

The P.D.M. was a much more integrated and cohesive political organization than the C.O.P., but because it did not have among its members the National Awami Party or the Awami League it was completely irrelevant in East Pakistan — except that one of the N.D.F. leaders owned the *Pakistan Observer*, an English daily published in Dacca which opposed the government when it suited its purpose. It also over-publicized the P.D.M. and gave it an entirely false image.

The P.D.M. also accepted that all majority decisions were binding, making it a reactionary combination *par excellence*.

While the P.D.M. did attempt to hold a number of meetings, it could not attract mass support because of the political character of the worthies who led it. This shows very clearly that the people were not interested merely in opposing Ayub; they wanted the opposition to Ayub now to be different from what it had been in the past. This the P.D.M. were incapable of providing. Besides, as the anti-Ayub and anti-dictatorship fervour of the masses increased, the P.D.M. leaders remained isolated. The most intelligent of them, Mumtaz Daultana of the Muslim League, admitted to the author that, "We never thought that the people would rise themselves, but neither did Bhutto. I met him on October 14th, [1968] and he didn't have a clue."[1] However, Bhutto did know that to join the P.D.M. would be the kiss of political death as far as he was concerned, and he scrupulously kept himself and his party aloof. Despite the fact that Mr Daultana thought that the people would not rise on their own, he and his party, the Council Muslim League, were aware to some extent of the people's feelings. They realized that twenty years of hardship, first under the parties now in opposition (with the exception of N.A.P.), and then directly under the army and bureaucracy, had left its mark.

In September 1968, the National Council of the Muslim League unanimously passed a resolution proposed by Sardar Shaukat Hayat Khan on behalf of the Working Committee. It was radical in its content, and a revolutionary departure for the post-Partition Muslim League. It called for nationalization of the banks, insurance companies, the major industries, all sources of energy, mines, " ... Textiles and all Agriculture-based industries, such as Jute, Sugar, Tea, Tobacco and Flour, shall be jointly owned and run by a co-operative of growers, entrepreneurs and labour."[2] It further called for a virtual state monopoly of foreign trade, the right of workers to bargain freely via their trade unions and to strike, and a taxation system designed to limit the maximum net income of any family, from any source, "so as not to exceed the equivalent of the income accruing from 250 acres of irrigated land, till each and every family in Pakistan

---

[1] Interview with author in Pakistan.
[2] *Decisions Taken and Resolution Passed at the Meeting of the Council of the Pakistan Muslim League held in September, 1968*, published by C.M.L., and included in the Appendix.

is assured a minimum income of Rs. 3,600 per year [£300 approximately]."[3]

The programme demanded a land-ownership ceiling of 250 acres of irrigated land, the setting up of co-operatives, and a minimum wage for agricultural labour; state-owned land could only be sold to agricultural co-operatives, and membership of co-operatives was to be confined to those who tilled the soil. In a complementary resolution on foreign policy the League demanded increasing friendship with China and the Arab world and an immediate withdrawal from CENTO and SEATO. It denounced Israel "as a creation and citadel of Western imperialism" and called upon the government to support the liberation movement in Palestine.

The programme surprised a large number of political activists, not least those belonging to the Muslim League itself. But the real reason for the programme soon became clear. It was nothing but a propaganda move, in belated recognition of the fact that the consciousness of the masses had been radicalized after the experiences of the last twenty years. The only slogans which interested them now were anti-capitalist, anti-feudal and anti-imperialist. To preserve even a vestige of credibility, the Muslim League had to adopt a radical programme. If it had put the programme into practice the League would have lost its only social base; the P.D.M. would have disintegrated immediately, as the extreme right wing would not have stayed within the same organization. However even the effects of propaganda were limited, as the League was so isolated from the people.

Mr Daultana and his friends realized this, and when they had convinced themselves that the revolt was not merely a "student affair" they decided to give the people the benefit of their leadership and actually emerged on the streets. A journalist in Rawalpindi was extremely surprised to "behold Mr Daultana leading processions to protest against those very gadgets of repression which he himself had used in his heyday though to a much lesser degree, to gag the press and fill the prisons with his political opponents."[4]

The decision had been made and the P.D.M. leaders had associated themselves with the movement; they had jumped on the bandwagon which, they thought, would take them straight to ministerial posts and maybe even Prime Ministirships. These men, who for the first ten years of their country's existence had exploited it on behalf of their class, and had even made a mess of that, were now denouncing

[3] Ibid.   [4] *Holiday*, December 22nd, 1968.

a dictator who had done exactly the same, with one difference—he had made an even bigger mess. One can understand the annoyance of the Central Intelligence Agency and the State Department with their successive clients.

Of the other components of the P.D.M., the only group worth mentioning is the Jamaat-i-Islami and its leader Maulana Maududi. Unlike the other political parties of the right, Maududi's followers did participate to a certain extent in the student rebellion when it first started. Their role was to shout pro-Islam slogans and burn family-planning clinics and denounce the Family Laws Ordinance. They excelled in preventing, or trying to prevent, militant students from marching on American-owned buildings or imperialist embassies. In the name of "democracy" they attacked Ayub for not being reactionary enough. But as the movement grew the influence of the neo-fascists on the students became negligible. Unfortunately they were the only disciplined and organized grouping in West Pakistan to operate in the student milieu; but even so their nauseating ideology and their violent methods alienated the vast majority of students.

The only party in West Pakistan which made any headway at all was the People's Party; admittedly, this was partly by default, but most of the credit must go to Bhutto. Bhutto was the only opposition leader who publicly opposed the regime when it was not yet fashionable to do so, and his stand won the People's Party a certain amount of support, particularly among students but also among the masses. Many political activists who had been disgusted by the pro-Ayub role of some of the other parties also joined Bhutto. But all these elements were in a minority. The most influential section of the party consisted of opportunists who had deserted the Convention Muslim League of President Ayub and joined Bhutto in the hope that he would soon gain power.

Like many others before him, Bhutto was intoxicated by the sight of thousands of cheering people shouting pro-Bhutto slogans; he mistook the deep and bitter opposition to Ayub as necessarily implying support for himself. This was by no means the case, as he eventually discovered. Some of his henchmen made matters worse by insisting that everyone address him as "Mr Chairman", and by establishing rituals of swearing allegiance to the Leader for some of the new recruits.

As we mentioned earlier, one of the main contributions of Bhutto and his party was to popularize the use of the word "socialism". From Bhutto's point of view this was a serious error, and he tried to wish it away by saying on numerous occasions that he meant the socialism which existed in Britain and in Scandinavia. He also tried to balance the anti-imperialist reputation he was acquiring by claiming that the United States had an "important role to play in Asia";[5] this was to convince the givers of aid that he was not the raving radical the Western press presented him to be. When the other parties were thinking of boycotting the election as it was to be held under the detested system of basic democracies, Mr Bhutto's candidature for the presidency was announced while he was still in prison. This merely confirmed the impression of many of his associates, and the announcement was greeted in Dacca with a mixture of cynicism and anger. A "special correspondent" wrote in his newspaper that: "The People's Party, which is in fact, more Bhutto's than people's is obviously more concerned about the candidacy of its party chief than of the interests of democracy."[6]

This incident reveals very clearly that for all the reformist consciousness of all the political parties, they could not allow themselves to visualize a situation where Ayub could be overthrown. There is no other explanation for all the talk about the 1970 "election".

The other two forces in West Pakistan were the two factions of the National Awami Party. The right-wing faction included in its ranks the nationalists from the Frontier and Baluchistan, and the Frontier N.A.P. was the strongest in West Pakistan. It was led by Wali Khan, whose father Khan Abdul Ghaffar Khan had been known as the Frontier Gandhi. He was a straightforward nationalist leader, chiefly interested in the breaking-up of One Unit and the establishment of an autonomous government in the Frontier Province. He knew even less about socialism than Mr Bhutto did. In the Punjab the mainstay of the party was Mian Mahmud Ali Kasuri, a rarity anywhere in the world of politics — an honest social-democrat.[7] The

---

[5] *International Herald Tribune*, February 21st, 1969. Interview with Selig Harrison.

[6] *Pakistan Observer*, January 15th, 1969.

[7] Kasuri was one of the leading radical lawyers in the country. The Ayub regime had made various attempts to buy him over, but he had consistently refused and emerged as one of the most principled critics of the dictatorship. On foreign policy his own position was one of support for the national liberation movements, and he was a judge at the War Crimes Tribunal convened on the initiative of Bertrand Russell which tried and found the United States guilty of war crimes in Vietnam. These facts are mentioned to refute the slander used against Kasuri in faction fights, that he was a "C.I.A. agent", and so on. Kasuri

right-wing N.A.P. also contained the few pro-Moscow Communists in West Pakistan who felt completely at home in struggling for bourgeois democracy in the company of feudal landlords from the Muslim League and fascists from the Jamaat-i-Islami. The aim of this party was to become part of the P.D.M., but at this stage the latter was not very interested. However Kasuri and Wali Khan were in the forefront of the anti-Ayub opposition, and Wali Khan had been arrested together with Bhutto.

The Left faction of the N.A.P. in West Pakistan contained all the pro-Peking Communists in West Pakistan and many of these were in leading positions in the party. Their attitude towards the upsurge was initially one of hostility, but as their party in East Pakistan had succeeded in projecting itself as the vanguard and had initiated a mass general strike, they backed the movement after some weeks had elapsed. Even then, because of their pro-Ayub attitude, they were not able to seize the leadership and were left in the rear of a massive popular upsurge.

Once they decided to participate in the struggle, their leaflets, pamphlets and journals contained some excellent anti-capitalist propaganda. But the old lessons learnt in the Stalinist school were hard to unlearn, and implicit in some of their propaganda was the idea that only the very big capitalists were the enemy, and that the bourgeoisie in general could still play a progressive role. However, the main emphasis was on ending feudalism and the rule of the monopoly capitalists. The party's position on American imperialism and its role in Pakistani politics was a hundred per cent correct, as was its opposition to the Jamaat-i-Islami. If the Left N.A.P. had opposed the Ayub dictatorship in a principled and consistent fashion there can be no doubt that it would have been able to give a vital lead to the masses in struggle, and would have been able to prevent the manœuvring of the right-wing political forces to contain the struggle.

In East Pakistan the situation was somewhat different. From the beginning all the political parties had associated themselves with the struggle. The pro-Peking N.A.P. had the additional advantage of having taken the initiative in calling for a strike against the dictator-

---

never pretended to be anything more than a social-democrat and to expect him to be versed in dialectical materialism was ludicrous. Criticism would have been more aptly directed against the pro-Moscow Communists working inside the right N.A.P. It should be added that those who slandered Kasuri were themselves in a weak position and had been politically discredited by their opportunist support for Ayub.

ship. The leader of the Awami League, Sheikh Mujibur Rehman, was imprisoned, and no other political leader could even challenge Bhashani's popularity with the people after he had led *gheraos* and been seen climbing up into trees to speak to the people. In the countryside Bhashani's strength was still unrivalled; thirty years of working with the peasantry had produced a strong peasant organization. Fortunately the peasant federation had not split despite the split in the parent organization, the N.A.P.

While the propaganda of the left-N.A.P. was carried out to a certain extent on class lines, the other two parties, the Awami League and the right-N.A.P., were concerned only with bourgeois democracy. The leader of the right-wing N.A.P. was a hardened pro-Moscow Khrushchevite Professor Mozaffar Ahmed. In an interview he told the author that his party believed that working through parliament was necessary at the moment.

> When I say objective conditions are ripe I do not mean ripe for socialism, but for bourgeois democracy. The political consciousness in Pakistan is not a socialist consciousness and therefore the revolution must come in stages. Of course we need a revolutionary party, but that is the next stage.

This was revisionism gone mad. In the circumstances it was only natural that the pro-Moscow N.A.P. clung to the skirts of the Awami League. This was a perfectly natural consequence of their political view, which envisaged an alliance with the bourgeoisie to fight for democracy. The question of democracy for whom never entered their minds. What this democracy was going to mean for the toiling masses was a question for the future, when somehow, miraculously, we had reached the "necessary stage" and every urban and rural proletarian in Pakistan had acquired a socialist consciousness. What bunk! Professor Ahmed had obviously not read any text by Lenin on the subject. In his polemics with the revisionists of his day Lenin was quite categorical on these questions. First on bourgeois democracy:

> Bourgeois democracy, although a great historical advance in comparison with medievalism, always remains, and under capitalism is bound to remain, restricted, truncated, false and hypocritical, a paradise for the rich and a snare and deception for the exploited, the poor ...[8]

[8] V. I. Lenin, "The Proletarian Revolution and the Renegade Kautsky". *Selected Works*, vol. 3. Moscow, 1968.

And he is equally vehement on the tasks of revolutionists:

> Kautsky does not display a shadow of an understanding of the truth that a revolutionary Marxist differs from the ordinary philistine and petty bourgeois by his ability to *preach* to the uneducated people that the maturing revolution is necessary, to *prove* that it is inevitable, to *explain* its benefits to the people, and to *prepare* the proletariat and all the working and exploited people for it.[9]

In January 1969 the leaders of the P.D.M. from West Pakistan came to Dacca in an attempt to form a united right-wing front to work in the entire country, and the Awami League and the pro-Moscow N.A.P. decided to join them in opposition to Ayub. Thus at a time when the Jamaat-i-Islami in West Pakistan was engaging in pitched battles against radical groupings, the "progressive" Sheikh Mujibur Rehman (who was in prison at this time, but not incommunicado) and the "Marxist" Professor Mozaffar Ahmed decided to join an opposition which contained the neo-fascists. The new, dynamic, united group was named the Democratic Action Committee (D.A.C.).

The skeleton programme on which the D.A.C. leaders agreed included demands for a federal and parliamentary form of government, adult franchise, release of all political prisoners (specifically Wali Khan, Bhutto and Mujibur Rehman) and the return of Progressive Papers Limited to its rightful owners. Despite the fact that the struggle had been going on for two months and the Ayub regime could not contain it, the D.A.C. leaders still had no concept of the national repercussions of the uprising.

On December 30th, 1968, the President while addressing the officials of his Muslim League said that "public demonstrations would never succeed in toppling his government and warned the Opposition that a collapse of the political system established by him would lead to civil war."[10] The people had become completely oblivious of all Ayub's threats, but the opposition parties understood what Ayub was saying to them. They realized that their own political system was scarcely distinguishable from Ayub's, and that their difference with Ayub was over the pace of reform, not over its nature. Hence the establishment of the D.A.C. and its future position

[9] Ibid.
[10] *Guardian*, December 31st, 1968.

as a stumbling-block in the path of the struggle. The headline of the Sunday newspaper *Holiday*: "D.A.C. – a Child of Intrigue",[11] aptly summed-up the new organization. No sooner had D.A.C. been formed than emissaries from the dictator made approaches to it and offered a negotiated settlement. Mr Daultana admitted that "By the end of January we began to receive reports that Ayub was prepared to talk. We thought it was too dangerous to talk to him and so we rebuffed him for two reasons. We mistrusted him and we knew it would finish us."[12] At that stage any political leader who even considered talking to Ayub was politically dead and the leaders of D.A.C. knew this well.

Students

While most of the political parties were preparing to reach a negotiated settlement with the dictator, the people who had been largely responsible for triggering off the movement were still engaged in struggle. When repression had clearly failed, the regime bought off some student "leaders", but the movement continued without them.

On December 6th, 1968, the Rawalpindi students held a student convention and declared that the struggle would continue until the demands of the students were met and an impartial commission set up to investigate police brutality and repression against the student movement. The police decided to break up the convention, and student militants maintain that more tear-gas was thrown into Gordon College on that day than had been used by the police throughout the struggle in Rawalpindi as a whole. As students attempted to leave the college precincts, they were baton-charged time and time again. The left-wing student leader, Raja Anwar, was beaten up so badly that he had to spend six days in hospital. At the same time the student leaders were approached by one of the President's sons, who offered them a private meeting with his father. The students refused. Various other approaches were made, but the government was able to buy only a couple of student leaders.

Once again the universities, colleges and schools were closed by the government, but this time the students were not to be tricked. Student leaders used to announce in the non-government newspapers

[11] cf. *Holiday*, January 12th, 1969.
[12] Interview with author.

when a demonstration was to be held, and an average of six thousand students used to assemble, have a discussion and march off. After December 25th, 1968, the isolation of the students in Rawalpindi was ended permanently. The masses had been convinced by the student actions that they meant business, and on December 25th a student demonstration of ten thousand was joined by twenty thousand workers, without the student action body making any appeals. Given the choice between the existing political parties and the students, the people opted for the latter, and student demonstrations attracted a larger number of workers than any political Party in West Pakistan. Also on December 25th, 1968, Raja Anwar announced the formation of a student-people alliance and declared that from then on students would work consciously among the masses in the cities and, still more important, in the countryside.

On the same day the students declared that they were not prepared to talk *at* the Ayub regime any longer: they would put their demands before a new, people's government—and their main demand now became that Ayub should quit. They were unclear as to the alternative, and preferred not to talk about it, but had in mind a National Government which would consist of all the opposition parties and would act as a caretaker government, and organize an immediate general election.

Throughout West Pakistan the fires still raged, but the student movement made no effort to co-ordinate, to set up a province-wide organization, or to send representatives throughout the province to organize and establish contacts with the various student groups. By the time the students decided to do this, it was too late. And not a single comprehensive programme containing the demands of the student movement of West Pakistan ever appeared. It is amazing that the struggle continued despite all the weaknesses of the students. It seems that since the chief object of hatred was Ayub, and since his removal had become the main demand, the students felt there was no need for ideological clarity on their part.[13]

---

[13] According to Raja Anwar the first ideological split in the student movement in West Pakistan (excluding Karachi and Sind) came when leftist students decided to invite me to come and "participate in the struggle". The right-wingers of all varieties then united against the leftists to oppose this suggestion, but the invitation was endorsed by a large General Assembly of students in Rawalpindi. "After that", said Rajar Anwar, "there was no looking back. From then on we were split permanently into rightist and leftists. The first wanting a return of the old politicians and us wanting socialism." Of course the left students were not well

In East Pakistan the situation was slightly different. A Student Action Committee had been established and its leaders had adopted an eleven-point programme of demands which was anti-capitalist in content. The first point dealt exclusively with educational demands and the remaining ten points dealt with the political demands of the people. The three dominant factors in the S.A.C. were E.P.S.U. (leftists), E.P.S.L., and E.P.S.U. (rightists). Much to the distaste of the Awami League leader, Sheikh Mujibur Rehman (who was still in prison, and his influence therefore much restricted), the leftists succeeded in pushing through demands for extensive nationalization and an anti-imperialist foreign policy. The students' eleven-point programme became the programme of the people. No political meeting could take place unless the eleven-point programme of the students was supported, and both the Awami League and the two National Awami Parties made public declarations supporting it.

The ideological traditions of the student movement in East Pakistan and the history of political struggle since Partition was obviously an important factor in the students' ability to formulate this programme. It was quite clear that East Pakistan was in the vanguard of the struggle, and that it was giving the lead to the entire nation; and in East Pakistan itself, the students dominated the political scene. The Student's Action Committee was to become the most powerful political organization in East Pakistan.

The People

The Student Action Committee in Dacca decided to join with the other opposition forces in the country and observe January 17th, 1969, as Demands Day. This was the first time such a co-ordinated action had been possible in both East and West Pakistan, and the first co-ordinated general strike in Pakistan on Demands Day brought the economic life of the country to a complete standstill. There were mass demonstrations in Dacca, Lahore, Karachi, Rawalpindi and the other main cities of the country. In East Pakistan the

---

organized. It was just fortunate that in Peshawar and in Rawalpindi, Qazi Anwar and Raja Anwar (not related by blood but by politics) both happened to be leaders of student unions and were both also radical. In Multan and Lyallpur there was a more conscious socialist organization; in Multan the Pakistan Student Movement (*tehrik-talba-i-Pakistan*) contained some excellent cadres, including Ali Gardezi and Karim Yar Abbasi. The influence of the local left-wing N.A.P. leader, Syed Kaswar Gardezi, had clearly proved beneficial.

police had been given instructions to try and disperse the marchers and, accordingly, "Demonstrating students were chased into the Dacca University campus and beaten up by the police, a number of whom were also injured, while staves and tear-gas were used to break up a parade in the city."

This new wave of repression by the government, which occurred just when it was saying that it was prepared to talk, did not endear it to the masses. In the cities, where the demonstrations seemed to be falling off, they resumed once again with renewed fervour. On January 25th there were furious street battles in Karachi, the largest industrialized city in the country with the largest single concentration of urban proletarians. The battles lasted eight hours on that particular day, but the workers and students were tired, as they had been fighting continuously for the two days previous to the 25th. Workers, students and unemployed burnt buses, trams, petrol pumps, oil stations and government offices. Workers raided banks, brought safes out into the streets and blew them up. The class hatred of the Karachi proletariat was unequalled elsewhere in the country. Hundreds of people were injured and over five hundred arrested.

The government thought that by arresting the leftist student leaders of Karachi they would be able to control the upsurge. In fact exactly the opposite happened. Enraged by the arrest of their spokesmen, the workers and students fought even more violently. In one area of Karachi over a thousand students marched on the house of a prominent member of Ayub's Muslim League who, seeing the crowd approaching, shot and critically wounded a student. The next day ten thousand students marched on the mansion. An army unit was stationed outside, with a young officer in command. He asked the students what they had come to do, and they told him that they had come to set fire to the mansion. After they had explained their reasons, the army officer was suddenly observed to order his unit to another area. The mansion was burned to the ground.

In other parts of Karachi, too, the army was called in to "restore order" as the police had lost control of the situation. A curfew was imposed for forty-eight hours, but even that failed to stop the street-fighting. Elsewhere in West Pakistan the upsurge continued. In the provincial capital of Lahore, students attacked the offices of a pro-government newspaper and set it on fire. Over fifty thousand students and workers marched through the streets, burning cars, battling with police and laying siege to government offices. As night fell in Lahore on January 26th, a large fire was seen burning near the building which houses the Supreme Court of Pakistan; it seemed almost as though it had been lit to highlight the servile role played by the majority of Supreme Court judges during the ten years of Ayub raj. In Lahore, Karachi and Rawalpindi students stopped cars carrying leading civil servants, pulled them out and forced them to shout anti-Ayub slogans. Not a single bureaucrat refused, much to the amusement of student onlookers. In Lahore the most senior police official was stripped of his uniform and forced to march at the head of a large student demonstration.

By now some professional people were beginning to follow the example of the students. Journalists, teachers, doctors, nurses, engineers, architects and prostitutes participated in demonstrating throughout West Pakistan. *The Times* wrote editorials implying and hoping that the worst was over and that the situation was returning to normal, but the conflict showed no signs of receding.[14]

The intensity of the struggle in West Pakistan began to worry the ruling class seriously. From January 17th, 1969, onwards the movement against the dictatorship had continued to gather momentum and fiercer street battles had become the order of the day. The bureaucracy used all its legal powers to try and contain the turmoil, but it seemed as if the days of bureaucratic manœuvrings backed by force were over. The people were determined to let nothing stand in their way. A strong force of police and army units were permanently stationed outside the Dacca Government House where Ayub's provincial satrap resided. During the day he had become a prisoner there, guarded by the people to see that he did not escape their clutches; it was only at night when the masses rested that the prisoner could travel under cover of darkness.

The bureaucracy could see no way out except by further repression. Even the respectable bourgeois leaders of the Democratic Action Committee were forced by the strength of the people to postpone their secret negotiations with government spokesmen. This was

[14] *The* [London] *Times*, January 4th, 1969. Commenting editorially the newspaper still seemed to think that Ayub would be contesting the 1970 "general election" and implied that his only serious opponent was Air Marshal Asghar Khan. It referred to Maulana Bhashani as "that hangover from the past", but in deriding Bhashani's age it did not understand that Bhashani was the only political leader in Pakistan who had the support of the workers and the peasants and who posed clear-cut class demands. Far from being a "hangover from the past", Bhashani was a spokesman for the future; for a Pakistan which was run by the workers and peasants under a socialist system of government.

unfortunate, because if only the D.A.C. had tried to meet Ayub at the height of the upsurge they would have signed their own political death warrant; they could not have deceived the people then as they could at a later stage.

The three days from January 24th to January 26th witnessed an orgy of bestiality by the state. Throughout East Pakistan the police killed demonstrators and the reaction of the government-controlled press to the killing so infuriated the students that on January 24th they set fire to the *Morning News* and *Dainik Pakistan* offices in Dacca. It was a salutary lesson; the same journalists who had prostituted themselves in praising the dictatorship were frightened into reporting the upsurge in a slightly more objective fashion than before.

Four people were killed in Dacca that day, one of them a fourteen-year-old schoolboy. The father of a dead student told a large student meeting, "Today I have lost one child, but in his place I have got a thousand children amongst you students. Go forward." The Students Action Committee called for a general strike in Dacca to protest against the killings, and once again the masses responded. Dacca was cut off from the rest of East Pakistan and from West Pakistan. Even the telecommunications services were suspended. A newspaper reported the day's events thus:

In Dacca city the strike began successfully, with all shops, bazaars and establishments closed. All transport remained off the streets. There was also a complete strike in the industrial areas around Dacca. Workers and peasants from outside Dacca came to the city for the demonstrations planned for the day. Some of them carried ploughs and sticks with them. Later pickets went to government and semi-government offices, calling on the employees to join the strike. Most of the employees in most of the offices including the East Pakistan Water and Development Authority, the East Pakistan Industrial Development Corporation and the G.P.O. responded to the call, but trouble began when pickets arrived at the East Pakistan Secretariat (the offices of the bureaucrats—T.A.) and it later culminated in the police firing ... This happened when the first group of demonstrators walked up to the gate of the secretariat and gave a call to the employees to come out and join the strike. The E.P.R. and police closed the gates and warned the demonstrators to disperse, but they refused to do so and continued to picket the secretariat. The police resorted to tear-gas. The demonstrators retaliated with bricks. Tear-gas shells fired by the police were also hurled back at the E.P.R. and the police inside the secretariat. Then the police opened fire. The second firing took place at 12.15 p.m. Undeterred by the first firing the crowd which swelled in numbers became frenzied and tried to approach the gate in the midst of heavy tear-gas shelling. They were hurling stones in reply to the tear-gas. At one stage the gate on the south side was seen burning. At that time the demonstrators took their positions near the gate. Meanwhile a fire brigade vehicle came to extinguish the fire but it was obstructed by the mob. A section of the mob tried to snap the telephone and power wires at the south-east corner of the secretariat. By that time the riot vans of the police had made a round of the area, heavily drenching the crowd. The crowd retaliated with brickbats. For quite some time there continued a fierce battle with the demonstrators on one side and the police and East Pakistan Rifles on the other. Shooting was heard at that time and three people were killed. A section of the demonstration was further infuriated and they went to the east side of the secretariat and set four government vehicles on fire ... [15]

There had been similar outbreaks in other parts of East Pakistan, and students, workers and peasants had successfully defied the oppressors and held their own ground. During the night of January 23rd to 24th, twenty-five thousand students marched with torches in the streets of Dacca and pledged themselves to fight for total victory, which meant acceptance of their eleven-point demands. But for victory a revolutionary leadership was needed, and none existed. The movement was miles ahead of existing political leadership, and even the old Maulana had to keep running fairly fast to keep up with the demands of the masses.

The role of the student leadership was extremely important:

The students of East Pakistan have left the entrenched opposition parties behind both in their programme and action. They have taken upon themselves the most challenging task of leading a political movement. By their actions and determined movement, the student community have been able to infuse

[15] *Pakistan Observer*, January 25th, 1969.

unbounded courage among the common people. While the political parties are busy modifying their points and counterpoints, the students have inspired all sections of the people to come out in the streets under their own banner of the eleven-point programme. The demand charter placed by them exceeds the imagination of the orderly political parties. What the students are agitating for can very well form the basis of an anti-feudal, anti-capitalist and anti-imperialist democratic movement. Their programme and leadership have largely been accepted by the people of the country ... [16]

However, the S.A.C. was not itself united, and the political parties were already beginning to denounce the "ultra-revolutionary and adventuristic"[17] slogans of the student movement. The reformists were determined that the movement should now be controlled, and some of them undoubtedly sent messages to Ayub indicating that were he to make an offer of some sort they would respond. Ayub gave his reply through his favourite Pakistani journalist, Z. A. Suleri, who published a front-page article in the Rawalpindi *Pakistan Times*, indicating that the great man was now prepared to talk to the opposition leaders. A day later the Foreign Minister tried to cool down the leftists by announcing in Parliament that the Chinese leader Chou En-lai had accepted an invitation to visit Pakistan.[18] But the movement was too far advanced for these sops to be taken seriously. Something more was needed.

On February 1st in a broadcast to the nation the President announced that he was prepared to talk to the opposition leaders. For Ayub this was a dramatic concession to the politicians he had been deriding only a few weeks previously, and he did it for two reasons. First, he was being pressured by the army to negotiate with the responsible opposition leaders, and he could no longer depend on the automatic support of the army for his political tactics and strategy. Second, he was frightened that unless he came to an agreement with the D.A.C. the chances were that despite lack of organization the extreme left wing would win more support from the people. The task which faced him and the D.A.C. leaders was to isolate the Left by reaching an agreement. Also the bureaucrats closest to Ayub

[16] *Holiday*, January 28th, 1969.
[17] *Holiday*, January 28th, 1969.
[18] *Pakistan Observer*, January 31st, 1969.

knew full well that an offer to talk would cause some dissension within the ranks of the D.A.C. itself, and as a British newspaper reported:

> While the saner elements in the opposition see reason in President Ayub Khan's offer to discuss national problems with "responsible opposition leaders" extremists have denounced the President's move. It has been described as an attempt to "divide the people, slow down the tempo of the movement and push it into the background and allow it to bog down in the muds of expectations, suspense and doubt".[19]

There could be no doubt that Ayub's appeal was intended to prompt the bourgeois and feudal politicians to get together with him and prevent the system disintegrating. He was prepared to make major concessions to the students as far as their university demands were concerned, so long as they agreed to abdicate their wider responsibilities:

> So far as the problems of students are concerned, it has been acknowledged by educational experts, teachers, parents of students that the government have considered their difficulties sympathetically and have made an honest effort to solve them. Most of the students' demands have been accepted to end the present stalemate. The university ordinances are being repealed and new legislation is being enacted to meet the present needs. It is hoped that under the new system most of the difficulties of teachers and students will be removed, and that a new era will begin in the field of education in the country. The students should also now take full advantage of these facilities and attend to their studies as quickly as possible. I fervently hope that the parents of students and the teachers will also use their influence and take practical steps to improve the present atmosphere.[20]

But it was too late from Ayub's point of view. The student community could not be bribed or browbeaten into abandoning the political struggle taking place in the country. Of course, Ayub did not think that his appeal would have any effect in East Pakistan; he was really addressing himself mainly to the students in West Pakistan, but there, too, his appeals fell on deaf ears. Most of the militants in

[19] *Financial Times*, February 6th, 1969.
[20] *Holiday*, February 2nd, 1969.

opposition were not particularly flattered by Ayub's references to hooligans, anti-social elements, and riff-raff.

Ayub maintained that he was not opposed to peaceful protests, but that violence in the streets had to be firmly combated by the state, and this view was shared by many leaders of D.A.C. Many of these leaders had, much to the surprise of the people, and even of themselves, decided to defy Section 144 on January 17th, 1969 and to hold a demonstration. But they could not lead their followers to the logical culmination of the defiance: battles with the police.

A different mood prevailed amongst the students. They were also inclined to violate Section 144 but were unwilling to restrain their forward movement in the face of resistance. So they kept their forward thrust and continued their effort to break the police resistance. The subsequent developments followed one another in quick succession. The East Pakistan Rifles replaced the police and the students became more organized and violent and resorted to brickbatting and barricades in replying to the atrocities. The uprising finally reached a height when the people virtually took the entire movement in their own hands and did not wait for any directive from any political leadership, which was non-existent in any case.[21]

The D.A.C. leaders realized full well that the movement was beyond their control. For them as well as Ayub a compromise seemed to be the only way out. The D.A.C. put forward some pre-conditions, of which the most important was a withdrawal of the State of Emergency prevailing in Pakistan, under which many political workers had been arrested. Almost immediately the Law Minister announced that the Defence of Pakistan Rules would soon be lifted and that no fresh action would be taken under them. It looked very much as though these points had been agreed by both sides in private and were being used in a propagandistic way to deceive the public: the D.A.C. leaders were making it clear that they were not prepared to talk unless some of the "people's demands" were met; and the dictator for his part was appearing as a "reasonable" man who was accepting the main demand. The charade had been well planned.

The rightist N.A.P., a leading component of the D.A.C., had been a trifle reluctant to talk while their leader, Wali Khan, was still in prison, but assurances had been given that it was a matter of days

[21] *Holiday*, February 2nd, 1969, p. 8; an article by Badruddin Umar.

before the State of Emergency would be lifted and both Bhutto and Wali Khan released. The question of Sheikh Mujibur Rehman, however, was slightly more complicated. The Awami League threatened to withdraw from the D.A.C. unless it was represented at the Round Table Conference by Mujibar Rehman. The government promised that Mujibur would be "made available" which was an ironical situation as Rehman was charged with "conspiracy" and treason. Despite this the regime was offering to release him on parole! Initially the Awami League leader agreed to come out on parole, but an outcry from the people soon changed his mind. And then developments on the streets overtook the Round Table negotiations.

Throughout West Pakistan the revolt continued. While Air Marshal Asghar Khan called for a national government the people showed their resentment and complete lack of trust in the D.A.C. leaders by continuing their struggle on the streets. The most dominant chant was one of "No compromise and Ayub must go." On February 13th an angry demonstration consisting of students, workers and some members of the intelligentsia marched in Lahore to the showrooms of the Oxford University Press and burnt them down. The Press had published Ayub's appalling memoirs, and the students who had had the book thrust down their throats in schools and universities were now wreaking their vengeance. Every single copy of the book was destroyed and the Oxford University Press suffered damage of over twenty thousand pounds.

On the same day over thirty thousand railway workers marched on the main streets of Lahore. They had finally persuaded their pro-Chinese leaders to organize a demonstration. The workers carried red flags chanting such slogans as: "Solidarity with the Chinese people", "Destroy capitalism", "Keep religion out of politics". There were five other demonstrations by workers on the same day and traffic was at a complete standstill. The workers seemed to be in con-control of the city, and the correspondent of *The Times*, noticing them apparently for the first time, sent back a dispatch to London which included the following sentence: "With the entry of the working class into the revolt, hitherto limited to students and political parties, observers are beginning to doubt whether the government or the opposition can control the forces unleashed in Pakistan."[22]

In the other cities of West Pakistan, particularly Karachi and Peshawar, the police opened fire on demonstrators, and on February

[22] *The* [London] *Times*, February 14th, 1969.

14th at least six people were killed by the police; one of them was a sixteen-year-old student in Lahore. On the same day, the students sabotaged the signals near Lahore railway station, disrupting train services. These were the real answers to Ayub's offer of talks, and they were in striking contrast to the D.A.C.'s attitudes of compromise and reform. They had no one to articulate their demands, so they decided to remain on the streets till these demands were met.

In the meantime the situation had deteriorated to such an extent that the ruling class was considering the imposition of Martial Law. Ayub was in regular consultation with the Army and it is clear that political intrigue was taking place on two different levels. Ayub was negotiating with the D.A.C. on one hand and with the army on the other. The army itself was involved in talks with some of the political leaders. In the first week of February, according to some senior civil servants, the army was preparing to impose Martial Law and salvage Ayub. The date had been fixed and the relevant Martial Law regulations printed, but at the last minute the situation in East Pakistan forced the army to change its mind.

In East Pakistan, Mujibur Rehman was still in prison, and though he was prepared to be released on parole the voice of the people, heard in meeting after meeting in Paltan Maidan, said no. Maulana Bhashani declared that the people of East Pakistan would not let Mujibur go to Rawalpindi on parole. He must be released unconditionally and if it was necessary the people would tear the prison walls down. Mujibur had no option but to accept the people's demand and he now said that he should be released.

Meanwhile the leftist student leaders were mercilessly attacking the D.A.C.'s Bengali representatives and claiming that the dialogue between the bourgeois opposition and the regime had no mandate from the people and that there could be no discussion except on the basis of the eleven-point demands of the Student Action Committee. The students saw that a concerted effort was being made by the government and the opposition to take the movement down more respectable channels, and some of them resisted. As a result the demonstrations and strikes continued.

On Saturday, February 15th, Sergeant Zahurul Haq, one of the Bengali soldiers accused together with Mujibur Rehman of conspiracy in the Agarthala Case, died from bullet wounds. The prison authorities claimed that he had been trying to escape, but the other prisoners denied this and said that he had been shot down in cold blood. Whatever the facts about his death, the killing of Zahurul Haq had an explosive effect on the people of Dacca. Students clashed with the police many times and Maulana Bhashani called a funeral meeting on Sunday, February 16th, 1969. It was at this meeting that the eighty-six-year-old peasant leader ended his oration with the call, "*Bangla jago, agun jalo*" (Bengalis awake, and light the fires). No sooner had the Maulana said these words than smoke was seen rising from the city centre. It was pure coincidence, but the dramatic effect heightened the already tense atmosphere in the city. The building which had been set on fire was the new headquarters of the Ayub Muslim League, still under construction, but nonetheless considered worth burning. Later the house of Nawab Hasan Askari, one of Ayub's Dacca supporters and a provincial minister, was also set on fire, as was the house of the Central Information Minister, Khwaja Shahabuddin. The masses, too, were enraged by the killing of Zahurul Haq. Government property and official cars were set on fire, and the army had to be called out once again to "restore order". A day later the state of emergency was withdrawn and Bhutto, Wali Khan and other political prisoners were released. Again on February 17th there were violent demonstrations in Dacca, and the army imposed a curfew.

The next day a Professor at Rajshahi University was bayoneted to death by a soldier during a demonstration. When the news of this new killing reached Dacca the atmosphere became charged. A curfew was imposed on the city, but both the army and the bureaucrats in Dacca realized that it would be defied. Bullets had failed to frighten the movement; student leaders pointed out to the army that thousands of peasants died whenever there was a flood and it did not matter too much if a few hundred students died facing bullets in the struggle for freedom.

Before we can describe the events of the night of February 18th, 1969, we should mention the balance of class forces inside Dacca. In the centre of the city is Dacca University. It is largely residential, and most students belong to one of the eight Halls of Residence which surround the campus. Student leaders, even if they themselves don't live in the Halls, are usually to be found there.[23] There are between 5,000 and 6,500 university students in Dacca, and a solid phalanx

[23] The different Halls elect three representatives each to represent them on the Dacca University Central Students Union (D.U.C.S.U.) and the offices of President and Secretary of this body are rotated amongst the representatives of the different Halls. The S.A.C. which is set up during struggle consists of D.U.C.S.U. representatives as well as nominees from the other colleges and universities.

of them are to be found in the core of the city. The industrial workers are all concentrated in the suburbs just outside Dacca in Tongi, Tejgaon, Demra and Adamjeenagar. The industrialists thought that they could isolate their workers by herding them together in estates, but in fact this made it much easier for the workers to organize themselves politically outside working hours. So we can see Dacca as two concentric circles, the inner circle containing the students, and the outer the proletariat; between the two circles are the bourgeoisie and the petit-bourgeoisie and also, of course, the slum-dwellers and the city poor. Beyond the outer circle numbers of landless and unemployed peasants are encamped near the industrial belt of Dacca, and beyond them are the rural peasantry.

There had been no definite decision by either students or workers to defy the curfew, but there was a spontaneous feeling that this might happen. Soon after 10 p.m. the students in the Halls started chanting slogans against the army, and calling for the curfew to be defied. Gradually the petit-bourgeoisie climbed on their rooftops and began to echo the student slogans. Within an hour, virtually the entire city was chanting the same slogans, and gradually people realized that the curfew would be defied. The news spread to the industrial areas and the workers gathered together and started marching towards the city centre.

Inside the city the first group to defy the army were the slum-dwellers, whose misery had hardened them to face anything. They were joined by other sections of the city poor, and they all linked up with the workers. Finally the students joined in, and Dacca became a mass of moving people. In many cases army officers stationed at key points of the city, panicked and ran away. In others they behaved like any colonial army and shot the workers down in cold blood.

The leadership of the left N.A.P. was meeting at a house in Eskaton. The old Maulana was pacing up and down in the garden, frustrated by his inability to give the lead and weeping as he heard the sound of machine-gun fire; the other "leaders" were debating how to escape if the army should raid the house. At one stage workers ran into the house and asked Bhashani for guns to use against the army, but no guns existed – at any rate, none were made available. When the workers wanted to assert their political power they faced the barrels of the ruling class's guns.

Throughout the city staccato bursts of gunfire were heard. In the working-class suburbs of Dacca the curfew was being defied, and workers sabotaged railway lines to prevent trains from moving into Dacca. Many of them were ruthlessly gunned down.

Between midnight and 1 a.m. even government officials with curfew passes were not allowed into the streets. Some journalists who defied this order and sneaked out saw for themselves the bodies of dead workers and peasants being carried away and soldiers cleansing the streets of blood. According to unofficial estimates (there are no official figures), over a hundred people were killed that night. But the newspapers were silent. Once again the workers and the city poor, without any leadership whatsoever, had defied the ruling class and faced the bullets of the bourgeoisie.

A revolutionary leadership organized throughout the province could have used this opportunity to seize power and to wage an armed struggle in Dacca itself to defeat the oppressors. Instead, the Student Action Committee agreed to meet the local bureaucrats across a conference table; it smacked of the Round Table Conference suggested earlier on, but in a sense it was more important than that. The students demanded that the curfew be lifted and that all political prisoners should be released.[24] They warned the government publicly that unless the curfew was withdrawn they would defy it in no uncertain way. The General commanding the Dacca garrison is reported to have sent back an extremely pessimistic picture of the situation in East Pakistan to his Boss in Rawalpindi, and his dispatch was probably crucial at that particular juncture.

On February 19th Ayub summoned the three Commanders-in-Chief of the armed forces. No public reports of the meeting have yet been published, but the following estimate was obtained from sources close to Ayub. Evidently he asked the three Commanders to impose Martial Law in all the cities in East and West Pakistan, but the army chief, General Yahya Khan, refused pointblank. He had received a report from his man in Dacca which suggested that if Martial Law were imposed they might be able to contain Dacca, but could not give any assurance for the rest of East Pakistan. The officers Yahya had consulted had told him that they were not opposed to Martial Law to save the country, but that it would have to be a Martial Law

---

[24] The very fact that at this critical stage they could agree to talk to the hated local bureaucracy shows the reformist consciousness of a large majority of the student leaders. Mahbubullah admitted this freely, and said that he had subjected himself to strenuous self-criticism for agreeing to the meeting; but quite clearly it would have been wrong for him to split with the S.A.C. on this issue and isolate himself.

14

without Ayub. Yahya advised Ayub to accept all the conditions of
the political leaders of the D.A.C. and then withdrew from politics.

Once Ayub had lost the backing of the army he was completely
helpless, and had no other option left to him. On February 20th the
curfew was ended; on February 21st Ayub announced his withdrawal from Pakistani politics.[25] Any other decision would have
meant a bloodbath, not only in East Pakistan, but also in some areas
in West Pakistan, particularly the North West Frontier, Karachi and
Baluchistan. On February 22nd, Sheikh Mujibur Rehman was
released from prison and the Agarthala Conspiracy Case completely
closed. Whatever political intrigue preceded this decision, its great
importance lay in its effect on the Bengali masses, who saw it as a
great victory for their national movement.

The meeting in Dacca called by the S.A.C. to celebrate Mujibur's
release was attended by over half a million people. Mahbubullah
spoke at the meeting in no uncertain terms, and warned Mujibur and
his co-thinkers that the masses would not tolerate any attempt to bypass the eleven-point demands of the students. Mujib was forced to
say that he would fight for them. The E.P.S.U. leftists had every right
to be pleased with themselves. Both they and Mujib knew the truth,
but the latter had been forced to accept the eleven-points in front of
half a million people.

While there can be no doubt that Ayub's decision to "retire" from
politics was a tremendous moral victory for the people who had been
engaged in the struggle against him, his decision had a certain
negative effect on the mass movement. Once Ayub was "down", the
leaders of the bourgeois parties could claim that they were holding
discussions with him only for the purposes of taking over power and
establishing a bourgeois democratic form of government in Pakistan,

[25] Cf. *Black Dwarf*, April 18th, 1969. I wrote in a report: "By a strange
coincidence I arrived in Pakistan on the morning of February 21st, 1969. That
same evening Ayub was scheduled to broadcast to the nation. He had been
unable to meet the needs of a mass movement which had been active since
November 1968. He had offered too little too late and political activists waited
anxiously for his broadcast. The atmosphere was reminiscent of Paris last June
with students and workers waiting for de Gaulle to appear on the small screen. In
the evening he announced his 'irrevocable' decision to retire from politics. His
voice was distraught. He spoke in simple Urdu of his deep love for Pakistan
(cynics speculated as to which of his two favourite civil servants—Altaf Gauhar
or Q. Shahab—could have written the speech. A few private bets were placed.)
Ayub is down, but is he out? Excitement ran high in the streets of the main cities.
Crowds danced with pleasure. Few ponder about the future. The present is more
important. The struggle has been victorious."

and that now there was no question of a compromise whereby Ayub stayed in power. Hence they could and did ask the people to forget the streets and concentrate on the Round Table at the President's House in Rawalpindi.

In West Pakistan, Bhutto refused to sit at the same table with Ayub and would not attend the Conference. Whatever the real reasons behind this move, it had the positive effect of increasing the ideological cleavage between the reactionary and progressive students. The "leaders" arriving at Rawalpindi to meet Ayub were greeted by students chanting anti-D.A.C. slogans. A pro-Bhutto student leader, Hassamul Haque, was slapped at Rawalpindi airport during one such manifestation by a luminary of the local D.A.C. The neo-fascists in particular came out quite openly, and brazenly attacked the core of the anti-Ayub opposition. Their onslaughts on Bhutto and Bhashani were reminiscent of the Nazi propaganda written in *Der Stürmer* in the 'thirties. I had personal experience of the way they worked. Whenever I arrived at a railway station or airport I was greeted by a large number of left-wing students and a small group of fascists who had been sent to provoke confrontations.[26] At Multan airport the Jamaat-i-Islami supporters greeted me with the following slogan: "We shall make Pakistan another Indonesia!" or simply: "Kill Socialists". I replied at a large public meeting in Multan, saying that if socialists were slaughtered they would not die in their beds but would defend themselves to the death and would kill seven fascists for every socialist. This was taken out of context by the pro-Jamaat-i-Islami press and used as anti-socialist propaganda.[27]

[26] cf. *Holiday*, March 16th, 1969, p. 3. The newspaper printed photographs showing the neo-fascists attacking unarmed students who had come to receive me at Lyallpur railway station, and a report exposing the Jamaat-i-Islami tactics against the Left.

[27] For instance one newspaper carried a headline which read: "Tariq Ali says: 'We Shall Avenge Death of Indonesian Communists in Pakistan'." The reason why the Jamaat-i-Islami was annoyed by my tour of important West Pakistani cities was mainly because of my "international reputation", and also because I insisted on linking the struggle in Pakistan with the struggle elsewhere in the world. *The* [London] *Times* (March 5th, 1969) reported that, "Student leaders supporting the right-wing religious Jamaat Islami party were even more dismayed. 'He will destroy Islam', one of them said. Although Tariq Ali has the support of the majority of left-wing radicals, more moderate socialists believe that such an outspoken Trotskyite would antagonize orthodox Muslim opinion." The "moderate socialists" were, of course, supporters of Mr Bhutto and at one stage they hinted that because I was opposed to Bhutto's politics I must be a C.I.A. agent!

In East Pakistan, Bhashani was under some pressure from sections of his party to attend the Round Table Conference. When Mujibur Rehman had been released from prison he had gone to see the Maulana the same day to ask him to attend the conference. Mujibur, who had been Bhashani's political secretary in former years, reportedly called the old man his father and asked him to come for the sake of Bengal. The Maulana's instincts warned him against attending, and he replied that when his son was going, what need was there for the father to attend as well. Again, when a journalist asked him whether he would not be isolated if he refused to go to Rawalpindi and negotiate with the government, Bhashani replied, "Yes, I'll isolate myself from Ayub, his entourage and all the bourgeois political leaders. I will not, however, be isolating myself from the people." The support of the Marxist students of E.P.S.U. and the militant trade-union leaders from Chittagong helped Bhashani to stay away from Rawalpindi. Even so his refusal was conditional; he argued that if the regime accepted some of the basic demands of the peasants he would attend.

There was not a single reasoned, socialist critique of the Round Table negotiations between Ayub and the opposition parties. It was merely a pause in the upsurge. In West Pakistan the main demand had been the removal of Ayub, and Ayub had removed himself. The students' lack of an ideology, combined with the opportunist, social-democratic lead given by Bhutto, meant that the extra-parliamentary opposition in West Pakistan was now operating in a vacuum.

The atmosphere in West Pakistan had definitely cooled down, apart from airport clashes between Jamaat-i-Islami-Ayub supporters and left-wing students, and in the western part of the country the upsurge had definitely been halted. Only Karachi seemed at first to be completely unaffected by the news of Ayub's withdrawal; in a few cases the Karachi workers occupied factories and expelled the managers, and by March 17th there was a general strike which paralysed the docks and railways, and the red flag was hoisted on Valika Textile Mills. The only workers who did not come out on strike were the workers belonging to the P.I.A. (Pakistan International Airlines) Employees Union.

In East Pakistan the upsurge continued. Though the students had cooled down, the urban proletariat and the poor peasants continued the struggle. In some parts of the countryside the peasants attacked the offices of the petty bureaucrats who collected and registered taxes: peasants often had to pay the tax and then pay treble the amount as a bribe to the bureaucrat to register that he *had* paid his tax. Now the peasants surrounded the bureaucrat's office and demanded their money back—the bribe money only. In every case where the money was refused the office was burnt down. In North Bengal the peasants stopped all payments due to the government and some villages elected People's Courts to try the local "evil gentry". About a dozen revenue officers, bureaucrats and basic democrats were tried and executed.

The reports of mass and indiscriminate slaughters were in fact slanders to discredit the peasant movement and to frighten the middle classes. But even if the peasants had slaughtered all the "evil gentry" they would have deserved support. The situation was not a new one. It had been described brilliantly by a Chinese revolutionary in the 'twenties:

> The peasants' revolt disturbed the gentry's sweet dreams. When the news from the countryside reached the cities it caused immediate uproar among the gentry ... From the middle social-strata upwards to the Kuomintang right-wingers, there was not a single person who did not sum up the whole business in the phrase, "It's terrible". Under the impact of the views of the "It is terrible" school then flooding the city, even quite revolutionary minded people became downhearted as they pictured the events in the countryside in their mind's eye; and they were unable to deny the word "terrible" ... But as already mentioned, the fact is that the great peasant masses have risen to fulfill their historic mission and that the forces of rural democracy have risen to overthrow the forces of rural feudalism ... It's fine. It is not "terrible" at all. It is anything but terrible. No revolutionary comrade should echo this nonsense.[28]

In Dacca, however, many "revolutionaries" did take fright at what they referred to as peasant "excesses" and there were constant appeals for calm and quiet in the countryside. While the bourgeoisie was trying to patch up its differences at the meeting in Rawalpindi, the class struggle was accelerating. The *gherao* movement was also in full swing. Workers laid siege to factories and the management were virtually imprisoned inside. They were not allowed to leave the factory till they had agreed to wage increases which varied from 25 per

[28] Mao Tse tung, *Selected Works* (Peking, 1949), vol. 1, pp. 26–7.

cent to 100 per cent, depending on how many days the managing director had been deprived of food and water.

In this situation it was obvious to everyone that the government was going to be taken over by the army. One of Ayub's Cabinet Ministers had threatened as much at the Round Table Conference. The parties who had refused to attend the D.A.C.-Ayub parleys should have prepared the people for Martial Law, and called for a general strike to observe an anti-Martial-Law Day throughout the country. There can be little doubt that the strike would have been a massive success.

At this crucial moment, Maulana Bhashani left his political base in East Pakistan and embarked on a tour of the western province. In West Pakistan he visited three cities and made extremely inflammatory speeches, which caused his enemies to say that he was acting in league with the army and deliberately exacerbating the situation to provide an excuse for Martial Law.

But the conspiracy theory of historical development, despite its petit-bourgeois attractions, is usually false. The army had quite clearly made up its mind to "save the nation" once again. While they obviously used some of Bhashani's statements to scare the West Pakistani middle class, in their minds the matter was settled. It was only a question of preparing the prologue, and the fact that the upsurge seemed to be tailing off did not suit the plans of the Generals. Their aim was to put forward a picture of a country on the verge of destruction, and themselves as the saviours. Ayub had used the same method in 1958.

But the developed political consciousness of the masses now called for more elaborate and sophisticated stage management. The game proceeded on two different levels. Ayub was encouraged to go ahead with his Round Table Conference talks with the D.A.C. leaders on March 10th. By this stage he was a complete wreck, mentally, morally and physically. The humiliation of being forced to deal with men some of whom he had considered too insignificant to win over, must have been a painful blow. He knew that without the army he was politically dead, and he needed all the encouragement from his pet bureaucrats to continue the charade. The bureaucrats were also desperate to reach some sort of agreement, as they knew that a second Martial Law would weaken their position vis-à-vis the army; but even they knew that the odds were hopeless.

At the Round Table Conference Ayub accepted the major demands of the D.A.C., but would not agree that Progressive Papers Limited should be returned to its previous owners. The D.A.C. leaders, with the honourable exception of the pro-Moscow N.A.P. leader Mozzafar Ahmed, were quite happy to forget this particular demand. It would only have meant giving the newspapers back to the leftists. Better that the status quo be preserved. Mujibur Rehman had pressed both the eleven-point and his six-point demands at the conference. In private he is supposed to have told Daultana; "I'll accept every R.T.C. decision, but this is a prelude to an election and if I am seen to be giving up any part of my programme, Bhashani will win. I'll yield to you but after the elections. If you want to help me against Bhashani you'll help me now."[29]

Soon after the conference ended, Mujibur disassociated himself from the D.A.C.; but this was mere demagogy as the D.A.C. dissolved itself soon afterwards. Its task of forcing the movement to pause had been successful, and the ruling class were once more on top of the situation.

The army had already met Mujibur Rehman when he was in Rawalpindi and it seems clear that the Bengali leader was informed that some sort of an army take-over was imminent; Bhashani, too, seems to have been informed of this and accordingly he cut short his tour and returned to Dacca on March 25th, 1969. A few days before the junta took over, Ayub had replaced the two provincial Governors and replaced them with two less despised civilians. Both the new Governors seemed to think that the "trouble" was dying down and the provinces returning to calm. The West Pakistan Governor, Mr Yusuf Haroon, visited Rawalpindi to tell Ayub and the army chiefs that all was well. He was met by Air Marshal Nur Khan who asked him to present a different report. The new report stated that the situation was worse than before.

On March 26th, President Ayub asked the army to take over and handed over his powers to them. Senior officers had seen the whole revolutionary uprising as a serious challenge to the army and the social system in Pakistan, with which the army leadership was well integrated. They had to reassert their authority, but without Ayub, as he and his family had brought only disgrace to the army – with the assistance, of course, of the "cursed" bureaucrats.

So the long-expected Martial Law was declared. It was welcomed by all the bourgeois political leaders, including Bhutto. Bhashani

[29] Interview with author.

claimed he was opposed to it, and Mujibur Rehman remained silent. Ayub retired to his son-in-law's estate in Swat, but he continued to meet the new Boss, Yahya Khan. The three months of hard and sustained struggle had been betrayed first of all by the bourgeois leaders, and their actions had paved the way for another army takeover. "Instead of *society* having conquered a new content for itself, it seems that the *state* only returned to its oldest form, to the shamelessly simple domination of the sabre and the cowl."[30]

[30] Karl Marx, *The Eighteenth Brumaire of Louis Bonaparte* (Moscow, 1968), p. 13.

CHAPTER EIGHT

Pakistan and the Permanent Revolution

> "It is nonsense to say that stages cannot in general be skipped. The living historical process always makes leaps over isolated 'stages' which derive from theoretical breakdown into its component parts of the process of development in its entirety, that is, taken in its fullest scope. The same is demanded of revolutionary policy at critical moments. It may be said that the first distinction between a revolutionist and a vulgar evolutionist lies in the capacity to recognize and exploit such moments." Leon Trotsky, *Permanent Revolution*

When the Russian workers seized state power under the leadership of the Bolshevik Party in October 1917 and expropriated the capitalists inside Russia, the effect on the oppressed throughout the world was electric—as it was on international capitalism, too; the Russian revolution seemed like an earthquake which would swallow them all up in a matter of years. They sent their armies to aid the counter-revolution, but were forced to admit defeat. The Red army, organized and led by Trotsky, had become a powerful revolutionary force, thanks to the support it received from the workers and poor peasants.

Despite the hopes of the Bolshevik leaders, the revolution did not spread to Europe (with the short-lived exception of Bela Kun's Hungary). With the victory of the German counter-revolution and the murder of its leaders Rosa Luxemburg and Karl Liebnicht, the Russian revolution was completely isolated. This isolation was to have serious repercussions on developments inside the Soviet Union. The victory of the Stalin faction inside the Bolshevik Party and the proclamation that it was possible to achieve "socialism in one country" saw the beginning of the degeneration of the Russian revolution. Stalin had made a virtue out of an unfortunate and temporary necessity, and abandoned both theoretically and in practice the world revolution. The Soviet Union had become a dictatorship of the bureaucracy. Gradually all vestiges of internationalism were to be removed from the Soviet Union, starting with the expulsion of Leon Trotsky from the party both he and Lenin had led to victory and from the country he had helped save from counter-revolution, and ending with the liquidation of all the old Bolsheviks and even some members of the Stalin faction.[1]

But while permanent revolution had been defeated inside the Soviet Union and also in Europe, whose Communist Parties were under the control of the by now completely Stalinized Comintern; elsewhere the tide of revolution could only be halted temporarily. Despite Stalin's reformist and anti-revolutionary theories, he could not stem the advancing revolution in China, though he tried many times. While Mao sometimes agreed with Stalin in the field of theory, in practice he followed his own line, which was largely responsible for the success of the Chinese revolution in 1949.

Mao refused to liquidate the Chinese Communist Party by merging it with the Kuomintang, under the domination of Chiang Kai-shek. More important, he never allowed anything to interfere with the development of an independent Communist *army*, and because of this even the paper alliances which the Comintern forced him to enter into with Chiang Kai-shek, remained totally meaningless. Chiang himself had no doubts as to the class character of the Chinese party and army. Even when the country was under Japanese occupation, he continued to devote his energies to fighting the Communists, because for him the latter were a deep-rooted "cancer", while the Japanese were simply a "disease" which could be cured. The success of Mao's armies and the establishment of the People's Republic of China in October 1949 was a vindication of the theory of permanent revolution.

Even if Mao had wanted to, he could not have maintained for long an indeterminate social structure. China was, without doubt, a

[1] It is not considered necessary here to go into the causes which led to the degeneration of the Russian revolution. However, the subject is extremely important for all revolutionaries and the following texts are recommended; *The Revolution Betrayed*, *Permanent Revolution*, and *In Defence of Marxism* by Leon Trotsky (New York, 1965, 1969, 1965, respectively). In Britain the books are available from Pioneer Book Service, 182 Pentonville Road, N.1. Also *Soviet History Falsified: Why?* (Bombay, 1965), by Ernest Mandel, available at the same address. For a history of the fourth International which was founded by Trotsky in 1938 to combat the degeneration of the Stalinist Third International after the betrayal of the Spanish Workers the only available text is in French by a leader of the Ligue Communiste (the French Section of the Fourth International) and a one-time secretary of Trotsky: *La Quatrième Internationale* by Pierre Frank (Paris 1969). An excellent anthology called *Fifty Years of World Revolution*, edited by Ernest Mandel (New York, 1969), would also be useful for a general understanding of the development of permanent revolutionary forces throughout the world.

workers' state. It had removed the world's largest country from the sphere of world capitalism and laid the foundations of a future socialist society. The Chinese revolution gave a boost to the struggle in Vietnam and to revolutionary forces throughout Asia.

The victory of the Cuban revolution added a new dimension to the permanent revolution. The emergence of the first workers' state in the American continent, only a few miles off the shores of the citadel of imperialism, the United States of America, acted as a powerful stimulant to guerrilla struggles elsewhere in the continent. It also increased the pressure on United States capitalism and forced the "liberal" President Kennedy to attempt an invasion of the Bay of Pigs, which failed miserably, defeated by the power of the Cuban workers and peasants armed by the Castro government.

Now Castro, too, was faced with the logic of the permanent revolution. He was to discover that there was no third way; either Cuba was to return to its former position as a favoured client state of United States imperialism, or it had to break decisively with the past, expropriate the indigenous capitalists and the foreign exploiters and declare Cuba a socialist country. Castro chose the latter alternative; he realized that even though it meant tying Cuba to the Soviet bloc, this was a more progressive solution to Cuba's problems than any alliance with imperialism.

It could be argued that Fidel and Che were extremely irresponsible to organize a revolution in Cuba without waiting for either a socialist revolution in the United States or a political revolution in the Soviet Union; either would have helped the Cuban revolution develop in a pure fashion. But the Eurocentric "Marxists" who argue this reveal themselves to be completely out of touch with the realities of the daily struggles which are taking place throughout the semi-colonial world.

After the victory of the Cuban revolution the imperialists launched a counter-offensive, and in the early 'sixties the revolutionary movement in the exploited countries suffered some serious setbacks. Without wishing to digress into the details of the rise of military dictatorships and the slackening of the mass movements in Brazil and Argentina, it is necessary to link them to the overthrow of Lumumba, his subsequent murder in the Congo, and the downfall of Nkrumah and Ben Bella in Ghana and Algeria.

The last two cases should be studied in detail by those who preach the "stages theory" of revolution. The tragedy of Indonesia is another case in point: here a Communist Party (the P.K.I.) with a mass membership and control of both the trade unions and the peasant organizations carried its belief in the theory of "revolution by stages" to the point where the net result was the brutal massacre of over a million unarmed Communists and fellow travellers. The leadership of the Indonesian Communist Party were still hoping that Sukarno would save them, even after the murders had begun and the blood of their leading cadres was making Indonesia's streams and rivers run red.

The defeat of the P.K.I. and the murder of its leader, D. N. Aidit, was a tremendous victory for the forces of counter-revolution. It should have convinced every Indonesian revolutionary that there was no "third way": that when a powerful alternative to an existing oligarchy and a corrupt social structure exists in the form of a worker-peasant organization, then it is necessary to exploit the situation and prepare for a seizure of state power. If the P.K.I. cadres had been prepared for a struggle it it possible that the first steps might have been taken towards a socialist revolution in Indonesia, preceded by a civil war which might even have diverted some United States troops from Vietnam and opened a second front against imperialism in Asia. The lessons of Indonesia should be studied closely by all revolutionaries; mistakes were made there which no revolutionary movement can afford to make a second time. A nationalist petit-bourgeoisie cannot be relied on to lead the anti-imperialist struggle without a transition to revolutionary socialism. The Nassers, Sukarnos and Nehrus discovered that their era was over and that they were being overtaken by history, though this process has by no means been completed.

In 1967 the military defeat of Egypt and Syria in the Six-Day War was a further boost to the increasing force of counter-revolution. American imperialism thought that it could bring its successful world-wide counter-offensive to a climax by inflicting a crushing military defeat on the Vietcong armies in South Vietnam. But here they were in for an unpleasant surprise.

In Vietnam the N.L.F. leadership was not simply fighting imperialism; it was also carrying out a social revolution in areas under its control. The contrast between the superior social and political organization of the Vietnamese revolutionaries and the corrupt and decadent puppet regime backed by America's military might was never more apparent. The revolutionary fervour and unprecedented militancy of the Vietnamese workers, peasants and students in both North and South Vietnam blocked decisively the march of reaction in Asia. The Tet Offensive launched by the N.L.F. guerrillas in February and March 1968, revealed the enormous reserves of the Vietnamese. It was a military, political and psychological defeat for the United States and also the most influential factor in Lyndon Baines Johnson's decision not to seek re-nomination for the American presidency.

In Western Europe the Tet Offensive inspired massive demonstrations against American imperialism in virtually every capital in Europe, while in the United States itself the liberal democratic establishment, headed by Senator Eugene McCarthy and the late Robert Kennedy, decided that it was now opportune to make "opposition" to the war respectable. The realization that the Vietnamese were capable of inflicting defeats on American forces shattered the myths to which the American establishment had subscribed for a long time. At the same time the ruling class in the United States began to realize that even the immense resources which it controlled were not sufficient to finance simultaneously a "conventional" war in South-East Asia (Vietnam, Laos, Thailand), nuclear armaments in competition with the U.S.S.R., reforms at home which were badly needed to decrease the internal tensions, and of course the global responsibilities of American capital.

The offensive of the Vietnamese revolution in the first few months of 1968 was one of the main reasons for the sharp increase in radical consciousness throughout the advanced industrialized capitalist countries in Western Europe. The successes of the Vietnamese were largely responsible for breaking the ideological straitjacket of the cold war, in which capitalism had succeeded in confining its youth. There was a resurgence of revolutionary fervour in Europe, of which the most striking and stirring example was the May revolt in France, undoubtedly the most significant post-war development in Western Europe.

A student strike in France, symbolized by the fight on the barricades on the night of May 10th, had succeeded in triggering off a massive general strike. For several days it seemed possible that the bourgeois state would be overthrown and that the workers would seize power. The reactionary role of the French Communist Party, which has been brilliantly documented elsewhere,[2] was largely

---

[2] Ernest Mandel, "The Lessons of May", *New Left Review*, No. 52.

responsible for the failure of the upsurge to develop further. However, the united action by the French students and workers paved the way to similar movements in other countries, particularly Italy, and succeeded in frightening the ruling classes throughout the capitalist world. The spectre of a new French revolution began to haunt the bourgeoisie in Western Europe and the bureaucratic elites in Eastern Europe and the Soviet Union. Both groups saw the new revolution as affecting their interests and changing the balance of class forces in Europe.

France had been considered the most stable country on the continent by bourgeois sociologists and the State Department in Washington. The May explosion frightened them, not so much by its concrete achievements but by the power of its example. A few months later the most "stable" country in Latin America, and the only one in which it was considered "safe" enough to hold the Olympic Games, exploded in a mass upsurge of the Mexican students and workers. The revolt was crushed in the most brutal way. While the athletes exhibited their prowess in the Olympic Stadium, the Mexican regime was exhibiting its prowess in the art of repression by crushing the workers and students who dared question the benevolence of the government.[3] Pakistan, too, was considered to be a model country for the development of free enterprise, and the November explosion which continued for four months must have caused some anxious moments to the policy-makers in Washington.

But in Pakistan, as in Mexico and France, no revolutionary Marxist party with a base in the key sectors of struggle was ready to pose the question of seizing state power. This, then, is the immediate task for revolutionary Marxists in Pakistan — and of course elsewhere: to build a revolutionary party which will end the system of capitalist property relations and substitute a government of the workers and poor peasants. A study of the class forces in Pakistan will enable us to picture clearly the state of both the Right and Left formations in East and West Pakistan, and to determine whom they represent and what role they can play in the struggle for socialism.

Class forces in Pakistan

1. *West Pakistan* and its component parts: Punjab, Sind, Baluchistan and the North West Frontier Province

[3] *Black Dwarf*, October 15th, 1968.

i. *The landlord class*

In economically backward West Pakistan the feudal and semi-feudal forces still maintain their power. Under British imperialism the landlords were the most loyal and useful weapon against mass movements, and they kept the peasantry firmly under their control. The landlords were in fact *created* by the British in a countryside in which the land had been controlled by village communities or was owned by the farmer who tilled it. In 1793 the Permanent Settlement scheme of Lord Cornwallis created a class of permanent landlords; in most cases the tax collectors in the countryside were given large tracts of land by the British; they thus became the most loyal sector and faithfully collaborated with imperialism till it was forced into a tactical withdrawal. The results of the Permanent Settlement were far-reaching and a later Indian Viceroy assessed them thus:

> If security was wanting against extensive popular tumult or revolution, I should say that the Permanent Settlement, though a failure in many other respects and in most important essentials, has this great advantage at least, of having created a vast body of rich landed proprietors deeply interested in the continuance of the British Dominion and having complete command over the mass of the people.[4]

The "land reforms" which were carried out in West Pakistan by the Ayub regime have left intact the entire system of feudal relationships in the countryside. No more than 1·6 per cent of the cultivable land in West Pakistan was redistributed, and the agrarian problem is still as pressing as always.

After the Partition of India the landlords continued to exercise their power in West Pakistan, and they are undoubtedly the most backward and reactionary class in Pakistan today. Externally they are forced by their class background to harmonize their views with the policies of the international bourgeoisie. Internally they stand for a maintenance of the status quo and are opposed to land reform on principle, though now and again they are forced to make certain tactical readjustments. They have not always been free from party ties. Immediately after Partition they were in the Muslim League, and while the bulk of them have remained loyal to the League, others have supported right-wing deviations and set up independent formations, the most prominent of which was the former Republican Party.

[4] Lord William Bentinck, quoted in R. P. Dutt, *India Today* (London, 1940).

The staunchest defender of feudal property relations, apart from the feudal political parties, is the Pakistan army. Since 1947 the Pakistan army and its leadership has rested in the hands of the feudal and lumpen-feudal elements. The officer class has had strong links with the countryside, and many landlords have traditionally sent their younger sons into the army. Even more important nowadays, the army's influence ensures that retired army officers are given preference, along with former bureaucrats, whenever there are auctions of state-owned land; as a result, ex-army officers and ex-bureaucrats are a significant proportion of middle landlords in West Pakistan, and the ties between the army and civil service are very close. The army has grown to over five times its size since 1958, and there has been an influx of non-feudal officers, but it will be some time before they can gain positions of power.

The feudal landlords have also developed links with the bureaucracy and the national bourgeoisie, and the network of inter-relationships which exists renders an overthrow of feudalism impossible within the existing framework. However, the feudal landlord belongs to a class which is historically finished, and it is only a matter of time before the class he represents is swept off the stage of Asian history.

ii. *The "national bourgeoisie"*

The bourgeoisie as a class is the upholder of the capitalist, "free enterprise", mode of production. The main characteristic of the bourgeoisie in West Pakistan is its relative inexperience; it has been in existence only since the establishment of Pakistan in 1947. But its inexperience manifests itself chiefly in its conduct of politics; it has undoubtedly made enormous progress in the sphere of industry.

The social groups which now comprise the bourgeoisie in Pakistan played a decisive part in the political struggle against British imperialism and in the setting up of a separate Muslim state, but once their narrow class interests had been satisfied they became a counter-revolutionary and anti-progressive force in Pakistani politics. Moreover it is perhaps anomalous even to consider the Pakistani bourgeoisie as a "national bourgeoisie" in any meaningful sense. They are tied financially to American finance-capital, and should therefore be categorized as the Pakistani section of international capitalism.

The near-monopoly positions of the robber baron industrialists enabled them to obtain profits which were as high as 80 per cent to 100 per cent, but without their links with foreign capital they could never have achieved this "success". This dependence of the capitalist class, and in fact of the entire economy, on foreign capital has been increasing rather than decreasing over the last decade. The statistics provided by the Government of Pakistan are revealing. They show that the total capital imports have increased by 100 per cent from 1955 to 1965, and the projected increase from 1965 to 1970 was given as another 100 per cent. About 32 per cent of the total development expenditure of Pakistan is shown to be directly dependent on foreign aid which could be used only in consultation with American economic advisers supplied by the Development Advisory Service (D.A.S.) based at Harvard University. Thus the actions of the Pakistani bourgeoisie were in most instances taken on instructions they received from the monopoly capitalists in the "advanced" capitalist world.

However, the lessons taught by the D.A.S. have been in the best traditions of monopoly capitalism. In 1968, as we mentioned earlier, the Chief Economist of the Pakistan Planning Commission revealed during the course of a speech that twenty leading industrialist families controlled 66 per cent of the industrial assets of the country, 70 per cent of insurance and 80 per cent of banking interests. At the same time over 25 per cent of the labour force was unemployed (including seasonal unemployment) and the Pakistani worker one of the worst paid in the world. The disparities were becoming sharper every day, but the D.A.S. could only note in its annual review for 1967-8: "Although the President's illness created a period of uncertainty, progress in economic policy and performance was excellent."

Despite its economic strength, the Pakistani bourgeoisie has not been able to develop a strong social base. It has had to rely on the bureaucracy to preserve and defend its class interests and this has prevented the emergence of a classic bourgeois party in Western Pakistan. The strength of the bureaucracy and the weakness of the political parties in Pakistan has created a situation where the bourgeoisie feels that the bureaucracy and the army will continue to fight for its interests, while its own political activity is usually confined to giving large bribes to all the parties it believes to have a following, simply as an insurance for the future. The links between the bureaucracy and the bourgeoisie are becoming even closer now because many bureaucrats are personally involved in financial deals to make money in collaboration with the bourgeoisie. The stability of the bureaucracy, in contrast to the shifting political parties, helped to attract the industrialists and strengthen the ties between them. Obviously, in these conditions an alliance of the "national" bourgeoisie and the revolutionary socialists is not on the agenda.

iii. The petit-bourgeoisie

This class is far from being united or cohesive, and can be divided into the upper and lower petit-bourgeoisie. The former includes many businessmen who have been ruined by the soaring costs of inflation, or who have obtained and lost import and export licences; they are determined to try and get rich again, and this colours their political outlook. Their economic status is close to that of the middle bourgeoisie (except in exceptional circumstances), and they are suspicious of the revolutionary movement. Some of them are large shopkeepers in the cities, others are small moneylenders in the countryside. Of late they have been joined by the petty bureaucrats, technocrats and small building contractors, office clerks, small lawyers and school teachers in the higher wage brackets.

In the countryside the rich peasants comprise the bulk of the upper ranks of the petit-bourgeoisie. They work on their own land, but they use their surplus money or crops to hire landless labourers to work for them and help increase their surplus, so that they can buy still more land. They are opposed to the big landlords, and in favour of land reforms which will break up the big estates so that capitalist property relations can be extended to the countryside. They will therefore give limited support to movements which they believe can achieve this. However, the limits to their desire for social reform are narrow and well defined, and while opposed to feudalism they are the main social force which props up the big bourgeoisie. When the anti-Ayub movement in Pakistan was at its peak and had become consciously anti-capitalist, the upper petit-bourgeoisie together with the big bourgeoisie and the feudal landlords welcomed the intervention of the Pakistan army, as they believed that at that juncture it was the only force which could preserve the system. Ideologically they are represented to a certain extent by the People's Party led by Mr Bhutto, and in the North West Frontier Province and Baluchistan by the pro-Moscow section of the National Awami Party.

The lower petit-bourgeoisie, who constitute the majority of this class, fall into two main groups. First, there are those who are economically self-supporting and self-sufficient. They would like to get rich, but economic conditions make it impossible. The peasant who tills his own land and just manages to eke out an existence is the best example of this class. However, because of the general economic situation he is constantly being forced to work harder to earn the same money, and in times of economic crisis he will at best have to do part-time work on someone else's land to make both ends meet or at worst sell his land and join the ranks of the landless labourers. Experience has made him hostile to the "rich", but before he joins any movement to unseat them he has to be convinced of the likelihood of its success, as if it fails he has everything to lose and nothing to gain. However, as a group they are not hostile to the revolutionary movement. In the cities the bulk of the students are in a similar situation, as are the lower ranks of teachers and university lecturers.

Second, there are those who are on the lowest rung of the petit-bourgeois ladder: the left-wing of the petit-bourgeois. It includes sections of students, office peons, shop assistants and small handicraftsmen. Their standard of living is constantly falling and their economic status is little different from that of the higher paid proletarians. In times of extreme reaction they are subject to bourgeois pressures, but normally they support the actions of the workers and poor peasants, and in a revolutionary struggle they will fight shoulder to shoulder with them. As a class they have become extremely responsive to socialist ideas, though in certain circumstances they can be used as tools of the bourgeoisie to promote chauvinism and communalism; but then this is true also for sections of the working class. They support the left faction of the National Awami Party in West Pakistan and also the right faction in certain areas of the Punjab.

iv. *The peasants/semi-proletarians*

The peasantry comprise the large majority of the population of West Pakistan. The "semi-proletariat" consist of the semi-owner peasants and the poor peasants who between them constitute a majority in the countryside. Most poor peasants are sharecroppers, and they cultivate land owned by a landlord who has the right to one-third or even one-half of their yield. Others are agricultural labourers, who have no land but are paid to work for the landlord or the rich peasant. These are the rural proletariat.

The owner-peasant who needs to work on a rich peasant's land some of the time in order to maintain his own land can be described as a semi-proletarian. The owner-peasant who neither does extra work nor employs extra help is the middle peasant.

Since a large majority of the population of West Pakistan lives in the countryside, it is worth making a breakdown of the rural social structure.

a. *Big Landlords* own more than 100 acres of land and number 63,348, according to the Census of Agriculture published in 1963–4. Between them they own 15,162,470 acres, which constitutes 31·2 per cent of the total area under private control. These landlords represent statistically 1·25 per cent of the total number of landowners in West Pakistan, and of them 6,061 landlords, 0·12 per cent of all the landowners, own 11·5 per cent of the total area.

b. *Rich peasants/kulaks* own between 25 and 100 acres of land and number 286,470. The area they own amounts to 10,616,308 acres, or 21·9 per cent of the total, and they represent 5·66 per cent of the total ownership of land in West Pakistan. They are the bastions of the rural bourgeoisie, and while the possibility exists that during a revolutionary upsurge they might send armed followers to raid a big landlord's estate to revenge themselves for their comparatively inferior social position, they will rarely, if ever, join hands with the peasant-proprietors or the poor peasants to overthrow the forces of feudalism in the countryside. They are much more likely to collaborate with the political party representing their class interests to change the existing order in the countryside. Very likely the landless labourers they employ will eventually rise in revolt against their poor treatment and conditions and burn the houses of their employers. It is possible that in a situation where there is a very strong peasant association the rich peasant might join it, either to prevent being isolated or in an attempt to try and control the association and render it harmless.

c. *Middle peasants* own between 5 and 25 acres. The total area under their control is 15,438,138 acres, representing 31·7 per cent of the total in West Pakistan, and the peasants themselves constitute 28·65 per cent of the total owners. However, the statistics do not reveal what percentage of the land owned by the middle peasants and the peasant-proprietors is in fact cultivable, or what difficulties are involved in ensuring a regular water supply.

d. *Poor peasants* own less than 5 acres of land and number 3,266,137, constituting 64·4 per cent of the total owners and owning a total area of 7,425,614 acres, or simply 15·25 per cent of the whole. When these figures are studied in detail, a figure emerges of 742,216 peasants who own *less* than one acre of land and as a result have to cultivate land belonging to the middle or rich peasants to stave off starvation. The figure 742,216 does not include the families of these peasants, and even an extremely optimistic view would multiply the figure by three, though in reality the average family is much larger. These peasants are the semi-proletarians about whom Mao Tse tung waxed so eloquent in his celebrated studies on the peasantry.[5]

e. *Poor peasants/sharecroppers and rural proletarians*. There are over two million landless peasants in West Pakistan who are tenant-sharecroppers and who cultivate more than half of the cultivated land in the province. The best part of the produce is appropriated by the landlord; the peasant sells the remainder at the local market, which is manipulated by the local landlord who buys the peasant's raw produce at artificially low prices and then sells it back to the peasant at extortionate rates. This is only a minor example of the oppression inflicted on the peasant by the landlord; in some areas the landlord still has the *droit de seigneur* over a peasant's bride. The rights of these tenant-peasants are virtually non-existent. In 1952 in the Punjab region of West Pakistan over 200,000 peasants were ejected from their land by the combined force of the landlords and the local police. In 1969 a majority of these peasants were still in constant risk of eviction.

However, compared with the rural proletarian the tenant-peasant is living in a paradise. He has no land at all and is forced to work for landlords and rich peasants. His existence is little better than that of a slave, and the money he earns is hardly enough for him to feed himself, let alone his family. He is forced to work for 112 hours a week. There are 700,000 of these serfs in West Pakistan—and this figure does not include their families. Their discontent, which for the moment they have no option but to suppress, will one day explode so violently that they will tear down and destroy everything and anything that stands in their way. They will not distinguish between big landlord and rich peasant. Anyone who is not for them will be against them. The anger, bitterness and despair which has been building up over the years will be the motive force of the revolution in the countryside, and the peasant uprising in West Pakistan will make the

[5] Mao Tse tung, "Analysis of the Classes in Chinese Society", and "Investigation of the Peasant Movement in Hunan" in *Selected Works* (Peking, 1949), vol. 1.

revolts of the Chinese peasantry in the 'thirties and 'forties pale by comparison.

Even if the bourgeoisie succeed in abolishing the big landlords as a class, they will substitute for them a new class of rich farmers who will own "economic" holdings and will continue to exploit the poor peasants in an even more brutal fashion. The agrarian revolution can only be successful when the entire system of capitalist property relations is abolished in both the towns and the countryside. The bourgeoisie is not capable of effecting this revolution in the countryside, as the development of both the Russian and Chinese revolutions has shown. The poor peasants in Pakistan will play an extremely important role in the coming Pakistani revolution, and those Menshevik-minded reformists who ignore them do so at their peril.

v. The proletariat

According to the last Census, in 1961, the urban population in Pakistan had grown from 7,839,000 in 1951 to 12,255,000 ten years later, an increase of 56 per cent. In West Pakistan it had grown from roughly 6 million to 9 million, an increase of 59·7 per cent. The distribution of population in West Pakistan in 1961 was 75·5 per cent in the countryside and 24·5 per cent in the towns, and the figure is bound to have increased since then according to the pace of industrialization.

The West Pakistani proletariat is concentrated in manufacturing industries, mining, communications, transport. At the moment there is a heavy concentration of workers in Karachi, Lahore and Lyallpur, though with the proposed machine-tool complex near Rawalpindi, that city, too, will become extremely important.

The urban proletariat, small though it is in comparison with the rural peasantry, is a necessary component for the leadership of the revolution. It is only when the rural and urban proletarians unite behind a revolutionary party led by their best class-conscious cadres that we will be able to achieve a revolution in Pakistan.

The rate of development of the industrial sector in West Pakistan has been fairly high, and there has been a corresponding increase in the numbers of the Pakistani working class. There can be no doubt that the capitalist class of West Pakistan is aware of this, and has been carefully consolidating its economic and political strength. However, the rapid pace of industrialization has not resulted in an increase in the standard of living of the Pakistani worker. On the contrary, industrialization has taken place under the direction of the givers of foreign loans, and the tax exemptions, tariff protections, export bonus schemes and so on that they have provided have benefited few but the Pakistani capitalist, who also enjoys the right to charge the highest possible price for the goods he manufactures. Even Gunnar Myrdal was forced to acknowledge the truth of this situation, and though he continued to see Ayub as the best alternative, he nevertheless described in Volume 1 of his *Asian Drama* the growth of Pakistani capitalism:

> Large amounts allotted for development projects benefitted financial backers of ruling parties. Inflation was countenanced while the Rupee's high international rate was maintained, distorting priorities and encouraging less essential types of consumption. Large investments took place in residential construction for the upper classes; fortunes were accumulated by building shoddy hotels, running cinemas, money-lending and dealing in import or export licences. Evasion of taxes was rewarded by government subsidies to defaulters. Smuggling, black-marketing, auction of licences and permits for replenishing party funds, bribery and corruption were rampant ... [6]

Myrdal is describing the situation on the eve of Ayub's Martial Law, but it is beyond all doubt that it became ten times worse during the "decade of development". The workers in the towns, the urban equivalent of the rural proletarians, are paid subsistence wages; they live in hovels, their children die for lack of food and medical aid and they themselves cannot afford to be ill. Some are unemployed for years at a stretch.

Despite the harsh labour laws of the Ayub regime and the legally institutionalized wage-freeze, the Pakistani workers have fought back, displaying a pugnacity reminiscent of the Russian workers before 1905. Though they lack an organization on a provincial level, the workers have used their own imagination and initiative and have won a number of important victories. Their participation in the struggle against the Ayub dictatorship, and their decision to continue to strike after the March 1969 Martial Law of Yahya Khan (the penalty for striking ranges from twenty-five years' imprisonment to death), shows the maturity of the urban proletariat. The workers'

[6] Harmondsworth, 1968, vol. 1, p. 305.

organizations are extremely weak in West Pakistan and there are very few trade-union leaders who command any real respect. In most cases the employers and the government have succeeded in foisting stooge trade unions in key sectors. However this situation is changing, mainly because of the pressure of the workers themselves. The task of harnessing the growing consciousness of the proletariat to the building of a strong revolutionary party, has at the present moment assumed a crucial importance.

2. East Pakistan

The situation in East Pakistan is in some respects so completely different from West Pakistan that it warrants dealing with the class forces in East Pakistan separately. Where the two provinces coincide, what has been said for the West holds true for the East. But first of all, two important aspects of the class structure must be confronted by any revolutionary socialists trying to analyse the situation in this province.

i. The "national bourgeoisie"

This does not exist as an economic force because East Pakistan has not been allowed to produce its own indigenous capitalist class. The big industrialists established in East Pakistan are all non-Bengalis, and there is not a single Bengali family among the infamous twenty families which control the country's economy. Bengali politics – in East Bengal at any rate – have traditionally been dominated by the upper petit-bourgeoisie. In the absence of a Muslim feudal or capitalist class it was the Muslim petit-bourgeois who led the struggle for Pakistan in Eastern Bengal; in their eyes it was a way of getting rid of the hated Hindu entrepreneur who dominated Bengali finance and exercized political power in league with the landlords.

In East Bengal the establishment of Pakistan has simply resulted in non-Bengalis, mainly from West Pakistan, filling the place of the departed Hindus. The industrialists used the foreign-exchange jute earnings of East Pakistan to industrialize West Pakistan, and this exploitation was bound to provoke a nationalist response. The national question, therefore, has been in the forefront ever since Partition. The Bengali petit-bourgeoisie has felt deprived of its rightful inheritance. In addition, the bureaucracy and the army, which have always dominated Pakistani politics in one way or another, had few Bengali members – considering that the majority of the population of Pakistan lived in Bengal the representation was really pitiful –

and were seen in Bengal as instruments of the class rule by West Pakistani magnates.

The West Pakistani rulers added insult to injury by constantly scheming to deny East Pakistan majority representation in the Central government; it was precisely to prevent this that Ayub took over in 1958. The demand for "autonomy" continued to increase in popularity and efforts by the Central government to deal with the situation by repression ended in failure.

The Awami League is the party of the urban upper petit-bourgeoisie, and its propaganda on the national question has won it considerable support in the major cities of East Pakistan. The lower petit-bourgeoisie seems to articulate its demands through the pro-Peking National Awami Party, which is a mixture of populism and petit-bourgeois nationalism. It has significant peasant support in North Bengal and some influence amongst the trade unions. The "Communists" who work within the party refuse to build strong and independent working class organizations; they declare that in Pakistan the situation is not ripe to build a proletarian party, and ask their co-thinkers to work within bourgeois parties. The total bankruptcy of this Menshevik-type revision of Marxism-Leninism should have been apparent during the December 1968–March 1969 uprising, when for a few days the students were in complete control of Dacca and a strong working class response could have resulted in worker-student councils being established to administer the city. The students who stress the need for building a proletarian party are denounced by our latter-day Mensheviks as "adventurist, Trotskyist and Guevarist". They are accused of over-optimism and an incorrect estimate of the revolutionary possibilities.

ii. *The agrarian question*

Although the population of East Pakistan is larger than that of the West, the geographical area is much smaller, and the high population density puts continual pressure on the land. (The total surveyed area in West Pakistan is just over 104 million acres and in East Pakistan it is just above 21 million acres.) Most of the feudal landlords in East Bengal were Hindus, and in an attempt to deprive them of their land the East Pakistan government passed in 1950 the East Pakistan Acquisition and Tenancy Act, which forbade holdings of over 33 acres and abolished the agency of the middlemen who used to collect rent from the peasants on behalf of the landlords. As a result of this measure most of the Hindu landlords left East Bengal for India, and their land was given to the peasants who were working on it or redistributed. Feudalism, therefore, does not exist in East Pakistan.

However, the number of poor peasants is constantly on the increase. Peasants owning less than 5 acres account for the largest area of land (9,254,734 acres), and of this total 3,529,995 acres are held in holdings of less than $2\frac{1}{2}$ acres. Over 4 million peasants and their families are in this category, while in comparison to West Pakistan the figure of tenant-sharecroppers is low — only 100,000. Landless labourers account for 1·4 million peasants and their families in addition to 3·2 million peasants who are forced to do similar work on a less regular basis. Thus we see that the number of landless labourers and those owning a small area of land is roughly equal.

The peasants with small landholdings are being forced to sell parts of their land in order to pay land tax and other debts. The holdings suffer a further division when a peasant dies, as his land is divided amongst his children and the result is several virtually worthless holdings. In many cases the new owners have no option but to sell their land to the rich peasant. The number of landless peasants is therefore rapidly increasing and these rural proletarians are employed regularly for only four months of the year.

The poor peasant who owns a small landholding is exploited by the state, which levies taxes on his land and on every commodity he produces, including the house or hut he decides to build. If he cannot pay his tax the government confiscates and auctions his land, and to prevent this the poor peasant will increase his indebtedness tenfold. The rural creditors are in most cases a small group of non-cultivating small landlords who own holdings of over twenty-five acres and have received direct benefits from rural development schemes in East Pakistan.

Though the situation has undoubtedly worsened over the last nine years, even the 1961 census provided a grim picture of the Bengali countryside. While 52 per cent of the peasants tilled their own land, a large majority of them were poverty-stricken smallholders. The average family farm is 3·5 acres, but 51 per cent of the farms are less than 2·5 acres. Landless labourers are 26 per cent of the total cultivators, though by now the figure must have risen by at least another 10 per cent.

While the strength of the peasant organizations is minimal in West Pakistan, in the East they are fairly strong and have an active tradition of militancy. The only viable organization is the peasant group led by Maulana Bhashani, which is supported and sustained by both pro-Moscow and pro-Peking sections of the National Awami Party. But even this is not capable of rising to the needs of the peasants in this phase. A militant peasant organization is required whose main task is to struggle for the peasants and at the same time constantly politicize their militant consciousness.

The situation in the East Pakistani countryside is extremely serious at the moment. A report published in November 1969 by the Forum Research Unit reveals that East Pakistan has been in the grip of a famine for the last three years:

> The arithmetic of this famine is quite simple. Three years ago there was an unexpectedly large fall in rice production, down from 103 lakh tons in 1965–6 to only 94 lakh tons in 1966–7. If a 3 per cent rate of population growth is assumed the requirement in 1966–7 was 114·6 lakh tons [a lakh is equivalent to 100,000 units]. The deficit of over 2 million tons was met partly by the net release of 11·66 lakh tons of rice and wheat by the Food Department ...

However, this was accompanied by a rise of 30 per cent in the price of rice, and large numbers of peasants went hungry. There has been no serious attempt by the government to ease the situation, and peasants continue to starve to death. A natural calamity like a cyclone or a flood could result in a famine of massive proportions which would lead to the death of hundreds of thousands of poor peasants.

iii. *The proletariat*

The urban population in East Pakistan has grown much more slowly than its counterpart in West Pakistan, and the reason for this is partly because of the low level of industrialization, but also because the First and Second Five Year Plans (1955–60 and 1960–5) allocated more funds for developing the Western sector than for the East, and the actual expenditures were even more unbalanced than the planned expenditures. Once West Pakistan was developed industrially it continued to attract capital. A better organized transportation system and other facilities helped this process considerably, and the continued transfer of capital resources from East to West Pakistan further increased the imbalance.

East Pakistan's jute supplies have provided the province with a favourable balance of foreign trade, but government policy has encouraged most of the foreign exchange to be spent in West Pakistan. Internal trade has also had its effect and goods manufactured in West Pakistan are sold at high prices because of transport costs. The third Five Year Plan proposed an increased allocation of 8 per cent more development funds to East than to West Pakistan, but this figure is irrelevant when it comes to reversing the trend of increasing inequality. The increase in urban population in East Pakistan from 1951 to 1961 has been from 4·4 per cent to 5·2 per cent as compared to 17·8 per cent to 24·5 per cent in West Pakistan. While there has obviously been an increase since 1961, the proportion has probably not risen by very much. The per capita income in East Pakistan is much lower than in West Pakistan, but the difference between the wages of East and West Pakistani workers is not very great. In both cases, though wages have risen between 1954 and 1964, the increase has not kept pace with the cost of living.

The Spring 1969 issue of *Pakistan Left Review* documented some interesting figues in this connection. It reported that the average monthly income of a working class family in East Pakistan was Rs. 78 (£7) per family or an average monthly income per head of Rs. 17 (just under £2). In West Pakistan the situation was only marginally better, with an average monthly income per head of Rs. 17·4. The problems faced by the proletariat in both parts of the country are therefore essentially the same. A greater degree of industrialization would not increase the average wage of the Bengali proletarian by more than a few paisas.

What then is the most immediate task?

An analysis of the class forces in both East and West Pakistan shows quite clearly that although the objective conditions for a revolutionary movement are mature what is lacking is a revolutionary party. The existing political parties are totally incapable of solving the fundamental contradiction in the countryside. The pro-Moscow- and pro-Peking- orientated Stalinists have completely abandoned the task of constructing independent vanguard parties because they believe in the theory of revolution by stages and in the completely discredited theory of the "independent" role of the Pakistani bourgeoisie.

The most immediate task facing Pakistani revolutionaries, therefore, is to build a revolutionary party; without one, a seizure of state power by the poor peasants and the proletariat is out of the question. Of course, a revolutionary party is not built simply by abstract propaganda, but in the heat of a struggle; nevertheless, in order to lead the struggle and win over its most advanced participants to the idea of a revolutionary party, it is important to have a nucleus of revolutionary Marxists grouped around a revolutionary programme.

Experience has shown us that all efforts to collaborate with the bourgeoisie in this task have led to tragic disasters. The massacre of the Chinese proletariat in 1927, the betrayal of the Western European proletariat in Spain and France in 1936 and France and Italy in 1946–8, were the results of *incorrect* (only in the case of China) and anti-revolutionary formulations (in every other instance) on the part of the Stalinized Comintern and the Soviet bureaucracy. Three more recent examples are the Geneva Accords of 1954, which were signed by the Vietnamese under Russian pressure, and which constitute the main reason why the Vietnamese revolution is still having to fight in the South; the massacre of the Indonesian Communists in 1965, because of a policy of collaboration with the Sukarno regime and the Indonesian leadership's complete failure to prepare the P.K.I. for the class struggle ahead; and, finally, the total and abject surrender by the French Communist Party in France in May 1968.

These experiences have taught us to formulate some specific points regarding the functions of a revolutionary party in the exploited world:

1. To form an independent political force of the urban and rural proletariat, and to combat the ideological influence of the urban and rural bourgeoisie within the proletarian movement.
2. To give critical support to any *real* anti-imperialist move by the local bourgeoisie (nationalization of Mexican oil, Suez Canal, Bolivian tin, foreign banks, etc.) while constantly explaining the limitations of the class which is compelled, owing to its own inner contradictions, to carry out these policies.
3. To represent the most radical and energetic force within the anti-imperialist movement not only by actions of solidarity with the national liberation movements in the three continents, but by linking these movements to the revolutionary struggle against one's own bourgeoisie, whatever stance it might be adopting at a particular moment.

4. Constantly to alert the toiling masses that a struggle against the bourgeoisie and upper petit-bourgeoisie is essential for a genuine rebirth of the nation; and to remember that the bourgeoisie is incapable of mobilizing the masses for the final thrust against imperialism. In some cases it is not even capable of making initial thrusts.
5. To fight on these political lines for the hegemony of the proletariat in the revolution. In concrete terms it means the victory of the proletarian party in gaining the leadership of the toilers in both town and countryside and leading them to overthrow the bourgeois state and establish the new socialist order.

At the moment there is only one international organization which is advancing this line on an international scale: the Fourth International. However, these rules were not established by Trotsky or the Fourth International. They were the touchstone of Bolshevik policy even before the 1905 revolution in Russia, and the differences of opinion between Bolshevik leaders did not include any doubts about these fundamentals, but were on the question of an intermediate stage between the tasks of the bourgeois-democratic revolution (i.e. the solution of the agrarian problem), the victory of the socialist revolution and the establishment of the dictatorship of the proletariat. This question became somewhat academic after the seizure of state power by the Bolsheviks in 1917 and the question was resolved in the course of history. There could be no intermediate stage. This was stressed still further by the victory of the Chinese and Cuban revolutions.

Many people will no doubt argue that the workers and peasants are still under the influence of bourgeois ideologies, and that they will not be able to understand the complexities of scientific socialism. This is undoubtedly correct, but at the same time it cannot be denied that the workers have been engaged in important struggles throughout East and West Pakistan from November 1968 onwards, notwithstanding the new Martial Law of General Yahya Khan. These struggles have been uncoordinated and sporadic but they have been of a mass nature.

A strategy for the transitional stage before the seizure of power must be formulated. We have seen from the preceding analysis that the most burning questions of the day in Pakistan are linked to the bourgeois-democratic revolution. As we have said, revolutionary history has taught us that revolution *cannot* be accomplished by the bourgeoisie, and that the only party capable of leading the workers and peasants forward to the stage where these tasks can be achieved is a revolutionary party of the rural and urban proletariat. The bourgeois-democratic revolution will therefore also lead to a socialist revolution and to the establishment of a workers' and poor peasants' state.

To help in the work of building a revolutionary party, and coordinating and making more cohesive the struggles of the Pakistani masses, the following demands are suggested as a basis for discussion.

Transitional and democratic demands

1. *The nationalization of all foreign enterprises without confiscation and the confiscation of all foreign assets*

The anti-imperialist fervour of the Pakistani masses has often been diverted into harmless channels by the ruling class, who often use anti-imperialist rhetoric themselves to deceive the masses (e.g. "friendship with China"). This must be mercilessly exposed, and this demand utilized to prove to the masses that the government is incapable of taking any concrete anti-imperialist action to improve the living standards of the working masses.

2. *The national question*

This has emerged as an extremely important facet of Pakistan's political life because of the economic and political exploitation of East Pakistan by West Pakistan capitalists. The right of self-determination must, therefore, be guaranteed to East Pakistan, and it is the duty of all West Pakistani socialists to support this demand. At the same time the revolutionaries in East Pakistan should distinguish their support for national self-determination or autonomy from that of the Bengali upper petit-bourgeoisie by stressing that meaningful autonomy is only possible within a socialist framework.

3. *All repressive laws should be repealed*

The struggle for civil liberties in both the towns and the countryside is an important part of the struggle for socialism. It helps us expose the façade of "democracy" and to show that in countries like Pakistan the bourgeoisie is incapable of guaranteeing complete civil liberties to the people.

4. *Rights of minority communities*

The rights of these communities should be defended by every socialist. It is only when the ruling class is faced with a crisis that it tries to divert attention from the real causes of the crisis by looking for scapegoats and lamenting strife, not only setting Muslims against non-Muslims, but also non-Bengali Muslims agains Bengali Muslims. The duty of socialists is both to expose and fight this, however difficult the conditions may be.

5. *The agrarian question*

1. WEST PAKISTAN

a. Feudalism in the countryside should be abolished by expropriating the estates of the landlords without any compensation.

b. Land to the tiller. Sharecropping should be completely abolished, and the peasants engaged in this medieval practice should be given ownership of the land on which they have worked all their life.

c. All peasant debts should be immediately annulled.

d. The maximum landholding should be fixed at 25 acres of cultivated land in West Pakistan.

e. A minimum wage should be fixed for rural proletarians, and their working hours restricted to 40 per week with a compulsory day of rest.

f. Surplus land expropriated from the big landlords should be used to resettle landless peasants and the rural unemployed in a system of co-operative farming.

g. Marketing facilities should be controlled by the state, and all hoarders and food speculators punished by having all their land confiscated.

h. The water supply should be rationalized and the tube-wells placed under the direct control of elected peasant representatives to ensure a water supply for all. The water rates should be fixed according to the amount of land owned.

i. Moneylending by private individuals should be outlawed, and the state should institute a system of cheap rural credit at low rates of interest.

j. The auction of state lands should be stopped and these lands should be distributed amongst the landless peasants. All land given as a reward for services rendered to government servants, ministers, army officers, should be immediately confiscated and distributed among the poor peasants.

k. Chemical fertilizers and seeds should be distributed only through co-operative societies at cheap prices.

l. Every village should have at least one school and one medical centre, and there should be at least one hospital and technical college for every sixty villages. The number of agricultural universities must be rapidly increased.

2. EAST PAKISTAN

a. Land tax should be abolished completely and replaced with an agricultural tax which should be assessed on the amount of raw material marketed.

b. The marketing of jute should be nationalized and the peasant paid a fair price in proportion to the price of jute on the world market.

c. The fisheries should be brought under state control.

d. The tea plantations should be nationalized and the foreign plantation owners expelled without any compensation. The same demand applies for the sugar-cane workers though in this case the owners are indigenous.

e. The minimum landholding should be $12\frac{1}{2}$ acres and uneconomic holdings should be welded together in co-operative farms which will lead to collectivization. This will of course go with common pooling of implements, animals, etc.

f. A minimum wage should be guaranteed to the increasing number of landless peasants and their hours of work established during employment. Their wage should be sufficient to cover essential expenses for the months during which they are unemployed.

6. *Nationalization of key and basic industries without compensation*

We have already outlined the monopoly conditions which exist in Pakistan. The soaring profits of the capitalist class should be contrasted with the wages of the Pakistani working class. The needs of any effective system of planning necessitate the removal of these industries from the control of a small handful of capitalists. This should go hand in hand with the nationalization of banks, insurance companies and the system of credit. However, we differentiate ourselves from the reformist by rejecting all talk of compensation; by not equating the nationalization by a bourgeois state with a change in the social ownership of the means of production; by continually calling on the masses to rely on their own strength and by linking the question of expropriation with the rights of the workers to control the means of production. The best transitional demand for the latter is a demand for *Workers' Control* in the nationalized industries.

7. *Right of full employment and the right to collective bargaining; sliding scale of wages and sliding scale of hours*

Revolutionary socialists must struggle to combat the rising prices and the increase in unemployment which is characteristic of semi-colonial societies. The rising prices must be followed by automatic rises for the workers in the same proportion. In times of recession the capitalists are forced to cut down on the number of workers they employ. The slogan to advance in this connection is one of sliding hours for *all* workers. It is the duty of trade unions and other mass groupings to bring the unemployed and employed workers together and to demand that work be divided. Employers are expert at dividing the workers' movement, and will no doubt be able to circumvent these demands unless they are fought by a strong trade-union movement which is capable of immobilizing the factories or occupying them till their demands are met. It is also necessary to support the economic struggle of the working class and the fight for democratic rights. The weakness of the trade unions must also be corrected and efforts made to set up a viable trade-union organization on a national scale.

8. *The creation of factory committees*

The phenomenon of weak trade unions combined with spontaneous militancy should lead to the growth of factory or strike committees. The new development in anti-capitalist consciousness is manifested in factory occupations and *gheraos*. In these situations the workers should elect factory committees to negotiate on their behalf, particularly where a trade union is weak, or non-existent, or controlled by the capitalist; an elected committee can become an important force in the factory. The very existence of such committees undermines the power of the capitalist.

9. *Students should control their universities*

The student movement should be allowed to control the political courses and education they receive at the universities. They should have joint committees of staff and students, elected on the basis of one man, one vote, to run the universities. They should also be guaranteed post-graduation jobs and in general the demands outlined in the eleven-point programme of the Students Action Committee of Dacca should become the demands of the entire student movement. (Appendix IV.)

10. *Support for all anti-imperialist and anti-capitalist struggles*

This involves demanding a foreign policy which recognizes the N.L.F. of South Vietnam and withdraws recognition from the puppet government; which will withdraw from CENTO and SEATO and break off relations with Iran for supporting Zionism in the Middle East. Material and moral support should be sent to the liberation movements in Asia, Africa and Latin America. Our foreign policy should offer unconditional defence of the Soviet Union, China and other workers' states against imperialism, but at the same time complete support for the struggle to establish socialist democracy and combat the bureaucracy in the workers' states. As far as India is concerned, we should distinguish between the reactionary Indian government and the Indian masses whose interests are not different from those of oppressed masses throughout the world. We must support all the anti-capitalist manifestations of the Indian workers and peasants. We must demand the right of the Kasmiri people to self-determination and support the struggle of the Nagas for national independence.

11. *And, lastly, for a workers and poor peasants' government in Pakistan*

We must make it absolutely clear that the nature of the demands outlined above is such that no bourgeois government can even begin to implement them. From the struggle for these demands there will emerge a mass revolutionary party which will lead the way to a socialist revolution; only a socialist revolution can solve satisfactorily the contradictions in the countryside and the towns. Class-collaboration has proved fatal in the past, and historical conditions have developed in such a way that there is not even the objective possibility for collaboration with the bourgeoisie on an international scale. There is only one answer – Forward to Socialism.

Military rule or people's power?

This question will rapidly become meaningless, because in the long term this is not the choice the people will have to make. The choice will be between socialist revolution – that is, people's power – or complete and utter disintegration. Military rule is class rule, and in the case of Pakistan the strength of feeling on the national question is such that military rule, however well disguised, will never be acceptable to the people of East Pakistan. In the West, too, there is growing disillusionment and the general malaise will undoubtedly affect the peasants in uniform who form the backbone of the Pakistani army. In a situation where the deepening social crisis is affecting the majority of the population, it will only be a matter of time before the common soldiers are also affected. The question of military rule or people's power will then be solved by the abolition of a mercenary army and its replacement by people's militia. However, if events are not to overtake us we have to create and build the revolutionary vanguard which will enable us to achieve a socialist workers' and peasants' republic in Pakistan.

Chronology of the Uprising:
November 7th, 1968 – March 26th, 1969

(It will be useful to refer to the maps on pages 58 and 86)

1968
NOVEMBER
7th   Rawalpindi: 2,000 Gordon College students demonstrate against custom officials confiscating goods from Landi Kotal; 1 student killed; 3 buses burnt, 4 police wounded; schools and colleges closed.

8th   Karachi: 60 arrested; buses and cars burnt; 4 student leaders arrested; schools and colleges closed in Karachi and Hyderabad. Rawalpindi: troops called in; curfew imposed; students and police clash; 2 G.T.S. buses and two customs wagons burnt; Commercial Bank, National Bank, House Buildings and Finance Corporation and central post office damaged; many arrests. Lahore: schools and colleges closed.

9th   Rawalpindi: curfew extended; 2 killed; 12 cars and other private property burnt; 37 arrested. Mardan: G.T.S. bus damaged; 4 arrested. Lahore: railway station damaged; 1 bus burnt; traffic signals broken. Karachi: 2 arrested. Peshawar and Lyallpur: colleges closed. Lyallpur: students and police clash; 4 arrested.

10th Peshawar: 2 shots at Ayub's Muslim League meeting; 1 arrested. Nowshera handed over to military. Charsada sugar mill: 1 killed. Lala Musa: government property damaged. Rawalpindi: curfew ends; 20 lakhs property damaged.

11th Processions in Pindi, Sargodha, Lyallpur, Campbellpur, Jhang, Sukkur, Lahore 81 arrested; government property damaged.

12th Lahore: 5 arrested.

13th Bhutto and 11 other leaders arrested. Hyderabad: 2 arrested. Multan: 22 arrested; buses and government property damaged. Sargodha: 8 arrested; 26 Karachi Municipal Corporation vehicles burnt. Karachi: 27 arrested.

245

14th West Pakistan: over 100 arrests; processions; government and public property damaged.

15th Peshawar: general strike; 7 arrested. Arrests in Nowshera: 1, Lahore: 27, Karachi: 26, Abbotabad: 26, Mianwali: 2.

16th Arrests in Peshawar: 8, Dadu: 1, Multan: 59, Sukkur: 1.

18th Arrests in Jhang: 1, Mianwali: 2.

19th Dacca: students and lawyers protest against West Pakistan repression.

20th Khairpur: 25 students arrested.

24th Lahore: students lathi-charged; 10 arrested; private and public property damaged.

25th Protest day observed by P.D.M. Sukkur: 2 arrested; buses, buildings and railway station damaged. Quetta: polytechnic burnt; demonstrations lathi-charged and tear-gassed. Lahore: 25 arrested.

27th Peshawar: public and private property worth thousands of rupees damaged; 24 arrested. Bahawalpur: Convention League office burnt and 15 arrested. Arrests in Rawalpindi: 2, Abbotabad: 2.

28th West Pakistan: N.A.P. demonstrations in main cities. Arrests in Bahawalpur: 20, Peshawar: 18.

29th Rawalpindi: mob tear-gassed; private and public property damaged; military called in. Arrests in Rawalpindi: 20, Sahiwal: 33. East and West Pakistan: lawyers demonstrate. Lahore: 8 arrested.

30th Sargodha: 4 arrested. Lyallpur: university building damaged. Demonstrations in West Pakistan.

DECEMBER

1st Peshawar: 50 arrested. West Pakistan: lawyers demonstrate.

2nd Rawalpindi Cantonment areas: troops again called in. Lyallpur: 4 arrested. Demonstrations in various towns.

3rd Nowshera: 2 held.

4th Arrests in Lahore: 6, Sahiwal: 75.

6th Rawalpindi: student demonstrations; private property damaged; police use lathis and tear-gas; 8 arrested.

8th East Pakistan: 2 killed, many arrested; vehicles set on fire; 128 arrested, many injured; Rawalpindi newsman shot at. West Pakistan: demonstrations. Sargodha: 3 arrested. Hyderabad: 24,000 students demonstrate; many arrested.

12th   Karachi: 1 arrested.
13th   Chittagong: mob fired on, 12 hurt: over 700 arrested in East
       Pakistan. Sahiwal: 12 lawyers arrested.
14th   Sahiwal: 5 arrested. Chittagong: 1 killed.
15th   Arrests in Lahore: 20, Gujranwala: 36.
16th   Arrests in Gujrat: 1, Sahiwal: 5.
18th   Sargodha: 1 arrested.
19th   Arrests in Sialkot: 60, Dera Ghazi Khan: 55, Lahore: 11.
20th   Lahore: 13 injured by police lathi-charge. Arrests in Lahore:
       28, Kot Adu: 7, Sargodha: 28, Sellianwali: 35, Gujranwala: 5.
23rd   Rawalpindi: 24 arrested; G.T.S. branch office damaged.
24th   Sahiwal: 9 arrested.
26th   Rawalpindi: 1 killed, 2 injured. Lahore: 9 injured. Peshawar: 8
       arrested. Sargodha: 2 arrested.
27th   Bahawalpur: 13 arrested.
28th   Karachi: 4 arrested.
29th   Campbellpur: 12 arrested. Narail: 2 injured by police gunfire.
       Pishinin: 5 hurt and 21 arrested. Dera Ghazi Khan: 5 arrested.
30th   Dacca: 7 killed by police gunfire, 14 injured, 4 arrested.

1969
JANUARY
5th   Mueltan: 5 held. Peshawar: 5 held; Deputy Speaker's house
       stoned, buses stones.
6th   Multan: 2 injured, 25 arrested.
10th   Rival political parties clash, 3 injured.
12th   Peshawar: 3 arrested for blowing up Deputy Speaker's house.
       Multan: 20 arrested. East Pakistan: 4 arrested.
16th   Arrests in Sargodha: 1, Sialkot: 66.
17th   Dera Ghazi Khan: 2 arrested. Clashes in Dacca. Rawalpindi:
       31 arrested.
18th   Students and police clash, 1,000 injured, 32 arrested. Kohat: 6
       students injured by police firing. 10 arrested.
19th   Dacca:* 1 killed, 3 injured by police gunfire, 8 arrested.
20th   Dacca:* 1 killed, 25 injured by E.P.R. firing. Bannu: many
       arrested, student-police clashes, 6 injured.
21st   Rawalpindi: police-mob clash: post office, buses, police station,
       damaged; 14 injured, over 160 arrested.

* Signifies in East Pakistan.

22nd Hyderabad: 12 injured, 9 arrested, property damaged. Rawalpindi: more than 100 arrested; a newspaper office and other
properties damaged.

23rd Bahawalpur: 1 arrested. Multan: buses damaged; 12 arrested.

24th Dacca:* army called in for 24-hour curfew; 5 killed by police
gunfire, 60 rounded up, 100 injured; *Dainik Pakistan, Morning
News* offices, houses of three Members of Parliament of East
Pakistan, secretariat building, 15 houses, railway station, 40
shops, vehicles, burnt. Khulna:* 3 killed, 25 injured, many
shops burnt. Karachi: over 100 injured by police firing. 260
arrested.

25th Karachi: 24-hour curfew, 4 government cars, buses, a petrol
pump burnt; public-police clash; 200 arrested, 1 killed, 30
injured. Lahore: L.M.C. office and secretariat furniture, a bus,
tents of fruit-show burnt. Multan: 6 injured, 4 arrested.
Khulna:* 31-hour curfew; 5 killed, 12 injured by army bullets.
Narayanganj:* 16 injured. Dacca:* 23 injured.

26th Narayanganj* and Dacca:* 4 killed, Khulna:* 10 killed; 145
arrested, Member of Parliament's house and a bank building
damaged. Mymensingh:* 74 arrested for violating curfew.
Karachi: Karachi Development Authority office ransacked;
private property damaged; 80 arrested.

27th Karachi: 6 killed, 300 arrested; army called in; government
property damaged. Peshawar: army called in; 129 arrested.
Lahore: curfew; army called in; 2 killed; 2 wounded earlier
died. Dacca:* many arrested. Khulna: curfew re-imposed; 3
arrested; bombs and deadly weapons seized. Mymensingh:* 1
killed.

28th Lahore: hundreds of people arrested — arson and looting cases.
Karachi: violence. Arson increasing; 7 killed — violation of curfew; 9 injured by police gunfire. Barisal:* many arrested.
Dacca:* over 1,000 arrested. Karachi and Lyallpur: 10
arrested.

29th Gujranwala: army called in; curfew imposed; 3 killed, 10
injured; trains and government property damaged. Dera
Ismail Khan: 6 arrested. Lahore: 6 injured. Toba-Takesing
Chenab Express damaged and passenger hurt. Lyallpur: 2
arrested. Hyderabad: bid to burn cloth market; 15 arrested.
Sargodha: 5 arrested, 1 injured. Barisal:* 1 died. Khulna:* 157
arrested. Sylhet:* 1 killed, 28 injured in gunfire.

30th Dacca:* 1 killed, 3 injured, during police firing in Faridpur district. Mymensingh:* 45 arrested. Chittagong:* many arrested. Pabna:* 10 arrested. Kushtia:* 24 arrested. Comilla:* 9 arrested. Manshiganj:* some arrested. Bahawalpur: crowd attack Jahamian railway station. Lala Musa: town committees office damaged. Gujranwala: 28 arrested; 100 shops damaged. Total arrested 46. Karachi: police say 720 arrested.

31st Swat: many arrested. Larkana: Minister's house damaged; 3 cinemas and medical store damaged. Gujranwala: 200 arrested; Sialkot Rangers called in. Arrests in Chittagong:* 13, Sylhet:* 10, Khulna:* 4, Narayanganj: *100.

FEBRUARY

1st Pabna:* total arrests 128. Arrests in Rajshahi:* 6, Bogra:* 3. Gopalganj:* 1 killed, 3 wounded by police gunfire. Gujran-wala: 3 arrested. Rawalpindi: 3 buses damaged. Sialkot: demonstrators tear-gassed.

2nd Injured in Satkhira:* 10, Naggaon: 3, Sargodha: 35. Police clash with mob.

3rd Kabirwala: clash; school building set on fire.

4th Lahore: police lathi-charge; many students arrested.

5th Tangail:* 1 killed, 10 injured by gunfire; houses of Ministers burnt.

6th Lahore: dozens arrested.

7th Dacca:* 3 killed by police gunfire in Comilla, many arrested. Sargodha: 1 injured by police gunfire.

8th Lahore: student-police clash. Many injured.

10th Nowshera: 1 killed and 9 injured by mob violence.

12th Lahore: 3 arrested, 15 injured. Sialkot: many shops damaged.

13th Lahore: Oxford University Press set on fire.

14th Lahore: police gunfire, 2 killed, 60 arrested. Karachi: military called in; 4 killed, 50 injured, 100 arrested, property ransacked and burnt. Hyderabad: rival parties clash; 1 killed, 13 injured. Sargodha: cinemas, railcars and trains damaged. Chittagong:* Insaf and Unity offices (pro-government newspapers) set on fire.

15th Hyderabad: 100 shops burnt, 12 arrested. Dacca:* 2 conspiracy-case accused shot at, 1 died. Narayanganj:* 1 killed, 2 injured.

16th Dacca:* curfew; 1 killed, 35 injured; houses of ministers burnt, and public and private property damaged.

17th Chittagong:* shops and houses burnt. Rangpur:* 2 arrested. Karachi: curfew ignored; mob violence, 3 died; shops and vehicles burnt; more than 100 injured.

18th Dacca:* curfew violation; many buildings burnt; 1 killed, 27 injured, many arrested. Rajshahi:* 2 killed, Dinajpur:* 13 injured; houses and cars burnt; 18 arrested. Karachi:* 3 killed, about 300 arrested. Sargodha: 3 arson cases; 30 arrested.

19th Dacca:* 4 killed, 26 injured – curfew violation. Chittagong:* 2 private cars set on fire, 10 injured. Noahkali:* 3 killed, 14 injured by police; 32 arrested. Kushtia:* 1 killed, 4 injured, shops burnt. Abbotabad: 4 hurt as rival parties clash.

20th Karachi: 11 vehicles set on fire.

21st Khulna:* 9 killed, 50 injured by police firing; army called out; Sabur's house and other buildings burnt. Daulatpur:* 1 killed, many injured by police gunfire. Member of Parliament's house and Tehsil office burnt. Kushtia:* Union Council Chairman beaten to death. Pabna:* 2 killed in police firing.

22nd Barisal:* 3 killed, 6 injured by police firing in industrial area.

23rd Dacca:* 5 hurt in clash with E.P.R. men. Khulna: 2 more of those injured died.

24th Rangpur:* 3 injured in E.P.R. gunfire.

25th Round Table Conference. 1st meeting.

MARCH

2nd Lahore: 5 injured in rival political parties clash.

3rd Dacca:* 2 killed.

4th Dacca:* curfew in Bogra*; mob clashes; houses and government establishment burnt. Chandpur:* 3 killed, 500 houses burnt. Nawabshah: mob attack; train passengers injured; some arrested.

6th Sylhet:* 2 killed in Habibganj firing by Union Chairman. Peshawar: 6 killed, many hurt in Dir State. Karachi: 2 killed, 9 injured in Site by Chaukidar, firing; 36 workers arrested.

8th Dacca:* Jamalpur;* 8 killed; mob killed 5 criminals thrown into the fire and their houses burnt; 15 boats looted. Tangail:* victims of gunfire on February 5th, died.

9th Jamalpur:* 8 killed; houses and huts burnt. Lahore: Jamaat office ransacked. Rawalpindi: violent clash at Chaklala airport on Tariq Ali's arrival between left-wing students and workers and small group of rightist students. Lyallpur: 5 arrested.

11th Kushtia:* 20 houses burnt; 14 shops razed at Daulatpur. Rajshahi:* 478 houses burnt; arson and looting. Multan: demonstrators burn shops.

12th Sukkur: 100 shops burnt. Jamalpur:* 5 more killed.

13th Ayub's announcement at Round Table Conference: adult franchise and parliamentary system accepted. Dacca: 76 criminals killed in Marikganj; 225 houses of criminals burnt.

15th Noahkali:* 4 police officers killed; mob attacked police station. Jamalpur:* 7 more died, two burnt to death.

17th Dacca:* brothels set on fire, 2 cinemas ransacked. Chittagong:* ransacking of shop; mob attack.

18th Dacca:* police havaldar (sergeant) beaten to death in Rajshahi Division; 6 rifles snatched away. Parbatpur:* 5 killed, over 200 huts and 100 houses burnt. Curfew imposed.

19th Chittagong:* mass exodus from three Comilla villages. Dacca:* 2 killed by stabbing. Jamalpur:* 1 burnt alive and another crucified.

20th Karachi: 1 killed; workers clash; 14 hurt. Hyderabad: 2 hurt as rival political parties clash. Lahore: 7 arrested. Faridpur: 15 arrested.

21st Rajshahi:* 3 killed, 9 arrested. Karachi: Rs. 1,000 million lost due to strikes and damage. Srimangal: 3 criminals killed.

22nd Karachi: 30 killed, 40 held for rioting. Dacca:* 18 arrested.

24th Singhair: 1 killed, 200 houses burnt.

25th Dacca:* 1 killed, 3 injured by police gunfire. Kushtia:* 31 criminals arrested. Rawalpindi: Martial Law proclaimed; Ayub hands over power to General Yahya.

26th Karachi: 451 factories re-start work after 10 days strike.

This information is taken from the following newspapers: *Pakistan Times* (government owned); *Dawn* (pro-government); *Nawa-i-waqt* and *Pakistan Observer* (the last two are right-wing opposition papers in West and East Pakistan respectively). Some of the large-scale massacres in East Pakistan were not reported—in particular the number of workers killed in Dacca on the night they defied the military curfew. Also the number of "criminals" killed is vastly exaggerated, as a later investigation showed. In most cases these "criminals" were well established political thugs who had victimized the people on behalf of the government.

On Pakistan and National Unity

(Resolution passed by the Enlarged Plenum of the Central Committee of the Communist Party of India on September 19th, 1942, and confirmed by the First Congress of the Communist Party of India in May 1943.)

All-in national unity based on communal harmony and Congress-League joint front is today an urgent and pressing necessity to solve the present national crisis, to win National Government from the hands of the British imperialist bureaucracy and to defend our Motherland against the fascist aggressor. This has brought the controversy of Pakistan versus the unity of India sharply to the forefront. The Communist Party, therefore, lays down the main principles of the Communist policy on this issue.

1. The Communist Party draws together the toilers of all castes, communities and nationalities in common class organizations (trade unions, Kisan Sabhas, etc). It unites them politically as the vanguard of the united national front for achieving the freedom of our country and democracy. This is the cornerstone of the policy of achieving communal unity.

2. To build the united national front of the peoples of the various communities and nationalities that inhabit India, for the defence and freedom of our country, it is however necessary to dispel the mutual distrust and suspicion that exists among them. This is a remnant of memories of past historical oppression and of present social inequalities arising out of the feudal imperialist exploitation. For this purpose, the basic rights of the communities and nationalities must be made an essential part of the programme of the united national front.

3. The programme of the U.N.F. must declare that in Free India, there will be perfect equality between nationalities and communities that live together in India. There will be no oppression of one nationality by another. There will be no inequalities or disabilities based on caste or community. To ensure this the national movement must recognize the following rights as part of its programme for national unity:

(a) Every section of the Indian people which has a contiguous territory as its homeland, common historical tradition, common language, culture, psychological make-up and common economic life would be recognized as a distinct nationality with the right to exist as an autonomous state within the free Indian union or federation and will have the right to secede from it if it may so desire. This means that the territories which are homelands of such nationalities and which today are split up by artificial boundaries of the present British provinces and of the so-called "Indian States" would be reunited and restored to them in Free India. Thus Free India of tomorrow would be a federation or union of autonomous states of the various nationalities such as Pathans, Western Punjabis (predominantly Muslims), Sikhs, Sindhis, Hindustanis, Rajasthanis, Gujeratis, Bengalis, Assamese, Beharis, Orlyas, Andhras, Tamils, Karnatakis, Maharashtrians, Keralas, etc.

(b) If there are interspersed minorities in the new states thus formed their rights regarding their culture, language, education, etc., would be guaranteed by Statute and their infringement would be punishable by law.

(c) All disabilities, privileges and discriminations based on caste, race or community (such as untouchability and allied wrongs) would be abolished by statute and their infringement would be punishable by law.

4. Such a declaration of rights inasmuch as it concedes to every nationality as defined above and therefore, to nationalities having Muslim faith, the right of autonomous state existence and of secession, can form the basis for unity between the National Congress and the League. For this would give to the Muslims, wherever they are in an overwhelming majority in a contiguous territory which is their homeland, the right to form their autonomous states and even to separate if they so desire. In the case of the Bengali Muslims of the Eastern and Northern Districts of Bengal where they form an overwhelming majority, they may form themselves into an autonomous region—the state of Bengal—or may form a separate state. Such a declaration therefore concedes the just essence of the Pakistan demand and has nothing in common with the separatist theory of dividing India into two nations on the basis of religion.

5. But the recognition of the right of separation in this form need not necessarily lead to actual separation. On the other hand, by dispelling the mutual suspicions, it brings about unity of action today

and lays the basis for a greater unity in the Free India of tomorrow. National unity forged on the basis of such a declaration and strengthened in the course of joint struggle in the defence of our Motherland is bound to convince the peoples of all Indian nationalities of the urgent need to stick together and to form a Free Indian Union or Federation in which each national state would be a free and equal member with right to secede. They will thus see this as the only path of protecting the freedom and democracy achieved, and building on that secure basis a greater and grander unity of India than our country has ever seen.

In spite of the apparent conflict and seemingly insoluble difficulties, the burning desire for unity is taking firmer hold of the people who today follow the Congress or the League. Under the stress of the growing menace of fascist invasion and of the present national crisis, the leadership of the two organizations also have moved closer together and in the direction of the very solution given in this resolution. There is no room whatsoever for defeatism on the question of unity. The Communist Party calls upon all patriots to join hands with it in popularizing the principles laid down herein and thus speed up the realization of Congress-League Unity, which is today the only path of national salvation for our Motherland in the hour of her gravest peril.

(This resolution was adopted by the Muslim League in September 1968.)

Resolution on Economic Policy

Whereas it is necessary to establish in Pakistan a social and economic order based on the Islamic principles of equality and fraternity and social and economic justice, and to march purposefully towards the social and economic goals clearly set for the nation by the Founder of Pakistan, Qaid-i-Azam Muhammad Ali Jinnah;

And whereas it is essential to deal effectively with both the long-term and immediately pressing economic and social problems confronting the mass of the people in Pakistan;

Now, therefore, the Council of the Pakistan Muslim League hereby adopts the following Economic Programme as the firm and declared policy of the party, and directs that it be immediately incorporated in and made part of the Manifesto of the Party, as a solemn commitment to the People of Pakistan that the Pakistan Muslim League shall earnestly strive for the earliest implementation of the said Programme, to ensure the establishment of social justice and economic security for all the People of Pakistan in accordance with the relevant principles of Islam:

A Programme to Ensure the Establishment of Islamic Social and Economic Justice for all the People of Pakistan

(1) All sources of capital formation such as banking and insurance shall be nationally owned, in order to ensure that the entire resources of the community are fully utilized and are used in a manner best calculated to serve the interests of the whole community.

(2) Industries, such as iron and steel and non-ferrous metals, machine tools, chemicals and fertilizers, heavy engineering, ship-building, arms and ammunition and all armament for defence, motor-car assembly and manufacture and essential electrical equipment for power (production, distribution and use) shall be owned by the state.

255

(3) All sources of energy such as electricity, oil, gas and coal as well as atomic energy and all major means of public transport, such as railways, shipping, airways and road transport and all exploitation of mineral wealth shall be nationally owned. Textiles and all agriculture-based industries, such as jute, sugar, tea, tobacco and flour, shall be jointly owned and run by co-operatives of growers, entrepreneurs and labour.

(4) All industries owned by the State shall be managed by highly skilled and qualified personnel, subject to control by public representatives and not the bureaucracy.

(5) All major exports such as textiles, cotton, jute, tea, food-grains, minerals and precious stones and all major imports of capital goods, fertilizers, metals and machinery, electronic equipment, motor vehicles and tractors shall be handled by a state trading corporation in the best interests of the nation as a whole, thereby rooting out the malpractices which have led to a loss of our precious foreign exchange.

(6) The rights of all workers shall be guaranteed by law, entitling them to minimum wages, free organization of trade unions, the right to strike, insurance against unemployment and injury or death during the course of work, and other basic benefits. Industrial labour shall be allotted shares in all factories by utilization of their savings, provident funds and bonuses, which shall be fixed from time to time by the State, so as to provide them with an effective voice in the efficient running of their concerns.

(7) To avoid the concentration of wealth and to achieve maximum possible equality of income, the taxation pattern shall be so devised as to limit the maximum net income of any family, from any source or sources, so as not to exceed the equivalent of the income accruing from 250 acres of irrigated land, till each and every family in Pakistan is assured a minimum income of Rs. 3,600 per annum based on the 1964–5 price index, the word "family" denoting father, mother and minor children.

(8) Housing requirements for low income groups will be given assistance on a priority basis: 50 per cent of House Building Finance shall be earmarked for the builders with an annual income of up to Rs. 6,000 per annum, 30 per cent of those

earning up to Rs. 12,000 a year and the balance for those earning up to Rs. 24,000 a year.

(9) Education for low-income groups will be free up to the matriculation level, and greater emphasis will be laid on technical education by opening more polytechnic institutes. Free college or university education will also be provided, on the basis of merit, for low-income groups.

(10) Economic development shall be so planned that unjust and unreasonable disparities in prosperity and growth between and West Pakistan and between different regions within a Province are avoided.

(11) All remaining vestiges of feudalism shall be removed, so that no family (as defined above) owns more than 250 acres of irrigated land (equivalent to 18,000 produce index units) and 500 acres of unirrigated land in West Pakistan: there shall be no exemption from this rule on any ground (on account of gardens, studs, etc). Agriculturists shall be assured just returns for the produce if they conform to national crop plans to achieve self-sufficiency in food and the supply of adequate raw materials for national industries; they shall be given subsidies (for seeds, fertilizers and implements) and additional credit facilities. A price support policy shall also be adopted, while town dwellers earning up to Rs. 500 per month shall be provided foodgrains on a subsidized basis. Increased job opportunities shall be created so that no one goes hungry, especially in rural areas.

(12) Co-operatives and other forms of agrarian organization shall be promoted to prevent exploitation of the cultivators.

(13) A minimum wage shall be fixed for agricultural labour.

(14) Compulsory crop and cattle insurance shall be introduced.

(15) The land revenue shall gradually be brought in line with the income tax so as to exempt small landholders.

(16) State-owned land shall be sold to agrarian co-operatives (the membership of which shall be restricted to the tilling peasants) or shall be awarded only to those who have received awards for valour.

(17) Salaries of services, especially of technical personnel and teachers, will be fixed according to their merit, keeping in view the expense involved in achieving the special qualifications and responsibilities carried by such jobs.

(18) Every citizen of Pakistan shall be the beneficiary of a complete system of social security. The social insurance system will be intended to furnish every person, particularly low-income groups, with social security from the cradle to the grave. Emphasis shall be laid on the free availability of medical services to all those who cannot afford treatment, and on the care of poor orphans and widows and the physically handicapped.

(19) In order to ensure an honourable life to the families of soldiers or policemen killed or disabled in service, all officers and other ranks of the fighting services and the police shall be insured by the government at its own expense.

(20) Those privately owned industries, which shall be nationalized in accordance with the above programme, shall be compensated commensurate with the principles of justice and equity on the one hand and the successful implementation of the abovementioned programme of economic reforms on the other hand.

(21) All foreign capital owned by Pakistan nationals abroad shall be declared within a specified time limit and shall thereupon become subject to the control of the State Bank of Pakistan. All such capital not so declared within the time limit shall be frozen and shall be liable to be confiscated by government.

(22) The amount of foreign capital and foreign investment in Pakistan shall be determined in accordance with the national interest.

(23) The Quranic law relating to charges created on personal property, such as Zakat, shall be strictly enforced.

In spite of the above measures, the private sector shall still play a considerable role in the industrial and agricultural fields. However, it might be alleged that if and when the above programme is implemented, it will tend to deprive the individual of greater material incentives and limit his acquisition of private propety. The solution of these and many other questions can and shall be found if all the citizens of Pakistan begin to *live by* the fundamental principle of Islam that the moral, economic, social and political welfare of the *whole* of society should be an article of faith with *each* one of them: the only worthwhile incentive and the only abidingly adequate property is the clear conscience and peace of mind born of living in a just order and sharing equally in the sorrows as well as the joys of one's fellow men.

This resolution, proposed by Sardar Shaukat Hayat Khan and seconded by Mian Manzar Bashir, was unanimously sponsored by the Working Committee of the Pakistan Muslim League and unanimously passed by the Council.

East Pakistan Students All-Party Committee of Action eleven-point Demands:

1. (a) Restoration of provincialized colleges to their original status.
   (b) Extension in number of schools and colleges.
   (c) Night shift arrangements in Provincial Colleges.
   (d) 50 per cent reduction in tuition fees.
   (e) Bengali as medium of instruction as well as work in all offices.
   (f) Hostel charges to be subsidized by 50 per cent.
   (g) Increase in salaries of teachers.
   (h) Free and compulsory education up to class VIII.
   (i) Medical University to be set up and Medical Council Ordinance to be withdrawn.
   (j) Facilities for condensed course for Polytechnic Students.
   (k) Train and bus concessions.
   (l) Job opportunity guarantee.
   (m) Repeal of University Ordinance and full autonomy for universities.
   (n) Repeal of National Education Commission and Hamoodur Rahman Reports.
2. Parliamentary democracy on basis of universal franchise.
3. (a) Federal form of government and sovereign legislature.
   (b) Federal Government's powers to be confined to defence, foreign policy and currency.
4. Sub-federation of Baluchistan, North West Frontier Province and Sind with regional autonomy for each unit.
5. Nationalization of banks, insurance companies and all big industries.
6. Reduction in rates of taxes and revenues on peasants.
7. Fair wages and bonus for workers.
8. Flood control measures for East Pakistan.
9. Withdrawal of all emergency laws, security acts and other prohibitive orders.
10. Quit SEATO, CENTO and Pakistan-U.S. military pacts.
11. Release of all detainees and political prisoners including those of Agarthala Conspiracy case.

INDEX